# SOPHRON'S MIMES

# Sophron's Mimes

*Text, Translation, and Commentary*

J. H. HORDERN

OXFORD
UNIVERSITY PRESS

# OXFORD
## UNIVERSITY PRESS

Great Clarendon Street, Oxford OX2 6DP

Oxford University Press is a department of the University of Oxford.
It furthers the University's objective of excellence in research, scholarship,
and education by publishing worldwide in

Oxford New York

Auckland Bangkok Buenos Aires Cape Town Chennai
Dar es Salaam Delhi Hong Kong Istanbul Karachi Kolkata
Kuala Lumpur Madrid Melbourne Mexico City Mumbai Nairobi
São Paulo Shanghai Taipei Tokyo Toronto

Oxford is a registered trade mark of Oxford University Press
in the UK and in certain other countries

Published in the United States
by Oxford University Press Inc., New York

© J. H. Hordern 2004

The moral rights of the author have been asserted
Database right Oxford University Press (maker)

First published 2004

British Library Cataloguing in Publication Data

Data available

Library of Congress Cataloging in Publication Data

Data applied for

ISBN 0-19-926613-1

3 5 7 9 10 8 6 4 2

Typeset by Regent Typesetting
Printed in Great Britain
on acid-free paper by
Biddles Ltd, King's Lynn

060906

# PREFACE

PREFACES are conventionally places for self-justification. A book on Sophron may seem to require more defence than most. Yet if Sophron does not stand in the first rank of Greek authors, he remains a fascinating and clearly innovative writer and a valuable example of non-Attic classical literature. The late fifth century was a time of dramatic literary change, and not just in Athens; and the meagre fragments collected here bear witness to a vibrant literary world with traditions and influences quite different from those with which we are most familiar. But the book must in the end justify itself. I hope that the reader will come away sharing my feelings not only of regret that so much of the mimes has been lost, but also that a study of the fragments well repays the time expended on it.

It is a pleasure to acknowledge the various debts incurred in the production of this work. I am extremely grateful to the Alexander von Humboldt Foundation for providing a year-long Fellowship and then extending it for a further nine months, and to Prof. Bernd Seidensticker, who first supported my proposal and then proved a kind and sympathetic host at the Institut für klassische Philologie at the Freie Universität, Berlin. Colin Austin, Martin West (M.L.W.), and Richard Janko all read parts of the book in early draft form, and their suggestions are occasionally cited here. In particular, I am painfully aware that without West's rigorous assessment of the book's problems and correction of its many errors, it would be much more flawed than it is. Gregory Hutchinson kindly read an early article on Sophron, and so inevitably influenced this, the final product. I examined the Sophron papyrus at the Biblioteca Laurenziana in Florence by kind permission of Prof. R. Pintaudi, and the papyrus of Demetrius Lacon's *On Poems* at the Biblioteca Nazionale in Naples with the permission and assistance of the Director and staff. Richard Janko was once again instrumental in effecting an introduction. While I still thought of producing a completely new edition of the text, I also examined the Florentine epitome of Athenaeus, and that in the Bibliothèque Nationale in Paris. My final decision to reprint, in abbreviated and slightly revised form, the text and apparatus from R. Kassel and C. Austin's magisterial *Poetae Comici Graeci* (Berlin and New York, 2001) was made much easier by their generous permission and that of their publisher, Walter de Gruyter GmbH & Co. Further debts, both academic and personal, are owed particularly to Ian Repath, who provided stimulating conversation and excellent whisky; and to Ben Akrigg, Kate Cooper, and Jonathon Prag.

Finally, I am grateful to the Press for agreeing to undertake the publication of the book, and especially to Hilary O'Shea for being a considerate and helpful editor.

J.H.

# CONTENTS

# ABBREVIATIONS AND REFERENCES

## 1. Editions and Monographs

| | |
|---|---|
| Ahrens | H. L. Ahrens, *De Graecae linguae dialectis*, II: *De dialecto Dorica* (Göttingen, 1843) |
| Blomfield (1811) | C. J. Blomfield, 'Sophronis mimorum fragmenta', *ClJ* 8: 380–90 |
| Blomfield (1826) | —— 'Sophronis mimographi fragmenta', *Mus. Crit.* 2: 340–58 and 559–69 |
| Botzon (1856) | L. Botzon, *De Sophrone et Xenarcho mimographis* (Progr. zu Lyck) |
| Botzon (1867) | —— *Sophroneorum mimorum reliquiae* (Progr. zu Marienburg; Danzig) |
| Grysar | C. Grysar, *De Sophrone mimographo* (Progr. zu Köln, 1838) |
| Kaibel | G. Kaibel, *Comicorum Graecorum Fragmenta*, i: *Doriensum comoedia, mimi, phlyaces*², rev. K. Latte (Berlin, 1958) |
| Kassel–Austin (K–A) | R. Kassel and C. Austin, *Poetae Comici Graeci*, vol. i (Berlin and New York, 2001) |
| Norsa–Vitelli | M. Norsa and G. Vitelli, 'Da un mimo di Sophron', *SIFC* 10 (1932), 119–24; 'Ancora frammenti di Sophron', *SIFC* 10 (1933), 247–53; republished as *Papiri Greci e Latini* (= *PSI*) xi (1935), no. 1214a–d |
| Olivieri | A. Olivieri, *Frammenti della Commedia Greca e del Mimo nella Sicilia e nella Magna Grecia*², vol. ii (Naples, 1947) |
| Page | D. L. Page, *Select Papyri*, iii: *Poetry* (Cambridge, Mass., and London, 1941) |
| Pinto Colombo | M. Pinto Colombo, *Il mimo di Sofrone e di Senarco* (Florence, 1934) |

## 2. Other Works

| | |
|---|---|
| Albini | U. Albini, 'Il frammento 24 Kaibel di Sofrone', *Maia*, 13 (1961), 126–30 |

| | |
|---|---|
| Allen | W. S. Allen, *Vox Graeca: The Pronunciation of Classical Greek*³ (Cambridge, 1987) |
| Arena | —— *Iscrizioni greche arcaiche di Sicilia e Magna Grecia* (Milan, 1989– ) |
| Arena (1975) | R. Arena, 'Ταὶ γυναῖκες αἳ τὰν θεόν φαντι ἐξελᾶν', *PP* 30: 217–19 |
| Bechtel | F. Bechtel, *Die griechischen Dialekte*, 3 vols. (Berlin, 1921–4) |
| Bechtel, *Personennamen* | —— *Die historischen Personennamen des Griechischen bis zur Kaiserzeit* (Halle, 1917) |
| Bechtel, *Spitznamen* | —— *Die einstämmigen männlichen Personennamen des Griechischen, die aus Spitznamen hervorgegangen sind* (Abh. Ges. Wiss. Gött., NS 2, 5; Berlin, 1898) |
| Berk | L. Berk, *Epicharmus* (Groningen, 1964) |
| Bossi | F. Bossi, *Studi su Archiloco*² (Bari, 1990) |
| Buck | C. D. Buck, *The Greek Dialects*² (Chicago and London, 1955) |
| CA | *Collectanea Alexandrina*, ed. J. U. Powell (Oxford, 1925) |
| Cassio | A. C. Cassio, 'The Language of Dorian Comedy', in Willi, 51–83 |
| Cataudella | Q. Cataudella, 'Mimo e romanzo (Sofrone 22, 30, 145b, 39, 101', *RCCM* 8 (1966), 3–11 |
| Chantraine | P. Chantraine, *Dictionnaire étymologique de la langue grecque, histoire des mots* (Paris, 1968–80) |
| Chantraine, *Grammaire* | —— *Grammaire homérique*, 2 vols. (Paris, 1942–53) |
| Chantraine (1935) | —— 'Un nouveau fragment de Sophron', *Riv. Phil.* 9 (1935), 22–32 |
| Chantraine (1963) | —— 'Le Fragment 26 de Sophron et les noms grecs de la crevette', *Maia*, 15: 136–42 |
| Colvin | S. Colvin, *Dialect in Aristophanes: The Politics of Language in Ancient Greek Literature* (Oxford, 1999) |
| Crusius | O. Crusius, 'Über das Phantastische in Mimus', *Neue Jb.* 25 (1910), 81–102 |
| Degani, *Studi* | E. Degani, *Studi su Ipponatte* (Bari, 1984) |

| | |
|---|---|
| Denniston | J. D. Denniston, *The Greek Particles*[2] (Oxford, 1954) |
| Denniston, *Prose Style* | —— *Greek Prose Style* (Oxford, 1952) |
| *DGE* | *Dialectorum Graecorum Exempla Epigraphica Potiora*[2], ed. E. Schwyzer, rev. P. Cauer (Leipzig, 1923) |
| Dickey | E. Dickey, *Greek Forms of Address from Herodotus to Lucian* (Oxford, 1986) |
| DK | H. Diels and W. Kranz (eds.), *Die Fragmente der Vorsokratiker*[10] (Berlin, 1961) |
| Dover | K. J. Dover, *The Evolution of Greek Prose* (Oxford, 1997) |
| Dubois | L. Dubois, *Inscriptions grecques dialectales de Sicile* (Collection de l' École Française de Rome; Paris and Rome, 1989) |
| Dunbabin | T. J. Dunbabin, *The Western Greeks* (Oxford, 1948) |
| Eitrem | S. Eitrem, 'Sophron und Theokrit', *SO* 12 (1933), 10–38 |
| *FGrH* | *Die Fragmente der griechischen Historiker*, ed. F. Jacoby *et al.* (Berlin and Leiden, 1923– ) |
| Frisk | H. Frisk, *Griechisches etymologisches Wörterbuch* (Heidelberg, 1960–72) |
| Gallavotti | C. Gallavotti, 'Per il nuovo Sofrone', *RFIC* 61 (NS 11) (1933), 459–76 |
| Gow | A. S. F. Gow, 'Sophron and Theocritus', *CR* 47 (1933), 113–15 |
| Gow, *Theocritus* | —— *Theocritus*[2], 2 vols. (Cambridge, 1952) |
| Hauler | E. Hauler, 'Der Mimus von Epicharm bis Sophron', *Xenia Austriaca, Festschr. d. österr. Mittelschulen zur 42. Versamml. deutscher Philologen und Schulmänner in Wien* (Vienna, 1893), i. 81–135 |
| *HE* | *Hellenistic Epigrams*, ed. A. S. F. Gow and D. L. Page, 2 vols. (Cambridge, 1965) |
| Henderson | J. Henderson, *The Maculate Muse: Obscene Language in Attic Comedy*[2] (Oxford and New York, 1991) |
| Herzog | R. Herzog, 'Die Zauberinnen des Sophron', *Hess. Blätt. f. Volkskunde*, 25 (1926), 218 ff. |

| | |
|---|---|
| Hordern, *Timotheus* | J. H. Hordern, *The Fragments of Timotheus of Miletus* (Oxford, 2002) |
| Hordern (2002*a*) | —— 'Love Magic and Purification in Sophron, *PSI* 1214a, and Theocritus' *Pharmakeutria*', *CQ*² 52 (2002), 164–73 |
| Hordern (2002*b*) | —— 'Sophron, fr. 171, and Theocritus 15', *ZPE* 140 (2002), 1–2 |
| Hordern (2002*c*) | —— 'Word-order and ἐκλογή in Sophron and Demetrius, *On Poems* 2, cols. 55–60', *ZPE* 141 (2002), 75–82 |
| Hunter | R. L. Hunter, *Theocritus: A Selection* (Cambridge, 1999) |
| Hutchinson | G. Hutchinson, *Hellenistic Poetry* (Oxford, 1988) |
| *IEG* | *Iambi et Elegi Graeci*², 2 vols., ed. M. L. West (Oxford, 1989–92) |
| Kaibel (1899) | G. Kaibel, 'Sophron Fragm. 166', *Hermes*, 37: 319–20 |
| Kerényi | C. Kerényi, 'Sofrone ovvero il naturalismo greco', *RIFC* 63 (1935), 1–19 = 'Sophron oder der griechische Naturalismus', in *Apollon* (Vienna, Amsterdam, and Leipzig, 1937), 142–70, 269–71 |
| Kerkhecker | A. Kerkhecker, *Callimachus' Book of Iambi* (Oxford, 1999) |
| Kerkhof | R. Kerkhof, *Dorische Posse, Epicharm, und Attische Komödie* (Beitr. zur Altertumskunde 147; Leipzig and Munich, 2001) |
| Latte | K. Latte, 'Zu dem neuen Sophron-fragment', *Philol.* 88 (NS 42) (1933), 259–64, 467, 488 = *Kl. Schr.* (Munich, 1968), 492–8 |
| *LGPN* | P. M. Fraser and E. Matthews (eds.), *A Lexicon of Greek Personal Names* (Oxford, 1987– ) |
| LSJ | H. G. Liddell and R. Scott, *A Greek–English Lexicon*⁹, rev. H. Stuart Jones and R. McKenzie (with revised Supplement: Oxford, 1996) |
| Maas, *Kl. Schr.* | P. Maas, *Kleine Schriften* (Munich, 1973) |

| | |
|---|---|
| Norden | E. Norden, *Die Antike Kunstprosa* (Berlin, 1915) |
| *OCD*³ | S. Hornblower and A. Spawforth (eds.), *The Oxford Classical Dictionary*³ (Oxford, 1996) |
| Parker | R. Parker, *Miasma: Pollution and Purification in Early Greek Religion* (Oxford, 1983) |
| Pfeiffer | R. Pfeiffer, *History of Classical Scholarship from the Beginning to the End of the Hellenistic Age* (Oxford, 1968) |
| *PGM* | *Papyri Graecae Magicae*, vol. 1, ed. K. Preisendanz (Stuttgart, 1928); rev. edn., A. Henrichs (1973); vol. 2, ed. K. Preisendanz (1931) |
| Pickard-Cambridge | A. W. Pickard-Cambridge, *Dithyramb, Tragedy and Comedy*² (Oxford, 1962) |
| *PMG* | *Poetae Melici Graeci*, ed. D. L. Page (Oxford, 1962) |
| *PMGF* | *Poetarum Melicorum Graecorum Fragmenta*, i, ed. M. Davies (Oxford, 1991) |
| Poltera | O. Poltera, *Le Langage de Simonide: Étude sur la tradition poétique et son renouvellement* (Bern, 1997) |
| Reich | H. Reich, *Der Mimus* (Berlin, 1903) |
| Romeo | C. Romeo, *Demetrio Lacone: La poesia* (La Scuola di Epicuro 9; Naples, 1988) |
| Romeo (1981) | —— 'Sofrone nei papiri ercolanesi (P. Herc. 1081 e 1014)', *Proc. 16th Intern. Congr. Papyr.* 183–90 |
| Schwyzer | E. Schwyzer, *Griechische Grammatik*, 3 vols. (Munich, 1939–53) |
| *SH* | *Supplementum Hellenisticum*, ed. P. J. Parsons and H. Lloyd-Jones (Berlin and New York, 1983) |
| Thompson | D'A. W. Thompson, *A Glossary of Greek Fishes* (London, 1947) |
| Thumb–Kieckers | A. Thumb and E. Kieckers, *Handbuch der griechischen Dialekte*, i (Heidelberg, 1932) |
| *TrGF* | *Tragicorum Graecorum Fragmenta*, ed. B. Snell, R. Kannicht, and S. Radt (Göttingen, 1971– ) |

| | |
|---|---|
| West, *East Face* | M. L. West, *The East Face of Helicon* (Oxford, 1997) |
| West, *Studies* | —— *Studies in Greek Elegy and Iambus* (Berlin and New York, 1974) |
| Wilamowitz, *Kl. Schr.* | U. von Wilamowitz-Moellendorff, *Kleine Schriften*, 5 vols. (Berlin, 1935–72) |
| Willi | A. Willi (ed.), *The Language of Greek Comedy* (Oxford, 2002) |
| Wünsch | R. Wünsch, 'Zu Sophrons Ταὶ γυναῖκεc αἳ τὰν θεόν φαντι ἐξελᾶν', *Jb. cl. Ph.* Suppl. 27 (1902), 111–22 |
| Wünsch (1909) | —— 'Die Zauberinnen des Theokrit', *Hess. Blätt. f. Volkskunde*, 8 (1909), 111–31 |

Other abbreviations are as in LSJ or should be readily comprehensible. Fragments are cited from the standard editions. Hipponax is given, like other iambic fragments, from *IEG* rather than from Degani's Teubner[2] (Stuttgart and Leipzig, 1991).

# Introduction

TIME has not been kind to Sophron. Though he was much admired in the Hellenistic period, and read at least as late as the second century AD, his works all but vanish in the succeeding period. This is the first volume devoted exclusively to the mimes in over fifty years (although Kassel and Austin have recently produced their splendid new edition), and the first in English ever. This neglect results partly from the extremely fragmentary nature of the material (more fragmentary even than the remains of iambus or early lyric), partly from the obscurities of the genre and the difficulty of the language. Both hopefully find some elucidation here.

For us, Sophron's interest lies in the first place in his connections with later literature, most notably Theocritus and Herodas. This is perhaps as it should be; in antiquity Hellenistic poets and scholars were those most interested in the mimes. However, their wider importance should not be underestimated. Syracuse was after all a major cultural and political power from the early fifth century, possessing its own dramatic tradition and a poetic inheritance in other respects somewhat different from that we know from Athens. And Sophron's startling decision to write in Doric prose, at a time when prose was primarily reserved for historical and scientific investigation and its natural language was Attic-Ionic, suggests someone consciously asserting a local identity. By the time he was writing, Attic drama (or at least tragedy) had clearly already had a major impact on the wider Greek world, and was certainly popular in Sicily. Dithyramb, while not exclusively Attic in origin, seems to have acquired official form in Athens. Most dithyrambographers, the majority in fact from outside Athens, were either based there or at the very least frequent visitors. Possibly Sophron wished actively to oppose himself to some perceived cultural encroachment. The interest which other Sicilian or Sicilian-based writers show in local mythological traditions suggests a similar assertion of cultural pride and identity. At any rate, enough of his work survives to make Sophron an interesting and innovative figure in his own right, one who in several ways prefigures Hellenistic literary developments, and illumines an intriguing byway of Greek literary history for which we have, as for so much, sadly little evidence.

## I. LIFE AND DATING

Of Sophron himself we know little. The *Suda* (c 893) provides the essentials:

Cώφρων, Cυρακούcιοc, Ἀγαθοκλέουc καὶ Δαμναcυλλίδοc. τοῖc δὲ χρόνοιc ἦν κατὰ Ξέρξην καὶ Εὐριπίδην. καὶ ἔγραψε μίμουc ἀνδρείουc, μίμουc γυναικείουc· εἰcὶ δὲ καταλογάδην, διαλέκτωι Δωρίδι.

Sophron, of Syracuse, the son of Agathocles and Damnasyllis.[1] He lived at the same time as Xerxes and Euripides. He wrote men's and women's mimes; they are in prose, in the Doric dialect.

To this we can add nothing precise, and even these few points provide difficulties.

The *Suda* says that he lived at the same time as Xerxes and Euripides. To a Greek ear κατὰ Ξέρξην could hardly refer to any period other than that of the Persian Wars (though a second Xerxes ruled Persia briefly in 425/4 BC); but 'at the same time as Euripides' should mean the second half of the fifth century. The latter date is favoured by one further piece of evidence. Sophron's son, Xenarchus, also a mime-writer, is said to have made fun of the Rhegians at the behest of Dionysius, who became tyrant of Syracuse in 406, and overcame Rhegium after a period of hostility in 386.[2] We have little further information about Xenarchus, though his mimes were known to Aristotle (*Poet.* 1. 1447ª28), and even the tradition that makes him Sophron's son might be thought suspicious. Greek scholars delighted in inventing such connections to account for developments in literary history. Thus, the Sicilian comic poet Dinolochus is rather conveniently said to be the son of

---

[1] Agathocles is an immensely popular name (*LGPN* III.A lists 127 instances, nine of these in Sicily; it is equally common elsewhere in the Greek world). Damnasyllis is not otherwise attested, but this is not sufficient reason to doubt the *Suda*'s reliability; men's names in any case tend to outweigh women's names quite significantly in the surviving evidence.

[2] Xenarch. test. 2 K–A (Phot. p. 485. 21 = *Suda* ρ 121); Diod. Sic. 13. 95–6.

Epicharmus, 'or, as some have it, his pupil' (*Suda*, δ 338), though even his place of birth, like that of Epicharmus himself, was disputed.[3] The story about Xenarchus is also told of a certain Nymphodorus, a *thaumatopoios* according to Athenaeus in one passage, a mime-writer in another.[4] This may cast further doubt on the reliability of the tradition, though Dionysius gathered round him a large number of poets and entertainers, and no doubt they sometimes dealt with the same subject. But of course there is nothing intrinsically unlikely in Sophron's or Epicharmus' son following his father's profession: we know of several families of tragedians in Athens, including those of Aeschylus and Sophocles.

However, even if the familial connection is a fabrication, it probably reflects accurately enough the relative dating of Sophron and Xenarchus. The *Suda*'s reference to Xerxes is perhaps due to confusion between Sophron and Epicharmus (so Kaibel, p. 152 n.), who certainly belongs to the early fifth century, or to textual corruption. Botzon suggested emending to κατ᾽ Ἀ⟨ρτα⟩ξέρξην;[5] Artaxerxes succeeded the first Xerxes in 465 and ruled until 425 (the other Artaxerxes, who ruled between 405 and 359 BC, would clearly be too late).

Beyond this we have no real information; the fragments themselves provide no internal hints to historical context. Knowledge of Sophron's name and work is unattested until the fourth century. There is a dubious tradition that he was popular with Plato (see below, Sect. IV), who certainly may have come across the mimes during his visits to Sicily, but the earliest firm reference to them comes from Aristotle, who in the *Poetics* (loc. cit.) groups the mimes of Sophron and Xenarchus with Socratic dialogue (probably with particular reference to those of Alexamenus of Teos, who was allegedly the first to write such dialogues) as mimetic prose.[6] This is perhaps not surprising

---

[3] Cf. Aelian, *N.A.* 6. 51, who makes him Epicharmus' ἀνταγωνιςτής. For Epicharmus' birthplace, cf. Kerkhof, 55 f.

[4] Athen. 1. 19 F (citing Duris, *FGrH* 76 F 57); 10. 452 F (= Clearchus, fr. 93 Wehrli). For the relationship between mime and θαυματοποιία, see M. W. Dickie, *CQ*² 51 (2001), 599–603.    [5] Botzon (1856), 3.

[6] Arist. fr. 72 R.³ (ap. Athen. 11. 505 C) and an Aristotelian papyrus from Oxyrhynchus (P. Oxy. 3219) make the connection with Alexamenus (test. 2–4 K–A). Cf. M. W. Haslam, *BICS* 19 (1972), 17–38. L. W. Daly, *AJP* 103 (1982), 86–8, attempts to find echoes of Sophron in Aristophanes, but the parallels are slight and unconvincing.

despite the close contacts that existed between Sicily, especially Syracuse, and various mainland Greek states. There is also little direct evidence that Epicharmus' plays were known in classical Athens, though obviously frequent visitors to Sicily such as Pindar and Aeschylus must have been aware of his dramas, and Plato (*Theaet.* 152 DE) makes him known to Socrates as the father of comedy.[7]

Syracuse was a Corinthian foundation of the eighth century BC. Always a city of significance, it had been a tyranny from early in the fifth century, first under Gelon (tyrant of Gela from 491), and then under his brother Hieron from 478. After Hieron's death in 467, and the brief and disastrous rule of his brother Thrasybulus, a democratic government was established. By this stage, the Carthaginian threat had been defeated; the Sicels, another menace to the Greek states in Sicily, were finally overcome in *c.*450. The foundation for Syracuse's wealth and prosperity had been laid by the early tyrants, and under democratic rule the city rose further in power and influence throughout the island. We may assume that Sophron lived through the interstate conflicts that beset Sicily throughout the last quarter of the fifth century, and, indeed, the Athenian expedition against Syracuse in 415. But none of this turmoil appears to have been reflected in his mimes.

## II. THE MIMES

Sophron's mimes were short (we do not know how short) dramatic sketches in prose dealing with comic scenes from everyday life. They were divided into μῖμοι ἀνδρεῖοι and μῖμοι γυναικεῖοι, men's and women's mimes. This division, probably Sophron's own,[8] appears to reflect the sex of the main character only; minor characters of the opposite sex could evidently appear in either. The presence of masculine participles in fr. 11 (*Busied about the Bride*) indicates that men featured at least in part of a narrative,[9] though the main speaker was a woman. Herodas'

---

[7] Epicharmus mocked Aeschylus' use of the verb τιμαλφεῖν (fr. 221), and his *Persians* may have been a parody (see Kerkhof, 136). The internal evidence that Epicharmus was known to and influenced Old Comedy is itself insubstantial (Kerkhof, 51–5, 144–50; Pickard-Cambridge, 278, 285 f.).

[8] It is not an obvious one for a later editor to make.

[9] Masculine participles may perhaps occasionally be used as feminines

mimiambi also show a rough division into those in which women (poems 1, 4, 6) or men (poem 2) are the main figures, though several are of mixed character (3, 5, 7).

An interest in character-drawing is suggested by a brief reference in Diogenes Laertius,[10] but the extant fragments present more evidence for simple coarseness and bawdy humour. In one of the longer papyrus passages the speaker describes in comic terms the effect of an overwhelming bout of diarrhoea (fr. 4D), and hurling excrement probably featured as an element of sympotic activity in *Busied about the Bride* (fr. 11). Elsewhere the incontinence of old men may appear as a subject for humour (fr. 52). Sex is a common theme, particularly in the women's mimes. Women readying themselves for intercourse are described in metaphorical, but clearly obscene, terms in fr. 24. We hear two women discussing dildoes in frs. 23 and 25, and a pun on fellatio features in fr. 38. Male homosexuality appears to have been the subject of a whole play ( *You'll frighten off boys*).

Other mimes may have been less scurrilous. Many of the fragments from the women's mimes refer to cookery, though this reflects at least in part Athenaeus' interest in this material; we do not know if a whole mime dealt with the subject. The [*Women watching the Isthmia*] (the title is a modern reconstruction) probably just presented women attending a festival, and commenting on the offerings on display in the sanctuary. Among the men's mimes we find a debate between a fisherman and a countryman, probably about the merits of their respective ways of life (frs. 42–4). Largely, however, we hear only snatches. A tunafisher sets off to go fishing (frs. 45–8); frs. 67 and 68 perhaps come from a violent exchange between two speakers; a character complains of poverty or his own profligacy (fr. 71); old men lament the debilities of age (frs. 52, 54–6).

There is little of religion or cult; where these feature, it is largely as a subject for humour. Heracles is a popular god (frs. 59,

---

elsewhere in Greek (though the evidence is slight; see Fraenkel on A. *Ag.* 562), but it would be perverse to assume without further evidence that this is the case here or elsewhere in Sophron.

[10] 3. 18 δοκεῖ δὲ Πλάτων καὶ τὰ Cώφρονοc . . . βιβλία ἠμελημένα πρῶτος εἰc Ἀθήναc διακομίcαι καὶ ἠθοποιῆcαι πρὸc αὐτόν (cf. J. M. S. McDonald, *Character-Portraiture in Epicharmus, Sophron, and Plato* (Diss. Columbia, 1931)); but this is probably just a development of the tradition that Sophron influenced Plato.

68, 72, 134), as in comedy;[11] Poseidon was mentioned some-where, possibly in [*Women watching the Isthmia*] (frs. 125, 131, *171?). Dionysus makes an appearance only so he can be mocked for proverbial stupidity in his guise as Morychus (fr. *73). Zeus is the subject of a mock-heroic invocation (fr. 41); Artemis, whose cult was important in Syracuse,[12] features in two frag-ments, but for each we lack a context (frs. 41, 166). Other figures belong to the realm of popular superstition. Hecate is a source of humorous possession (frs. 3, 4A), and we meet bogies like Mormoluka and Epial(t)es (frs. 4B, 67–8). Ritual practices (again in frs. 3, 4A) are also those of personal, low-level religion; here too belongs the superstitious chewing of thorn-leaves to ward off evil (fr. 165). But there is no evidence that any of this was satirical; Sophron's characters occupy the religious sphere which they would have thought had most direct impact on their lives. State cult, like the Olympian gods, is something distant. There is nothing like the comic portrayal of gods we find in Epicharmus or Attic comedy. Equally distant is the world of heroic myth; the Trojans and Ajax only appear (in a less than creditable story) as a comparison for little boys throwing sticks and leaves at a group of men (fr. 31).

Interestingly, Sophron's world closely recalls that of Hipponax's iambi, where we find the same obsession with sexual activity, scatology, and bawdy and boisterous behaviour. Evidence for the invective element which characterizes iambus is lacking in Sophron, but Xenarchus' mockery of the people of Rhegium indicates that personal abuse would not be out of place in the mimes. Certainly we would expect Sophron to have known Hipponax's poems, and we cannot rule out the possi-bility that he was influenced by him; he will not, however, have been a direct model. More directly important, perhaps, are the non-mythological dramas (he will not himself have called them comedies)[13] of Epicharmus, written a generation before Sophron.[14] We have few substantial fragments of these, but cer-

---

[11] Cf. e.g. Ar. *Vesp.* 60; see Olson on Ar. *Pax* 741; G. K. Galinsky, *The Heracles Theme* (Oxford, 1971), 81–100.

[12] Cf. e.g. Pi. *N*. 1. 3.

[13] U. von Wilamowitz-Moellendorff, *Einleitung in die griechische Tragödie* (Berlin, 1889), 55; West, *Studies*, 34.

[14] See the brief discussion in Kerkhof, 129–33; Epicharmus' gods and heroes were also probably presented as ordinary folk (cf. Kerkhof, 128).

tain titles are reminiscent of those we find in Sophron. His
*Robberies* (Ἁρπαγαί) satirized deceitful female soothsayers (cf.
Sophr. fr. 3?), and we know of two debate poems, one of which,
*Earth and Sea*, recalls Sophron's debate between the fisherman
and the countryman. Common comic types appeared; parasites
allegedly made their first entry into Greek literature here (frs.
31–4),[15] and Athenaeus says he was the first to bring a drunkard
onto the stage (10. 429 A). One poem (*Thearoi*) contained people
commenting on the contents of a sanctuary (fr. 68), perhaps as
Sophron's [*Women watching the Isthmia*] did. Sophron clearly
will have known Epicharmus' work, and with more material
from both authors we could probably make closer connections.
But we cannot doubt that Sophron also had much that was
original.

　　Simple mimetic performances were a common feature of
Greek popular culture. From Sosibius[16] we hear of Spartan
performers called δ(ε)ικηλιcταί (ὡϲ ἄν τιϲ cκευοποιοὺϲ εἴπηι καὶ
μιμητάϲ, says Athenaeus; 'or, as one might say maskers and
mummers'),[17] who 'in vulgar language' (ἐν εὐτελεῖ τῆι λέξει)
would imitate someone stealing fruit or a foreign doctor.
Athenaeus' gloss of the Laconian word as μιμηταί is particularly
interesting. The fruit-stealer intriguingly recalls Hipponax's
portrayal of himself as a thief in his iambi (frs. 3a, 32, 79).[18] A
corrupt entry in Hesychius refers to another Spartan performer,
who wore grotesque women's masks and sang songs.[19] Such
simple performances no doubt featured in most areas. They are

---

[15] However, the report (fr. 33) that he actually used the word παράcιτοc is
almost certainly wrong (cf. Kerkhof, 165–71; G. Arnott, *GRBS* 9 (1968), 161–8;
Pickard-Cambridge, 273).

[16] *FGrH* 595 F 7, cited by Athen. 14. 621 D–F.

[17] Athenaeus provides various local terms which he equates with δικηλιcταί:
Cικυώνιοι μὲν γὰρ φαλλοφόρουϲ αὐτοὺϲ καλοῦcιν, ἄλλοι δὲ αὐτοκαβδάλουϲ, οἳ δὲ
φλύακαϲ, ὡϲ Ἰταλοί, cοφιcτὰϲ δὲ οἱ πολλοί. But his account of *autokabdaloi* and
*phallophoroi* (following the Delian historian Semus' *On Paeans, FGrH* 396 F 24)
points to a somewhat different type of theatrical performer (though it is
interesting that Semus says the *phallophoroi* wore garlands, women's robes, and
masks representing drunken men); cf. Pickard-Cambridge, 140 f.

[18] Pollux (4. 104) also mentions a Spartan dance which imitated men caught
in the act of stealing stale meat; cf. Pickard-Cambridge, 136.

[19] Hesych. β 1245 βρυλλιχιcταί· οἱ αἰcχρὰ προcωπεῖα περιτιθέμενοι γυναικεῖα καὶ
ὕμνουϲ ἄιδοντεϲ; also Hsch. (β 1243) βρυδαλίχα· πρόcωπον γυναικεῖον. παρὰ τὸ
γελοῖον καὶ αἰcχρὸν †ορροϲ τίθεται †ὀρίνθω τὴν ὀρχίcτραν καὶ γυναικεῖα ἱμάτια
ἐνδέδυται. ὅθεν καὶ τὰϲ †μαχρὰc βρυδαλίχαϲ καλοῦcι Λάκωνεϲ (previously Kaibel's
*Rhinthon* fr. 16, but see K. Latte, *Kleine Schriften* (Munich, 1968), 677 f.).

doubtless connected with later performers such as the magodist, a reciter of verse who, according to Aristoxenus (fr. 110 Wehrli), acted both male and female roles. Agathocles (ap. Athen. 14. 621 CD) adds that the magodist acted female roles in male costume, which probably means that he did not wear a costume or mask, but relied on characterization solely by voice and gesture. The characterization of figures in performances of iambus, such as the carpenter Charon (the speaker of Archil. fr. 19) or the girl in the Cologne Epode (Archil. fr. 196a) may have been similarly achieved, although both these figure are part of a wider narrative frame. Athenaeus comments that the magodists performed to the music of cymbals and tambourines, and that they portrayed, amongst other things, women playing the role of adulteresses, or pimps, or men going drunken to a komos. This all sounds rather like what we expect from Sophron.

But, by contrast, Sophron's mimes were primarily literary in character. It is scarcely credible that they would have survived, and received literary attention from Hellenistic and later scholarship (below, Sect. V. A), had they been simple little pieces of the sort outlined above. They were probably therefore intended for sympotic performance. Xenarchus' mocking of the Rhegians sounds suspiciously like sympotic entertainment for Dionysius' court, and we may perhaps further compare the erotic pantomimic ballet, described by Xenophon (*Symp.* 9. 2–7), depicting the love of Ariadne and Dionysus. The imagined context of individual mimes can of course vary. The setting for the purification of fr. 4A is indoors; the action in other mimes also probably took place inside (e.g. the sympotic revelry of *Busied about the Bride*; the seamstresses of frs. 1–2 chatting, perhaps over their work). An indoors setting is similarly provided for most of Herodas' mimiambi. Attic comedy, where the action always takes place outside, provides an interesting contrast. Of course none of this necessarily has any impact on actual performance, but it is hard to believe they were produced on a public stage.[20] Probably they were recited by only one or two people.[21] Some mimes may have

[20] Despite Solin. 5. 13 *quidquid Sicilia gignit sive soli sive hominis ingenio, proximum est his quae optima iudicantur . . . hic primum inventa comoedia, hic et cavillatio mimica in scaena stetit* (test. 12 K–A), who is making an unjustifiable inference from the mime of his own day.

[21] Troupes of mime-actors proper are first attested in the 3rd cent. BC; cf. C. Watzinger, *Ath. Mitt.* 26 (1901), 1–8.

been simple monologues, but dialogue is attested in several fragments. While a single reciter may occasionally have played two (or more) parts, this seems less probable for lengthier conversations. The poems of Sophron's later imitators, Theocritus and Herodas, may also have been meant, at least in part, for sympotic recitation,[22] and we hear of mimic presentations at dinners in Plutarch's day (*Quaest. Conviv.* 712 E).[23]

Aristotle's grouping of the mimes with Socratic dialogue may suggest that they were largely read by his time. Possibly they were never widely performed outside Sicily or long after Sophron's death. Sympotic presentation of course means that props, if used at all, will have been kept to a minimum; the materials mentioned for the purification of fr. 4A, like the magician's assistants, will have been imagined. The use of stage-properties seems to have been restricted even in some later stage-mime.[24]

Sophron's mimes are thus a long way from those later stage-plays which also go by the name μῖμος. Mime (with pantomime) was the most popular performance-genre throughout the Roman period, although, or perhaps because, it was associated with scurrility and obscenity. (As early as the second century BC, we hear, though in the unreliable Valerius Maximus (2. 10. 8), who was writing in the second century AD, of Roman mime-actresses performing a sort of strip-tease at the Floralia.) But these performances have little directly in common with Sophron's literary exercises.

[22] Sympotic performance for Theocritus and Herodas is the attractive suggestion of A. Cameron, *Callimachus and his Critics* (Princeton, 1995), 89–90. An argument can be made that their poems were meant in the first instance for a reading public (cf. Hunter, 11; Hutchinson, 241), but limited sympotic recitation or performance should not be ruled out on that account (see also R. L. Hunter, *Antichthon*, 27 (1993), 31–44, who thinks Herodas' mimes may have been staged; G. Mastromarco, *The Public of Herondas* (Amsterdam, 1984), also argues for more elaborate staging).

[23] Much has been made of Plutarch's distinction between two types of mime, called ὑποθέσεις and παίγνια, the first of which has prolonged action and numerous stage-properties, the second mainly concerned with low and trivial comedy (consequently neither is appropriate for performance at symposia); it is doubtful whether this has any relevance for Sophron. J. Davidson in D. Harvey and J. Wilkins (eds.), *The Rivals of Aristophanes* (Swansea, 2000), 41–64, argues that παίγνιον can refer to a type of 'lyrical mime' as early as the 5th cent.; but see my 'Gnesippus and the Rivals of Aristophanes', *CQ²* (forthcoming).

[24] Cf. P. Berol. 13927 (5th/6th cent. AD), a list of mime-titles with the stage-properties they require.

Several papyrus texts dating from the first century BC onwards have been more or less plausibly ascribed to Greek mime of this period.[25] Some of these are verse; others are prose and thus have a stronger claim to be considered mimic. One, an ostracon of the first or second century BC, portrays a drunken man trying to set out on a komos, while being restrained by a sober companion (*mim. fr.* 3). A second short prose fragment, heavily mutilated, apparently also involves a drunkard (*mim. fr.* 2). A longer prose monologue of the second century AD found in Oxyrhynchus has a scheming mistress trying to force one of her slaves to have sex with her; there are some similarities here to Bitinna in Herodas 5. Later she attempts, with the assistance of a parasite, to poison her husband (*mim. fr.* 7). The same papyrus contains an elaborate stage-text for a farce (the 'Charition mime'; *mim. fr.* 6), mainly prose but with occasional verse elements, based in part on Euripides' *Iphigenia in Tauris*. This requires a large cast and complicated staging, and was clearly much longer than any of Sophron's pieces. Finally, a short fragment (*mim. fr.* 10) depicts a quarrel between several people, apparently about a girl (who has perhaps been assaulted?).[26] A chorus is required by the Charition mime, and perhaps also by fr. 10. The Charition mime has been partly rewritten, in a different hand from the main one, probably pointing to the use of the papyrus as a performance text. The verso of fr. 10 is inscribed ἐκ βιβλιοθή(κης) Πρασί(ου) Ἡρακλείδης ἀ[πέγραψεν (suppl. Milne); Page concludes that 'evidently the texts of these wretched and ephemeral pieces were circulated for the delectation of the reading public', but this Heraclides may instead have been a mime-actor or stage-manager. At any rate there are few close similarities to Sophron's mimes among these pieces, beyond those which belong to a common comic inheritance, and their social context is quite different.

---

[25] Ed. I. C. Cunningham, *Herodas. Mimiambi* (Leipzig, 1987).

[26] Partial translations of most fragments, with useful discussion, in Page, 332–3 (fr. 3), 336–61 (frs. 6 and 7), 362–6 (fr. 10); summary and brief discussion in Cunningham, *Herodas* (Oxford, 1971), 7–10; general treatment in H. Wiemken, *Der griechische Mimus* (Bremen, 1972).

## III. STYLE AND LANGUAGE

### A. *Style*

What is perhaps most striking about Sophron is his decision to write in prose rather than verse (previous prose writing being largely restricted to philosophical or historical investigation), and that he wrote in Doric. Although there was some tradition of Dorian prose in Magna Graecia,[27] the influence of Ionian prose writing was so strong that even Antiochus of Syracuse's history of Sicily was written in Ionic, as were the prose works of Pherecydes of Athens, and Acusilaus of Argos. The later shift in the focus for written culture in the later fifth century is exemplified by Gorgias, who, although an Ionian from Sicily, nevertheless writes in Attic. Sophron's use of Doric is defiantly vernacular.

What evidence we have for Dorian prose is now largely limited to inscriptions, both formal and informal, which have their own conventions (though even simple inscriptional formulae can show surprising variability);[28] they will tell us something about dialect, but little about stylistic features in Sophron. Better comparisons can be made with the Ionian prose of the early mythographers and philosophers; roughly contemporary, Ionian writing such as Herodotus, parts of the Hippocratic corpus, and the new Sicilian oratory; and fourth-century Attic prose, which developed under the influence of the Ionian tradition.[29] Interestingly, what little we can gather of Sophron's style shows points of contact with all these, but particularly with writers of highly artistic prose such as Gorgias.[30] Other elements recall the poetry of Epicharmus.

### (a) *Syntax*

The longer fragments show relatively simple and short syntactic structure. Evidently we should not expect the language of the market-place and tavern to approach the complexity of Thucydides[31] or Demosthenes. A fondness for occasional short

---

[27] Cf. A. Cassio, *Tra Sicilia e Magna Grecia* (Naples, 1989), 145–9.
[28] See Dover, 13 ff.
[29] Cf. Denniston, *Prose Style*, 5; Dover, 83–5.
[30] For the development of Gorgias' prose, see Norden, i. 15 ff.
[31] Though even Thucydides' sentences are built up of shorter, simpler elements; cf. Dover, 28.

clauses, less frequently for extended sequences of short clauses, also characterizes Platonic prose,[32] no doubt reflecting the liveliness and rapidity of everyday speech.

Sophron's clauses are largely paratactic; the most common particles are δέ and γάρ,[33] less often καί.[34] Other particles are few, and the same ones (mainly δή, θην,[35] ἄρα, and γα) recur with monotonous regularity. The use of emphatic particles declines in Hellenistic prose, probably reflecting a similar decline in their use in popular language.[36]

There are a few relative pronouns; subordination is more usually achieved through the use of participles, but is not on the whole common.

## (b) *Antithesis and Symmetry*

Antithetical phrasing, though carried to an extreme by Gorgias,[37] is a common feature of much Greek prose and verse. Sophron has few extant examples, but cf. e.g. fr. 49 τρίγλας μὲν γένηον / τριγόλα δ᾽ ὀπισθίδια. The device is very important to Epicharmus; e.g. frs. 40. 4 (ὄστρεια συμμεμυκότα) τὰ διελεῖν μέν ἐντι χαλεπά, καταφαγῆμεν δ᾽ εὐμαρέα, 6 (cκιφύδρια) τὰ γλυκέα μέν ἐντ᾽ ἐπέcθειν, ἐμπαγῆμεν δ᾽ ὀξέα; 47 νεῖν μὲν οὐκ ἴcαντι, πεζᾶι δ᾽ ἐμπορεύονται μόνοι; 49, 50, etc.

A related, but more frequently attested, stylistic trick is the symmetrical balancing of clauses, as in frs. 4A. 2–4 (λάζεcθε δὲ) ἁλὸς χονδρὸν ἐc τὰν χῆρα / καὶ δάφναν πὰρ τὸ ὦας, and 9–10 ἔχε καὶ τὸ δάιδιον / καὶ τὸ λιβανωτόν; *136 νῦν τ᾽ ἦνθεc . . . / νῦν τ᾽ ἔπραδεc (also with homoioteleuton in the last two cases). Cf. Epich. frs. 32. 1–2 cυνδειπνέων τῶι λῶντι, καλέcαι δεῖ μόνον, | καὶ τῶι γα μηδὲ λῶντι, κωὐδὲν δεῖ καλεῖν; 18. 2–4 βρέμει μὲν ὁ φάρυγξ ἔνδοθ᾽, ἀραβεῖ δ᾽ ἁ γνάθος, | ψοφεῖ δ᾽ ὁ γομφίος, τέτριγε δ᾽ ὁ κυνόδων, | cίζει δε ταῖc ῥίνεccι, κινεῖ δ᾽ οὔατα, etc.[38]

---

[32] Denniston, *Prose Style*, 60 f.

[33] For Sophron's use of γάρ, see on fr. 4A. 8.

[34] For καί in early prose, see Dover, 71 f.

[35] On θην, see fr. 23 n.

[36] See J. Blomqvist, *Greek Particles in Hellenistic Prose* (Lund, 1969), 132 ff. A similar decline in particle-use can be seen in some late classical lyric; see my *Timotheus*, 53–5.

[37] Cf. Denniston, *Prose Style*, 12 f.; Norden, i. 16–23.

[38] Cf. Berk, 43–5 (antithesis), 45–6 (symmetry).

## (c) *Rhyme*

Rhyme, another Gorgianic trick, seems important;[39] while some instances might be thought accidental, others do not look unintentional. Note the internal rhyme ὀρῆτε/cβῆτε at fr. 4A. 12–14 (also lines 9–10); triple end-rhyme together with alliteration of μεγα- at fr. *9 κύων πρὸ μεγαρέων μέγα ὑλακτέων; the homoioteleuton -ωμάτων in fr. 29;[40] also frs. 95, 100, 105, *136, etc.

Rhyme also appears to feature strongly in some of Epicharmus' poetry; again, though some instances could be claimed as accidental, it is hard not to see design in a case like the following:

> καὶ χελιδόνες τε μύρμαι θ᾽, οἵ τε κολιᾶν μέζονες
> ἐντὶ καὶ cκόμβρων, ἀτὰρ τᾶν θυννίδων γα μήονες.   (fr. 55)

Other simple examples may perhaps be furnished by Epich. frs. 41. 2–3 (cκιαθίδες / παλοκουρίδες), 48. 1 and 3 (Φοινικικοῖc / θεοῖc), or 53. 1–2 (κάμμαροι / ἄλκιμοι). We can also see a taste for assonant line-endings (e.g. χάλκιαι and χάλκιοι in fr. 68. 1–2, βατίc, βάτοc, and βατίc in fr. 79. 1–3, though the second case of βατίc may be an error).[41]

## (d) *Alliteration and Assonance*

Alliteration, often doubted as an effective device in Greek verse, but more convincingly attested in prose,[42] makes an occasional appearance; cf. e.g. frs. *9 μεγαρέων μέγα,[43] 15 δοῦcα ἀπόδοc, and the repeated gutterals (κ, χ) in frs. 24, 25, 28. At fr. 48 λοξῶν τὰc λογάδαc the alliteration may be intended to suggest a supposed etymology; for this trick in contemporary poetry, cf. e.g. Melanipp. *PMG* 759 καλεῖται δ᾽ ⟨εἵνεκ᾽⟩ ἐν κόλποιcι γαίαc | ἄχε᾽ εἷcιν προχέων Ἀχέρων, 761 ἐπώνυμον . . . οἶνον Οἰνέωc; Licymn. *PMG* 770(b) Ἀχέρων ἄχεα πορθμεύει βροτοῖcιν. In Epicharmus,

---

[39] Denniston, *Prose Style*, 10 f.
[40] Cf. Norden, i. 48 n. 2.
[41] The rhyming in [Epich.] fr. 279, which on linguistic grounds is the least objectionable of the fragments quoted by Alcimus (ap. Diog. Laert. 3. 9–16; see Kerkhof, 76 ff., for discussion, though he thinks fr. 279 a forgery), may support a case for authenticity.
[42] Denniston, *Prose Style*, 127; cf. my *Timotheus*, 171 (on *Pers.* 78).
[43] Repetition of initial syllables like this is especially characteristic of Gorgianic prose (Dover, 152).

the point of such assonance is often simply comic; e.g. fr. 48.3 καὶ
cκάρουc, τῶν οὐδὲ τὸ cκὰρ θεμιτὸν ἐκβαλεῖν θεοῖc.[44]

Especially notable is the occurrence of assonance and alliteration in certain proverbial expressions (e.g. frs. 73 μωρότεροc εἶ
Μορύχου; 147 τὸν ξύοντα ἀντιξύειν; 168 μοῖτον ἀντὶ μοίτου); a
similar feature can be observed in the proverbial phrase at Epich.
fr. 211 ἁ δὲ χεὶρ τὰν χεῖρα νίζει. Such jingles were doubtless a
common feature of popular sayings (cf. also Epich. fr. 233).

### (e) *Use of Popular Sayings*

Sophron's use of proverbs and popular sayings stood out even in
antiquity. Demetrius (*Eloc.* 156 = fr. 105) notes his tendency to
use multiple proverbs in the same passage, and claims that
almost all known proverbs could be collected from his plays,
though this is no doubt an exaggeration. Proverbs particularly
belong to comedy (including Epicharmus, who shares at least
one proverb with Sophron (Epich. fr. 152), and it seems likely
that there were others they both used), and to writers such as
Theocritus and Herodas; interestingly, they seem to have been
less common in iambus. In Sophron they perhaps aimed to
reproduce the banal sententiousness of popular wisdom, or add
an element of humour. Demetrius (loc. cit.) thought that they
were 'naturally charming', but most are quoted without a
context and the precise effect is difficult to gauge.[45]

### (f) *Intentional Solecisms*

The grammarian Philoxenus, the source for fragments 33 and
34, claims that Sophron deliberately made his speaker commit
grammatical solecisms (the false form ὑγιώτερον in fr. 33, a messy
hanging participle in fr. 34) in order to imitate popular (female)
speech, which tends to be sloppy and frequently ungrammatical.
This intention doubtless also underlies the comic superlative
φωρτάτουc in fr. 1 (though Philoxenus sees no literary artifice
here), and may be responsible for other grammatically suspect
fragments (e.g. fr. 117).

The Greeks found the solecisms committed by non-native

---

[44] Cf. Berk, 47.

[45] Particularly common is the formation, adjective + genitive of comparison
(frs. 33, 62, 63, *103, 156?, 169); cf. P. Martin, *Studien auf dem Gebiete des
griechischen Sprichwort* (Progr./Diss., Gymn. zu Plauen i. V, 1889), 11.

Greek-speakers funny. Foreign characters also appeared in the mimes: the slave-girl Koikoa was a barbarian, and Sophron seems to make her produce false forms in some of the passages quoted by Demetrius (fr. 16). However, there seems to be nothing on the scale of the barbarized speech of Aristophanes' Scythian archer in *Thesmophoriazusae* or the terrified Celaenaean in Timotheus' *Persians*, whose utterance is a comedy of errors.[46]

## (g) *Prose Rhythm*

Thrasymachus of Chalcedon, a contemporary of Gorgias, was credited with the invention of 'prose rhythm'; we can see the impact it made in his own time in Plato's parody at *Phaedr.* 267 CD, and perhaps in the ornate rhythms of Agathon's speech in the *Symposium.*[47] It is certainly possible that Sophron was influenced by him, and various attempts have been made to identify prose rhythms in Sophron. However, while in several fragments homoioteleuton or symmetrical phrasing may point to natural divisions within sentences,[48] meaningful cola, such as we find in the later Asiatic style or in the elaborate rhythms of Ciceronic clausulae,[49] are difficult to identify. The problem is further complicated by the absence of any metrical controls to aid the analysis; we do not know, for instance, whether hiatus was permitted (e.g. in fr. 3), how stop + liquid combinations were treated, whether correption was admitted, and so on. Since early Greek prose will have taken poetry as a partial model, occasional metrical reminiscences, such as the dactylic rhythms in fr. 41, ought not to surprise. Anapaestic and dactylic rhythms can be identified in the prose of Pherecydes of Syros, possibly the earliest Greek literary prose to survive,[50] and we should expect to find similar passages in Sophron; but this not the same thing at all as having a technical theory or practice of prose rhythm.

In fact, the idea that Sophron wrote rhythmical prose essentially derives from Aristotle's grouping of the mimes with

---

[46] See my *Timotheus*, 204–8, with the references there.
[47] Cf. Norden, i. 43–4; Dover, 44, 169–70.
[48] Norden, i. 48; E. Hauler, *Verhandlungen der 42. Versamml. deutsch. Philol. u. Schulmänner in Wien* (Leipzig, 1894), 258. For peculiar and messy attempts to analyse some fragments metrically, see G. Perrotta, *SIFC* 22 (1947), 93–100, and, more recently, A. Saija, *Aegyptus*, 67 (1987), 27–32.
[49] Denniston, *Prose Style*, 13–14.
[50] Dover, 161–2.

Socratic dialogue (*Poet.* 1. 1447ᵇ10), and his statement in his *On Poets* that Plato's dialogues were half-way between prose and verse (fr. 73 R.³).[51] It is not at all clear that these two passages should be taken together to imply anything about prose rhythms in Sophron. In the *Poetics* Aristotle is simply talking about the difference between non-metrical (mime, Socratic dialogue) and metrical mimesis, and for him mimesis is the defining quality of 'poetry'; thus Empedocles, though he wrote in verse, is for Aristotle a natural philosopher rather than a poet. By contrast, Philodemus, probably arguing against the otherwise unknown Heracleodorus, wishes to restrict the use of the word ποήματα to metrical works, and so is particularly keen to refute the view that Sophron wrote 'verses'.[52] Heracleodorus took an extreme view of the works of Herodotus and Demosthenes as ποήματα since he defined a πόημα by its use of word-order and euphony rather than by metrical form; there is no evidence that he believed Sophron's works metrical.

## B. *Language*

Sicily was a linguistic melting-pot. The pre-Greek Sicels spoke a language which was probably Indo-European, perhaps connected with Illyrian (itself a shadowy tongue) or Italic (Thuc. 6. 2. 4 makes them come to Sicily from Italy). Trade no doubt brought influences from mainland Italy; colonization and conquest brought Phoenician and divers forms of Greek. But Sophron's native dialect will have been that form of West Greek current in Syracuse, ultimately deriving from Corinthian, though with several local elements.

There are relatively few surviving Syracusan inscriptions from the early period; what there is tends to be short, and often uninformative. Much the same can be said of the early Corinthian evidence.[53] Corinth forms a linguistic bloc with

[51] Cf. Norden, i. 44 ff. A scholion to Gregory of Nazianzus (6th cent. AD) says that the latter imitated Sophron in his use of poetic rhythms and cola; whoever is the source for this statement almost certainly had no direct access to Sophron's text.

[52] See R. Janko, *Philodemus. On Poems I* (Oxford, 2001), 155–9, and his comments on 1. 199 ff. The various ancient sources which refer to Sophron as a ποιητής (cf. Kassel–Austin on test. 19), or to his works as δράματα (cf. fr. 105), will ultimately depend on the Aristotelian usage.

[53] Cf. Bechtel, ii. 209–12.

Phleius, Cleonae, and Sicyon, and additional inscriptional evidence comes from these sites, and from Corinthian colonies like Corcyra. However, when dealing with material from the later period we must allow for elements intruding from Koine or other dialects,[54] and even early inscriptions are not necessarily dialectally consistent.[55] Many fragments of Sophron and Epicharmus are quoted by our sources, particularly the grammatical writings of Apollonius Dyscolus, as evidence for Syracusan or wider Sicilian Doric usage. But often this will mean little more than that the word or form was attested in their works. Few grammarians had access to much other material. Nevertheless, their general assumption is that Sophron, though writing in a literary manner, did not use a literary dialect like that found in Greek poetry, and his language certainly shows marked divergence from the literary Doric of, for example, Stesichorus and Pindar. Some features can be paralleled from Theocritus, who wrote a literary Doric with Syracusan/West Greek elements. Closer is Epicharmus, but his language contains elements foreign to Syracusan; most of these seem to derive from epic or Rhodian (e.g. infinitives in -μειν), the latter probably due to influence from Gela, which was a Rhodian foundation.[56] There are, perhaps surprisingly, no obviously Rhodian elements in Sophron.

One particular problem faces us when looking at Sophron's dialect. Poetic texts have metrical controls which can guarantee one form against another; thus, we can tell that Epicharmus wrote μέcαι at fr. 122. 6, rather than μέccαι as we would expect, because the metre demands the first form. No such guarantees are offered for a prose author. An additional difficulty is raised by the question of the alphabet. Greek alphabets differed widely from region to region in the archaic period and classical periods. Many of these did not distinguish orthographically between the three *e*- or *o*-sounds. Thus, in Athens only in the late fifth century was a script, East Ionian in origin, adopted which could distinguish between ε, η, and the 'spurious diphthong' ει (to be distinguished from genuine diphthongs written in the same way): all had previously been represented by the same letter. The

---

[54] The later Corinthian inscriptions have considerable Koine admixture (Buck, 165).  [55] Dover, 86.

[56] Bechtel, ii. 213; but see Cassio's recent doubts (pp. 54–5).

same applied to the three equivalent *o*-sounds. We do not know what an early Syracusan text will have looked like. While Corinthian inscriptions show early use of orthographic equivalents to *EI* and *OY* for the spurious diphthongs, the simple forms (equivalent to *E* and *O*) are still used to represent two different sounds (ϵ and η, o and ω). It is hard to doubt that Sophron will have written in his local alphabet; one presumes, therefore, that at some stage the mimes must have been rewritten in the East Ionic alphabet which became standard for later Greek soon after it was adopted in Athens. That there were errors in transcription is by no means inconceivable, and the recovery of original forms thus often uncertain.[57]

In what follows I largely note only the most significant differences from Attic-Ionic. Further individual points will be found scattered throughout the commentary.

## (a) *Phonology*

### 1. *Vowels*

(i) Original *ā* is retained throughout as in all dialects outside Attic-Ionic.

(ii) -ϵo- is usually uncontracted (as in Epicharmus); instances of ov for ϵo and ϵv are probably mostly due to influence from the later Koine on manuscript transmission. A shift from ϵo to ϵv is also a feature of other Doric dialects (e.g. Megarian, Delphian, and others), and is attested as early as the sixth century BC in Corinthian in the name Θϵυγένϵϲ;[58] instances of ϵv in the MSS of Sophron (e.g. fr. 36 δϵυμένα, and doublets such as τϵῦϲ alongside τέoϲ) may thus be genuine.

(iii) ϵ + ϵ produces η in fr. 11 προῆχϵ, where *s* originally separated the vowels, but ϵι in θωκϵῖτϵ (frs. 4A. 6, where it is corrected in the papyrus from -ῆτϵ; 60), ἐϲϲϵῖϲθαι (fr. 57), ὠναϲϵῖται (fr. 121), and in Epich. fr. 153 πνιξϵῖϲθϵ, where the vowels were originally separated by a glide (*y*).

(iv) ϵ + η is uncontracted in fr. 155 δϵήϲϵι, but contracted to η in the same verb at fr. 45 δῆϲθϵ.

(v) α + ϵ > η (e.g. frs. 4A. 13 ὁρῆτϵ, 20 ἐλωβῆτο), as generally in West Greek dialects (Bechtel, ii. 224).

---

[57] See also Cassio's brief but excellent discussion (pp. 58–62) of the problem in relation to Epicharmus.      [58] Bechtel, ii. 221–2.

(vi) ε + α > η in some West Greek dialects, and appears e.g. in frs. 113 δελήτιον,[59] 24 κρῆς = Att. κρέας.[60]

(vii) Secondary ε̄ and ō ('spurious diphthongs' caused by lengthening and represented in Attic and several other dialects by ει and ου, elsewhere by η and ω) are largely represented in the MSS as ει and ου (fr. 4A. 3 has χῆρα < *χεϲρ-,[61] but fr. 15 χειρὸϲ; forms with ει are standard in Epicharmus, but there is inscriptional evidence for forms with η[62]). In Corinthian, the pronunciation of secondary ε̄ and ō coalesced very early with original ει and ου due to monophthongization of the diphthongs (Buck, 30–1).

(viii) Occasionally the long vowels η and ω are shortened in hiatus with short *o*; fr. 118 χρέομαι < χρήομαι (and cf. Theocr. 2. 5 ζοοί, Epich. fr. 53. 2 λαγοί < *λαγοοί < λαγωϝοί).

(ix) Crasis: the crasis of καὶ + ἐ- produces η rather than Attic ᾱ (frs. 11 κἤπειτα, 52 κἠγώ, 115 κἠπιθυϲιῶμες).[63] In the quotation at fr. 16C, Demetrius twice (or perhaps thrice) writes this crasis as κά-. This could easily be emended, but since the speaker is almost certainly the barbarian slave-girl Koikoa, it is tempting to see them as deliberate errors (see ad loc.).

## 2. *Consonants*

(i) Fr. 136 ἦνθεϲ = ἦλθεϲ. -νθ- for -λθ- (not a general feature of West Greek, but common to some West Greek dialects, including Corcyran)[64] in the aorist forms of ἔρχομαι also occurs at Epich. fr. 97. 7, 11 (papyrus; ἦλθεν is transmitted in the MSS at fr. 213), and in Theocritus. It occasionally occurs in other words (Epich. fr. 49. 2 φίντάται = φίλτ-;[65] Theocr. 5. 76 βέντιϲτοϲ = βέλτ-).

---

[59] Cf. Alcman (?) *PMGF* 167 βλῆρ = Att. δέλεαρ.
[60] Epicharmus has the uncontracted form in frs. 84 κρέαϲ, 122. 2 κρέα, in both cases required by the metre. But κρῆϲ is Doric, again supported by the metre, at Ar. *Ach.* 795 (the Megarian is speaking), and possibly at Theocr. 1. 6, where MSS have κρῆϲ, but editors print κρέαϲ, the latter slightly favoured by the metre (see Colvin, 177, 243; Hunter ad loc.).
[61] Cf. Lesb. χέρρεϲ.
[62] Buck, 28–9; Thumb–Kieckers, 211; Bechtel, ii. 229.
[63] Buck, 80; Thumb–Kieckers, 212. Thumb–Kieckers see a distinction in Epicharmus between the crases formed by καὶ + ἐ- in open and closed syllables, noting that MSS have κέμβάφια at fr. 63 (closed syllable); Ahrens emends to κῆ-, which Kassel–Austin print. The crasis is written κῆ- in the MSS at fr. 60 κῆκτραπελογάϲτοραϲ.         [64] Buck, 64–5.
[65] Cf. the Syracusan name Φίντων (Bechtel, ii. 236).

(ii) Where Attic, and usually Ionic, has c from original τy and θy in ὄcoc, ὁπόcoc, μέcoc, most dialects, including Corinthian, have cc; cf. fr. 112 ὄccωι, Epich. frs. 68. 4 ὄccον(?), 114 ὄcca. We find ὄca at frs. 31 and 87, probably the result of later scribal normalization. Epicharmus, however, writes μέcaι at fr. 122. 6, and the metre precludes cc; the form, presumably here chosen essentially for metrical reasons, will obviously have been known to Epicharmus from epic, whose influence on his language is attested by various other forms.[66]

(iii) Original χy, κy produce ττ in Attic (so also in Cretan, Boeotian, and at least parts of Euboean), cc in Ionic and West Greek; Sophron has cc in frs. 80 ἧccων (Att. ἥττων), 112 δαδύccεcθε.

(iv) ρc > ρρ in frs. 59, 116 κάρρων and Epich. fr. 163 κάρρονεc; Epich. fr. 223 has θαρρεῖ (not θάρcει). Early inscriptions show ρρ and ρc existing side by side (Bechtel, ii. 235).

## (b) *Morphology*

(i) Dative plurals of the o-stems are formed in -οιc.[67]

(ii) The dative plural of the consonant stems is -εccι (frs. **8, 124, 151; cf. Epich. fr. 18. 4),[68] characteristic of Aeolic and some Doric dialects, and attested in Cyrenaean and various Corinthian colonies (Buck, 89), where it may have an Aeolic origin (cf. Thuc. 4. 42. 2 on Aeolic elements in Corinth, though the presence of an 'Aeolic substrate' in the Peloponnese in general is much disputed).

(iii) Personal Pronouns: common to West Greek and literary Doric are the genitives in -εοc[69] (expanded from the forms in -εο) and datives in -ιν. Forms in -εν probably derive from earlier -ειο, which by loss of iota becomes εο > εν (as in Ionic; the contraction produces Att. ον). Unattested in Sophron are the West Greek

---

[66] Cf. Bechtel, ii. 233–4.

[67] Epicharmus has a few cases of -οιcι (frs. 48, 53, 99); the presence of -οιcι in Cretan shows it could be Doric, so it may be correct for Syracusan of the early 5th cent. (Bechtel, ii. 249) or perhaps due to epic influence. There is no attestation in Sophron.

[68] This probably develops from universalizing the dat. pl. ending -εc-cι of the s-stems. Buck (p. 89) mentions the possibility that -εccι derives from analogy to the dat. pl. endings of the first and second declensions (-αιcι, -οιcι), taking them as if formed on the nom. pl. -αι, -οι; but in this case we might expect the neuters to produce a dative -*α-cι.

[69] Cf. also ἐμίωc and τίωc in Rhinth. fr. 10 (Tarentum).

enclitics in -οι (Buck, 98). There are various doublets; at least some of these may have existed side by side (τέος, τεῦ, etc.) where they do not result from Koine influence in later manuscripts.

(*a*)  1st-pers. sg.: N. ἐγών (but ἐγώ once at fr. 52); A. ἐμέ (also με at frs. 28, \*171. 4);[70] G. ἐμεῦ (and ἐμέος, ἐμεῦς in Epicharmus; also ἐμοῦς under influence from later Koine), μεθέν (fr. 19)[71] is an oddity which Apollonius quotes to illustrate Syracusan ἐμέθεν (see ad loc.); D. ἐμίν, μοι.

(*b*)  2nd-pers. sg.: N. τύ; A. τυ (from the nominative);[72] G. τέος, τεοῦς,[73] τεοῦ (and τεῦς in Epicharmus, at Theocr. 2. 126, in a poem based on Sophron, and elsewhere: see Gow ad loc.). Dative coι is attested in fr. 16A, parallel to μοι, if this is not normalized, a paraphrase, or deliberately non-Doric; we would also expect a dative τίν, like ἐμίν.[74]

(*c*)  3rd-pers. sg.: A. νιν; D. οἱ.

(*d*)  1st and 2nd-pers. pl.: ἁμές, ἁμέ; ὑμές, ὑμέ, as in all dialects outside Att.-Ion. (-εις, -έας > -ᾶς). Uncontracted genitive ὑμέων at frs. 45, 85.

(*e*)  3rd-pers. pl.: A. ψε; D. ψιν (perhaps produced by metathesis of the consonants in the familiar forms, cφε and cφιν).[75] Epicharmus has fr. 113. 381 ψε (papyrus) alongside fr. 108. 2 cφιν. At fr. 86 Apollonius says ὦν is equivalent to αὐτῶν; however, Wilamowitz (*Kl. Schr.* II. 134 n. 1) thinks this an error, and reads ὧν (= οὖν).

(iv) Reflexive Pronouns: combinations of αὐτός used reflexively are a feature of several West Greek dialects (Buck, 99). Fr. 18 has αὐταυτᾶς = ἐμαυτῆς. This form of intensified pronoun is widely attested for Corinthian, and especially Sicilian, dialects; Archytas of Tarentum has αὐταύτου and αὔταυτον (DK

---

[70]  Epicharmus also has ἐμεί (fr. 140); cf. Alcm. *PMGF* 70(b) τεί.

[71]  Forms in -θεν are also in literary Lesbian (ἐμέθεν, cέθεν, Ϝέθεν), Homer (alongside the other genitive forms; cf. Chantraine, *Grammaire* i. 243–4), and in Epidaurian inscriptions (Bechtel, ii. 254).

[72]  Buck, 98. The accusative is enclitic according to Apollonius (= Sophr. fr. 78); cf. Epich. fr. 34. 1, Ar. *Eq.* 1225 (a line in Doric probably taken from Eupolis' *Helots*). In fr. 77 τυ for τοι (Bekker) may be correct.

[73]  Cf. Theocr. 11. 25, 18. 41.

[74]  τίν is also dative in Alcman and Pindar.

[75]  Buck, 74. Theocr. 4. 3 also has ψε, said by the scholia (p. 135 W.) to be Doric, and in a papyrus at 15. 80 (spoken by a Syracusan in Alexandria; codd. cφε).

47 B 2, 3), though both are conjectures, and in inscriptions Heraclea and Aegina have αὔταυτον.[76] Twice we find such intensified forms in the Pseudepicharmea (frs. 244. 16; 278. 7).

(v) The Article: the nominative plural definite articles are τοί, ταί (common to West Greek). The masculine genitive singular is twice τῶ (frs. 56, 86), but τοῦ elsewhere (frs. 82, 96, *171?), with corresponding genitive endings for nominal forms. Epicharmus has τῶ in papyrus at fr. 135. 1, but τοῦ, also in papyrus, at fr. 113. 249 and fr. 186.

(vi) The demonstrative τῆνος (fr. 56; rather than (ἐ)κειν-, κῆν-) is usual in Sicilian Doric literature (as in Delphian, Megarian, Argolic, and Heraclean; Buck, 101).[77] οὗτος has an unusual feminine οὗτα in fr. 4A. 8; but Corinna has οὗταν (*PMG* 654 iii 4) and the neut. pl. οὗτα is attested in inscriptions. The masc. pl. is τοῦτοι at fr. 23.

(vii) Verbs:

(a) 1st-pers. pl. -μες instead of -μεν.

(b) 3rd-pers. pl. -ντι (e.g. frs. 31 βαλλίζοντι not -ουσι; 24 κεχάναντι). The corresponding form of the verb 'to be' ἐντί (= εἰσί) is found at frs. 23, 25, but fr. 154 has εἰσιν (restored to ἐντι by Botzon (1867), 19).

(c) The 'Doric Future' in -σέω (and medio-passive -σέομαι/ -σοῦμαι) is largely confined to West Greek; cf. fr. 57 ἐσσεῖσθαι < *ἐσ-σέ-εσθαι (ἐσσεῖται is also Homeric; cf. [Epich.] fr. 280. 2) against Attic ἔσεσθαι (i.e. ἔσομαι).

(d) The subjunctive of εἶμι, εἴω (fr. 47) rather than ἴω, can be compared to Gortyn. ἐνσείει, Hom. φήηι (not φῆι), Boeot. καθιστάει, Delph. διδώη.[78]

(c) *Other Features*

(i) Apocope (loss of the final vowel) of κατά and ποτί before a dental (frs. 4A. 1 κάτθετε, 5 πὸτ τάν etc.) is particularly common in West Greek dialects and Doric generally (cf. esp. Epich. frs. 31. 2, 51. 1, 88. 3 κατθέμειν, 74 ποτθιγεῖν etc.). Apocope of other prepositions also occurs (e.g. frs. 4A. 4 πὰρ τό; 162 ἀνδούμενοι).

[76] Bechtel, ii. 255–6.
[77] Epich. fr. 88. 2 has accusative κῆνον, which is suspect, though less so in Epicharmus than it would be in Sophron. Cf. Gow on Theocr. 7. 104.
[78] Thumb–Kieckers, 215; Bechtel, ii. 264.

(ii)  Adverbs:

(a)  in -ει (πεῖ, εἴ; cf. Epich. frs. 32. 3, 97. 16 τηνεῖ) are generally the West Greek equivalent of Att.-Ion. forms in -ου.

(b)  in -υc (πῦc; cf. Epich. fr. 97. 11 ὕcπερ) are found in Argolic (*IG* 4. 498. 4 πῦc) and Rhodian (ὅπυc), though are not otherwise attested for West Greek. The form πῦc at fr. 75, though doubted by Ahrens, could nevertheless be correct. Related forms in -υι are found in Cyrenaean and other Doric dialects, and in Lesbian (τυίδε; cf. also Hes. *Op.* 635). See also fr. 75 n.

(c)  in -ω (with ablatival sense); cf. αὐτῶ, πῶ, τουτῶ. By contrast, in Epicharmus adverbs in -ω are instrumental (πώποκα, ὧδε).

(iii)  West Greek -κα = Att.-Ion. and Arc.-Cypr. -τε, Lesb. -τα; cf. frs. 15, 23 ποκά (also οὔποκα, τόκα in Epicharmus). ὅκκα < ὅκα κα is only attested in literary sources (Epich. frs. 26, 131, 163; Sophr. fr. 45; anon. Dor. fr. 17).

## (d) *Lexicon*

We might expect Sophron's language to display various lexical elements from Sicel, Punic, or Italic, just as we find various items of Asiatic vocabulary in Hipponax. However, this is not generally the case. κάρκαρον (fr. 145 = Lat. *carcer*; cf. Rhinth. fr. 17) and πατάνα (fr. 12; cf. Lat. *patina*) could be Sicel, borrowed thence into Italic and Greek, or possibly Italic borrowings into Greek (the etymologies are unclear),[79] and a series of words for weights and coins have Italic cognates; cf. ὀγκία (the usual form in Sophron and Epicharmus; other sources have οὐγγία or οὐκγία) ~ Lat. *uncia*; λίτρα and Lat. *liber* both probably derive from an earlier Italic *liθra; νούμμος (νόμος is the form in Sophron and Epicharmus) ~ Lat. *nummus*; Sicilian μοῖτον (fr. 168) ~ Lat. *mutuum*.[80] Most are probably in origin Sicel words which spread

[79]  For a brief discussion of the problem, see L. R. Palmer, *The Latin Language* (London, 1954), 43–6. Bechtel, ii. 286, thinks *patina* is borrowed into Latin from Greek; Epicharmus used the word πατάνεψις 'dressed in a πατάνα' (fr. 216).

[80]  Latinate forms are more noticeable in Rhinthon and other later Sicilian/Italian Greek authors; cf. e.g. πάνια or πανία (Rhinth. fr. 1 = Blaesus fr. 1 = Dinolochus fr. 6; cf. Messapian πανός) < *panis* or *pane*; κάλτοι (Rhinth. fr. 5) < *calcei* (?); φαινόλα (Rhinth. fr. 7) < *paenula*. κράββατον (Rhinth. fr. 11) is a loanword of uncertain origin, but Lat. *grabatum*, *grabatus* is probably a borrowing through Greek.

to Greek and Latin through trade. Punic has left almost no trace, although Maas suggests a Punic (or Italic) origin for ϲιληπορδεῖν (fr. 163).[81]

There are numerous *hapax legomena*; mostly these are simple dialectal variants belonging to Syracusan. Many are just different forms of familiar words, brought about by metathesis (e.g. δρίφοϲ for δίφροϲ, or the vocalic metathesis in fr. 110 βιπτάζω for βαπτίζω; cf. Epich. fr. 177 κοκρύδεϲ for κροκύδεϲ) or other familiar linguistic processes. Others are lexical alternatives based on familiar stems but with different formations, either verbal (e.g. fr. 4. 16 πυκταλ-εύω for πυκταλ-ίζω) or substantival (e.g. κυαθίϲ for κύαθοϲ). These may also have been current in mainland dialects like Corinthian or related West Greek dialects, but the evidence is lacking. Most do not belong to the category of words we expect to find in formal or even informal inscriptions, and thus we cannot know whether they were usual in Syracusan or even there thought to be more typical of lower-class speech.

(e) *Accentuation*

Doric accentuation is a thorny problem. We have various statements in ancient grammatical sources which provide a limited account, and some papyri of Dorian poetry are partly accented, though not always consistently.[82] But we know too little to provide a complete account; what follows is restricted to the most important points outlined by the grammarians.

(i) In Attic-Ionic a long accented penult is properispomenon when the vowel of the last syllable is short, and paroxytone when long; thus δῆμοϲ, but δήμου, and ϲωτήρ, but ϲωτῆρα (whence this rule is known as the ϲωτῆρα rule). According to various sources Doric lacked this rule;[83] thus it had forms such as παῖδεϲ, παῖδα, and χεῖρεϲ, rather than παῖδεϲ, παῖδα, and χεῖρεϲ. This rule is only applied inconsistently in the Doric papyri, though this does not necessarily mean that the grammarians were wrong. The fact that Doric lacked the ϲωτῆρα rule generally need not mean that it always applied the precise opposite of the rule.

---

[81] *Kl. Schr.* 214–18.

[82] The grammatical material is collected and discussed in Ahrens, 26–35; for the papyrus evidence, see M. Nöthiger, *Die Sprache des Stesichorus und des Ibycus* (Zurich, 1971), 83–6.

[83] e.g. Choerob. *An. Bekk.* 1236 (= i. 386 Hilg.), ap. Ahrens, 29 n.10, with further references there.

(ii) The nominative terminations -οι/-αι were not treated as short for accenting purposes, as they were in Attic. Thus, nominative plurals of the first and second declensions were paroxytone where elsewhere we find them proparoxytone or perispomenon (so ἀνθρῶποι, ἀγγέλοι, ἀγκύραι not ἄνθρωποι, ἄγγελοι, ἄγκυραι).

(iii) Similarly, the 3rd-pers. pl. act. imperfect and aorist (< -*οντ, -*αντ) were paroxytone like the other verbal plurals (i.e. ἐλύςαν like ἐλύςαμεν, rather than ἔλυςαν as in Attic).

(iv) Certain, but apparently not all, monosyllables with long vowels, which were perispomenon in Attic-Ionic, were oxytone in Doric (e.g. cκώρ not cκῶρ, γλαύξ not γλαῦξ).

The papyrus accents fr. 4A. 12 πάcαι, but Kassel–Austin print πᾶcαι. However, πάcαι could be correct, given the tendency to paroxytonesis which the features listed above point to, though I have found no other instance in the Doric papyri. At line 9 we find δάιδιον (representing δαίδιον as often in papyri), for which Attic would have δαιδίον, and the papyrus accent is supported by a scholion to Theocritus.[84] Otherwise the papyrus accentuation is mostly unremarkable. There may be a few errors (e.g. fr. 4D. 39 -κολύμφευ |, where -κολυμφεῦ(μεc) is more attractive; 41 ἀποτόcιτουc, but we expect ἀποτοcίτουc). At 4A. 3 the grave papyrus accent χὸνδρον simply indicates that the accent on the first omicron was not acute (i.e. not *χόνδρον), a common phenomenon in papyrus accentuation.[85]

Apollonius says that adverbs in -ωc were oxytone in Doric, citing καλώc at fr. *21. This is supported by e.g. Theognost. p. 164, 18, who gives cοφώc and again καλώc as examples of the Doric accentuation; a papyrus text of Epicharmus (fr. 113. 132, 2nd cent. AD) has καλώc so accented.

---

[84] Schol. Theocr. 1. 50b (p. 48 W.) τὸ παίδιον· οὕτω Θεαίτητοc, ὡc τὸ παίγνιον, φέρνιον· Ἀττικοὶ δὲ [οὕτω] παραπλήcιον τῶι κλειδίον λέγουcιν; Herodian i. 357.

[85] A similar principle applies in the system of Vedic accentuation used in the Rigveda, where the syllables preceding and following the main accent (the udātta), an intermediate tone, are marked as respectively lower and higher, while the udātta itself is unmarked.

IV. INFLUENCE

Although Sophron merited detailed treatment by Apollodorus of Athens, and was still being read as late as the second century AD, there is surprisingly little evidence for his influence on writers much beyond the Hellenistic period. A relatively early (first in Duris, *c.*340–260 BC) and persistent tradition makes his mimes admired and imitated by Plato,[86] but there is no concrete evidence to support this. Some see an allusion to the mimes at *Rep.* 5. 451 C, where Socrates, turning the conversation to the status of women in his ideal city, says: τάχα δὲ οὕτως ἂν ὀρθῶς ἔχοι, μετὰ ἀνδρεῖον δρᾶμα παντελῶς διαπερανθὲν τὸ γυναικεῖον αὖ περαίνειν ('but maybe it is right that since we have gone through the male drama completely, we should also go through the female'). There is no obvious point to a reference to Sophron's work here, and the allusion is more likely to be simply to popular performances like those of the magodists. Similar popular entertainments are probably also meant at *Thesm.* 151–4, where Aristophanes makes the tragedian Agathon speak of δράματα γυναικεῖα and ἀνδρεῖα, and Sophron does not enter into it. One wonders whether the tradition was not originally hostile, linking Plato with a writer known for lascivious and immoral subject-matter, and some sources have the works of Sophron and Aristophanes found together by the philosopher's death-bed.[87] It may also be significant that Plato specifically criticizes mimetic performance at *Rep.* 3. 394 D–398 A, though he is there thinking in fact of tragedy and comedy.[88] But the fact that sources favourable to Plato, like Olympiodorus, also carry the story shows that, even if originally hostile, it was rapidly absorbed into the mainstream tradition. The similarity between Plato's dialogues and Sophron's mimes is basically restricted to

[86] See variously Duris, *FGrH* 76 F 72; Diog. Laert. 3. 18; Choric. 32. 14; Olympiod. *vit. Plat.* p. 3. 65 W.; Anon. proleg. in Plat. p. 7 (3. 11) West.; Val. Max. 8. 7. ext. 3; Quint. 1. 10. 17 (= test. 5–11 K–A).

[87] e.g. Olympiod. loc. cit.

[88] A less likely alternative is that it derives from a patriotic West Greek tradition similar to that promulgated by the 4th-cent. Sicilian historian Alcimus, which implausibly made Epicharmus' dramas the source for much Platonic thought; cf. [Epich.] frs. 275–80 (= Alcimus ap. Diog. Laert. 3. 9–17), with analysis in A. C. Cassio, *HSCP* 89 (1985), 37–51; further Kerkhof, 65–78; Pickard-Cambridge, 247–55.

their common use of prose and a dramatic setting, and while this may have been enough to sustain the tradition, it is worth remembering that prose had been standard in philosophical works from the archaic period.[89]

Sophron's literary influence is most immediately apparent in the mimes written by Xenarchus to entertain Dionysius' court. Unfortunately of these not a single fragment is extant. He may also have influenced the Roman literary mimographer Decimus Laberius, though the evidence for any close connection is slim (cf. on *Seamstresses*); Laberius is after all writing Roman mime, which develops from a largely independent tradition, probably linked to local Italian genres like Atellan farce, and was meant for stage performance.[90]

For us, however, Sophron's importance lies mainly in his impact on Hellenistic literature, particularly Theocritus, who was no doubt in part patriotically motivated in choosing another Syracusan writer as a model for several poems; we may compare his use of Philoxenus' *Cyclops*, with its Sicilian connections,[91] in Poems 6 and 11. The Theocritean scholia point to close borrowings in *Id.* 2 and 15, though without the corresponding mimes it is difficult to assess the precise extent of the debt (see further my comments on *The women who say they are expelling the goddess*, with fr. 4A, and [*Women watching the Isthmia*]).[92] Certainly we would not expect Theocritus to be a slavish imitator. There may also be something of Sophron about poem 14,[93] though no direct influence can be observed. Lexical material shared by Sophron and Theocritus, while sometimes deliberate, may often just reflect a common linguistic heritage, as, for instance, in fr. 37, where it is almost certainly not of direct relevance that the word βαίτα also appears at Theocr. 5. 15.

Beyond such particular similarities, we can see broader connections between Theocritus' urban poems and Sophron's

---

[89] If the quotations in fr. \*\*172 are genuine Sophron, then they would provide clear evidence that Plato knew and quoted the mimes; but the arguments for those passages being his are weak (see ad loc.).

[90] Cf. the anecdote at Macrob. *Sat.* 2. 7. 1, which has Laberius performing one of his own mimes on stage (and thus losing his civic status as a member of the Equestrian order) at Caesar's behest.

[91] Cf. *CQ*[2] 49 (1999), 445–55.

[92] On Idyll 15, cf. also Hordern (2002*b*).

[93] So Hutchinson, 200.

mimes in their choice of characters and subjects belonging to the
lower end of the social scale, and the depiction, though in a
highly literary fashion, of the rough and tumble of day-to-day
Greek life. Theocritus is sometimes credited with introducing
literary imitations of 'popular genres' like the mime or goat-
herd's songs. But as we have seen, Sophron's mimes were from
the first literary in character; Theocritus' real innovation in his
urban poems is a piece of highly literary genre-mixing of the sort
we should expect from the Alexandrians, and not so very far
from Herodas' linking of mime with iambus.

While there is no other explicit testimony to Sophron's
influence on Hellenistic poetry, it is highly likely that his work
was known to Herodas. The latter probably claims Hipponax as
a direct model in poem 8 (disappointingly lacunose at the relevant point, but see Cunningham's commentary on the problem),
just as Callimachus does in his first iambus.[94] But a debt to
Sophron's mimes is clearly suggested by Herodas' use of the
term μιμίαμβοι to describe his poems,[95] and once again we see
an interest in everyday scenes and dramas, with lower-class
characters in comic situations. Women chatting amongst themselves about sex, procuresses, pimps—all these are familiar
figures. But they are also stock characters of much comedy;
closer connections are harder to establish. Herodas' two poems
dealing with dildoes (poems 6 and 7) may have been modelled on
something in Sophron's mimes (see on frs. 23 and 25), and his
depiction of two women sacrificing to Asclepius and inspecting
the god's sanctuary in poem 4 perhaps owes something to
Sophron's women at the Isthmia (see ad loc.). Yet without more
of Sophron, and lacking any substantial ancient tradition about
Herodas, we cannot be sure.[96]

There is little we can add to these details. The mimes have left
little mark on Callimachus' iambi, where we might expect to see
some impact. Sophron seems to have included a schoolmaster in

---

[94] Cf. Kerkhecker, 17–18, 28–30; and also Iambus 5 with Kerkhecker's
comments ad loc.

[95] Cf. Cunningham's edn. (Oxford, 1971), p. 3.

[96] Hutchinson, 240 n. 43, speculates that Sophron may be the source for the
oath μὰ τὰς Μοίρας, found only at Herod. 1. 11, 66, 4. 30, and Theocr. 2. 160 (the
last of these poems was certainly based on Sophron), and for the exclamation μᾶ
(often in Herodas; Theocr. 15. 89). These are possibilities, but no more than
that.

one of his mimes (fr. 153), and we may think of Callimachus' pederastic teacher (Iambus 5), as well as of Herodas' Lampriscus (poem 3), but such connections can be tenuous at best. Sophron was not an important author for the Second Sophistic, and although it is tempting to see the influence of the mime in the form of Lucian's *Dialogues*, Socratic dialogue is clearly more directly important.[97] He does not merit an epitaph or laudatory epigram in the Anthology, though more obscure figures are so honoured and we know that a statue could be found in Rome in Tatian's day (*ad Graec.* 34. 2). Discussing the origin and history of Roman satire in the sixth century AD, John the Lydian claims (*Magistr.* 41 p. 42. 16 W.) that Persius tried to imitate Sophron in his satires; the evidence for this assertion is unknown, and a supposed parallel to fr. 91 at Persius 4. 39 f. (*quinque palaestritae licet haec plantaria vellant | elixasque nates labefactent forcipe adunca . . .*), hesitantly adduced by Botzon,[98] of doubtful value. John's account of the development of satire is in any case farcical, apparently dependent on a desire to link it with early Italian Greek philosophy: it has no real scholarly value, and we do not even know that he actually knew the mimes at first hand. His claim that Persius achieved 'the obscurity of Lycophron' as a result of his imitation looks suspiciously like a misunderstanding of Statius' description of Sophron as *implicitus* (*Silv.* 5. 3. 156 ff.). Finally, it is worth noting that Choricius of Gaza, at roughly the same period, used Sophron's popularity with Plato as a defence of the scandalous contemporary stage-mime against Christian hostility (= fr. 102); but his interest is not really in the texts themselves, which again he may not have known personally. The literary record is otherwise silent.

## V. THE HISTORY OF THE TEXT

### A. *Transmission*

The survival of the text is fairly certain at least until the second century AD, when we have in a sillybus (a papyrus tag attached to the outside of a roll with the work's title and author) for the

---

[97] But *D. Meretr.* 1 looks back to Theocr. 2, and perhaps thence to Sophron's original mime (frs. *5–*9).

[98] Botzon (1867), 16.

women's mimes evidence for a copy at Oxyrhynchus.[99] The text probably comprised no more than two book-rolls, one containing the men's mimes, the other the women's. The main surviving papyrus fragments (frs. 4A–D), also from Oxyrhynchus, date to the first century AD, and at roughly this period Statius' father taught Sophron in Naples and Rome, together with a remarkable array of archaic, classical, and Hellenistic poets. Statius mentions him in the company of Callimachus, Lycophron, and Corinna, describing him as *Sophrona . . . implicitum* (*Silv.* 5. 3. 156 ff.), which suggests that by this stage he was felt to be a difficult author, probably with reference to his dialect.

Sometime after Sophron's death the mimes were introduced to Athens (by Plato, according to some sources).[100] Certainly Aristotle was familiar with the mimes, and we can hardly doubt that he had a text. Possibly they were still performed in symposia, but the few isolated references do not suggest wide familiarity.

In the second century BC, the mimes were the subject of a monumental work by Apollodorus of Athens, the follower of Aristarchus who also wrote on Epicharmus (and perhaps edited the plays). Athenaeus (3. 89 A; 7. 281 E; 309 C; cf. also fr. 161) cites this work as Περὶ Cώφρονοc, and Pfeiffer therefore took it to be a monograph 'with interpretations in the Περί-style'.[101] But a ὑπόμνημα τῶν Cώφρονοc ἀνδρείων is mentioned as the source for fr. 69, Athenaeus (7. 281 E) says that the third book of Apollodorus' work was on the men's mimes, and the quotations of Apollodorus at frs. 62–3 suggest a detailed commentary with lemmata. A fourth book is mentioned in a scholion on Aristophanes (schol. *Vesp.* 525b Ἀπολλόδωροc καὶ ὅτι τὸ ποτήριον μεcτὸν πάλιν ἀπεπλήρουν, δεδήλωκεν ἐν τῆι δ′ περὶ Cώφρονοc);[102] perhaps this was on the women's mimes, though that leaves the first two books unaccounted for. They may have contained

---

[99] P. Oxy. 301 = E. G. Turner and P. J. Parsons, *Greek Manuscripts of the Ancient World*[2], *BICS* Suppl. 46 (London, 1987), no. 8.

[100] e.g. Diog. Laert. 3. 18.

[101] Pfeiffer, 264.

[102] Apollod. *FGrH* 244 F 15. W. J. Koster (*Scholia in Aristophanem*, II/i: *Scholia in Vespas* (Groningen, 1978), 84) marks a lacuna after Ἀπολλόδωροc, possibly rightly, but the reference to the commentary on Sophron shows that he is in any case the source for what follows.

monograph material, with detailed commentary reserved for books 3 and 4, but the small biographical tradition about Sophron suggests that biography was not one of Apollodorus' interests, and two books on the subject would seem excessively detailed treatment. The work is cited several times on the meaning of obscure words. Apollodorus showed in his work *On Gods* and on the Homeric catalogue of ships a taste for etymologizing explanations of the names of gods and places, and a similar tendency is revealed here. His explanation of the name Cothonias (fr. 44) looks likely in view of the 'speaking names' we find elsewhere in Sophron, and his commentary perhaps lies behind Demetrius Lacon's account of the name Koikoa (fr. 16); but absurdly fanciful is the etymological explanation for the word μαcτροπόc 'pimp' at fr. 69, where Kassel–Austin plausibly see Apollodorus' hand. He is also quoted by Athenaeus to explain the meaning of a proverb, and by the Homeric scholia on Sicilian weights and measures (frs. 67, 161).

We can connect a number of other fragments with his work. The Etymologicum Genuinum,[103] in a discussion of the word ἠπίαλοc and related forms, cites the use ἠπιάληc for ἐπιάλτηc; in cod. A and most codices of the Etymologicum magnum the source for this usage is given in abbreviated form as Ἀπολλω; cod. B, and cod. M of the *Et. magn.*, have Ἀπολλώνιοc, but it is at least possible that we should read Ἀπολλόδωροc.[104] Apollodorus is cited by Photius (λ 97 = *Suda* λ 121 = *FGrH* 244 F 287) for the sense cιτεύω for λαρινεύω, which should almost certainly be related to fr. 99. And he is an explicit source for the lexical note at fr. 109 and the explanation of a Sicilian proverb at fr. *170. No doubt much of his work was devoted to explaining lexical obscurities and unfamiliar phrases; possibly many other fragments that we have from grammatical sources ultimately depend on Apollodorus himself.

Whether Apollodorus also edited the mimes is unknown, though he may have produced an edition of Epicharmus.[105] An intriguing note in Hesychius preserves what looks like a textual

[103] Et. gen. AB (*Et. magn.* p. 434,6) ap. C. Theodoridis, *RhM* 122 (1979), 12 f. (= fr. 67).
[104] Reitzenstein ap. Kaibel (fr. 68); Theodoridis, loc. cit.
[105] Pfeiffer, 264.

variant, or at least disagreement about the text: where some
(rightly; see the commentary) explained δι᾽ ἀτέλειαν as (διὰ) τὸ
ἄπρακτον, 'others write δι᾽ ἀγγελίαν' (fr. 133). Unfortunately we
do not know who these others were, nor precisely with whom
they were disagreeing, but Apollodorus must be a strong candidate for the orthodox reading. The debate, exemplified by
Philodemus and his opponents, about whether Sophron' mimes
were to be classified as ποήματα is hardly likely to have focused on
textual readings.

Beyond this we can say little. The mimes' unfamiliar dialect
and strange vocabulary will have made them difficult reading
even for an educated reader. The Christian Church was opposed
to the later Greek and Roman mime,[106] and its hostility will
easily have extended to Sophron's scurrilous playlets. When
Choricius of Gaza used Sophron's popularity with Plato in his
defence of the mime from Christian attack in the sixth century
(= fr. 102), he may have known little about him beyond that
dubious tradition.[107] I very much doubt he could have had a text
open before him at this late stage.

## B. *Text*

Most fragments of Sophron's mimes survive as quotations in
various authors, especially in anthologizing writers such as
Athenaeus, and in divers grammatical monographs and lexico-
graphical compendia. At least some material contained in these
works will have come to them at second hand; this, together with
the unfamiliar dialect, provides natural ground for corruptions
to flourish.

Apart from these quotation-fragments, we have one main
papyrus (fr. 4), consisting of four separate pieces all belonging to
the same ancient copy. This is an expensively produced text with
sizeable margins and scholarly annotation. Errors appear to have
been kept to a minimum. The hand is a neat, clearly legible book-
hand, dating to the first century AD, with finials on most straight
strokes (so, for example, on *A, Γ, Δ, K, M, N, Π, T*, etc.). Epsilon
is rounded, the tongue not usually attached to the bowl. Sigma is
lunate, as we would expect for the period. Mu is made in three

---

[106] Cf. Reich, i. 109–81.
[107] On Choricius and the mime in 6th-cent. Gaza, cf. U. Albini, *SIFC* 15
(1997), 116–22.

strokes; omega in two. The script is largely bilinear, though the vertical of phi extends below and above the line. There are numerous accents and lectional signs, and occasional corrections in the same hand as the main script. An asterisk at fr. 4A. 3 directs the reader to a commentary, probably Apollodorus. There are fragmentary and illegible scholia on the second fragment, presumably also derived from Apollodorus or some later commentator.

The fragments were originally published in two articles by M. Norsa and G. Vitelli in 1932–3, and then republished in *Papiri Greci e Latini* (1935) as *PSI* 1214. I examined them at the Biblioteca Laurenziana in July 2000, by kind permission of Professor R. Pintaudi, and append here a brief description.

Fr. A: 13×19 cm. A large upper margin of 3.7 cm., and a generous intercolumnium ranging between 4 and 6 cm. Column i has 20 lines. Nothing can be made of the isolated letters, the beginnings of three lines only, which constitute col. ii.

Fr. B: A small scrap, 4.3×6 cm.

Fr. C: 6.1×8 cm, with a large lower margin of at least 4.5 cm.

Fr. D: Another largish fragment, 14×12.5 cm, with a left margin, evidently an intercolumnium, of a maximum of 4 cm.

Three other papyri are of relevance. A papyrus scrap (4.5× 5.5 cm.) of the second century AD (*PSI* 1387, ed. V. Bartoletti, vol. 14 (1957), 29 = fr. *171), written in a small, elegant, uncial script, contains the last six lines of a column of Doric prose. There is a generous lower margin (at least 2 cm.), and some lectional signs. Sophron has a strong claim to authorship.[108] There is also a brief reference to Sophron in P. Oxy. 2429 (= fr. 140), a commentary on Epicharmus. Finally, six columns of Demetrius' *On Poems* (P. Herc. 1014) contains discussion of mime, apparently restricting itself to Sophron; these I examined at the Biblioteca Nazionale in Naples in May 2002, by kind permission of the director of the Officina dei Papiri. The papyrus, like all those at Herculaneum, was carbonized during the eruption of Vesuvius; generally column tops and bottoms are poorly preserved. The hand probably belongs to the late second century BC.

My text, apparatus, and numeration are based on those in Kassel–Austin's recent edition. I have reduced the size of the

---

[108] P. Maas, ap. Bartoletti, p. xvi; cf. Hordern (2002*b*).

apparatus, providing only the more essential details, and also of the text in some instances. Mostly these omissions are insignificant, but Kassel–Austin should always be consulted for a full account. I have given a much fuller version of Demetrius' discussion as fr. 16, since I believe that this probably deals with Sophron throughout. The text is based on Romeo's edition, but there are substantial new readings, and some suggested emendations based on Hordern (2002c), where I discuss Demetrius' argument in greater detail. There is one certain new fragment (fr. 30A), and I have also, after some hesitation, included some passages quoted by Plato, assigned to Sophron by Wilamowitz, as fr. **172, though in fact I very much doubt that they are his.

# A NOTE ON THE TEXT AND TRANSLATION

Full bibliographical references for each fragment (as opposed to the abbreviated forms given in the text) can be found in Kassel–Austin, whose edition should also be consulted for other details, such as names of modern scholars, mentioned in the apparatus. 'Wil. ap. Kaib.' refers throughout out to the views of Wilamowitz reported by Kaibel in his edition but not published elsewhere.

The asterisk before a fragment number usually indicates that the fragment is not explicitly attributed to Sophron by our source. Two asterisks points to greater uncertainty in the attribution.

For most fragments I provide a full translation of the Greek testimonia. In some cases, however, where translating all the original material would involve wearisome and pointless repetition, I have restricted the translation to the most important sources.

# SIGLA

| | |
|---|---|
| ạ | littera incerta |
| . | litterae deperditae vestigia |
| [ ] | textus papyri periit |
| ⟨ ⟩ | inserendum |
| { } | delendum |
| ` ´ | inseruit librarius |
| ⟦ ⟧ | delevit librarius |
| † | corruptum |
| :: | loquentium vicis |

TEXT AND TRANSLATION

*MIMOI ΓΥΝΑΙΚΕΙΟΙ*

## Ἀκέϲτριαι

### I

φωρτάτουϲ ἀεὶ καπήλουϲ παρέχεται

Et. gen. AB s.v. μακάρτατοϲ (Et. magn. p. 573,54) μεμπτέον Cώφρονα
λέγοντα (-νι -τι Reitz.) φωρ. — παρέχεται· οὐδὲ (-ἐν Α, -έποτε Reitz.) γὰρ
τὰ εἰϲ ωρ (ω Β, Et. Magn.) λήγοντα (-τα compend. AB, -τα ῥήματα Et.
magn., λῆγον Reitz.) ϲχηματίζουϲιν (παραϲχ- AB, παραϲχηματίζει Et.
magn., corr. Reitz.) ϲυγκριτικὸν καὶ ὑπερθετικὸν (-οἷϲ καὶ -οἷϲ Reitz.). ἔτι
ἁμαρτάνουϲιν οἱ λέγοντεϲ μακάρτατοϲ κτλ. in fine glossae Φιλ(όξενοϲ Α, om.
B, Et. magn. (fr. 347 Theod.).

φωρτάτουϲ Blomfield: φωροτ- codd.        καπήλουϲ Β, Et. magn.:
καπηλαϲ Α    παρέρχεται Hauler

### *2

ἄκουέ νυν καὶ ἐμεῦ, Ῥόγκα

Apoll. Dysc. pron., GrGr II 1,1 p. 65,13 Schn. ἐμεῦ· κοινὴ Ἰώνων καὶ
Δωριέων . . . ἄκουε — Ῥόγκα Cώφρων
νυν Latte: νῦν cod.    Ῥόγκα Wil. ap. Kaib.: ρωγκα cod.

### Ταὶ γυναῖκεϲ αἳ τὰν θεόν φαντι ἐξελᾶν

Apoll. Dysc. ad., GrGr II 1,1 p. 180,6 Schn. τὸ γὰρ οἱ τοί φαϲι Δωριεῖϲ
καὶ τὸ αἱ ταί . . . λέγω δὲ ὅτε κατὰ προτακτικὴν θέϲιν ἐϲτὶ τὸ ἄρθρον· ἐπεὶ ὅτε
γε καθ᾽ ὑπόταξίν ἐϲτι, τὸ τ ου πάντωϲ προϲτίθεϲιν . . . ὅθεν οὐδ᾽ ἐπίμεμπτον
ταὶ γυναῖκεϲ αἳ τὰν θεόν φαντι ἐξελᾶν.

### 3

ὑποκατώρυκται δὲ ἐν κυαθίδι τρικτὺϲ ἀλεξιφαρμάκων

Athen. 11. 480 Β κυαθίϲ· κοτυλῶδεϲ ἀγγεῖον. Cώφρων δ᾽ ἐν τῶι ἐπιγραφομένωι μίμωι Γυναῖκεϲ αἳ τὰν θεόν φαντι ἐξελᾶν (ἔλεξαν Α, corr. Blomfield)·
ὑποκ. — ἀλ.
κυαθίδι Α    τρικτὺϲ Schweigh.: -τοι Α: -τύα Jahn et Ahrens: τρίκοι᾽
LSJ s.v. τριττύα

## I. WOMEN'S MIMES

### Seamstresses

I

## (it) always has the most thievish shopkeepers

(*Etymologicum genuinum* and *magnum*) Sophron should be criticized for saying 'always — shopkeepers', since words in -ωρ do not have comparatives or superlatives. Indeed, those who say μακάρτατος ('most blessed') are making a mistake etc. . . . Phil(oxenus) (fr. 347 Theod.).

\*2

## now listen to me too, Rhongka

(Apollonius Dyscolus, *On Pronouns*) ἐμεῦ is common to Ionic and Doric. 'now — Rhongka'. Sophron.

### The women who say they are expelling the goddess

3

## buried deep in a cup is a triad of protective drugs

(Athenaeus) κυαθίς: a vessel like a cup. Sophron, in the mime entitled *Women who say they are expelling the goddess*: 'buried — drugs'.

42   SOPHRON

4

Fr. a. col. i    τὰν τράπεζαν κάτθετε
2    ὥσπερ ἔχει·
2    λάζεςθε δὲ
3    ἁλὸς χονδρὸν ἐς τὰν χῆρα
4    καὶ δάφναν πὰρ τὸ ὦας.
5–6    ποτιβάντες νυν ποτ τὰν | ἱςτίαν θωκεῖτε.
6–7    δὸς μοι τὺ | τὤμφακες·
7    φέρ’ ὦ τὰν cκύλακα.
8    πεῖ γὰρ ἁ ἄςφαλτος;
8    :: οὖτα. ::
9    ἔχε καὶ τὸ δάιδιον
9–10    καὶ τὸν | λιβανωτόν
10    ἄγετε δὴ
11–12    πεπτάςθων μοι ταὶ θύραι | πάςαι.
12–13    ὑμὲς δὲ ἐνταῦθα | ὁρῆτε
13–14    καὶ τὸν δαελὸν | cβῆτε
14    ὥσπερ ἔχει.
14–15    εὐκαμίαν | νυν παρέχεςθε
15–16    ἃς κ’ ἐγὼν | ποτ τᾶνδε πυκταλεύςω.
17    πότνια,
17–18    δείπνου μέν τυ κα[ὶ | ξ]ενίων ἀμεμφέων

[1–49] PSI 1214 (saec. Iᴾ) ed. Norsa–Vitelli SIFC 10 (1933) 119–
124. 247–253≅PSI xi (1935) pp. 115–120 cum tab. VIII (Fr. a)
[8] Ioann. Alex. De accent. p. 32,14 (post fr. 139) πεῖ γὰρ ἄςφαλτος,
Sophrone non nominato post idem fr. 139 Apoll. Dysc. adv., GrGr II
1,1 p. 207,17 et 210,2 Schn., ante fr. 139 p. 132,27 (τὸ παρὰ Δωριεῦςι) πεῖ
γὰρ ἁ ἄςφαλτος. Ammon. adf. voc. diff. 423 (γ [θ, GF]π; Sym.) =
Herenn. Phil. 157 τὸ . . . πεῖ τὴν ἐν τόπωι ςχέςιν δηλοῖ. Cώφρων (fr. 5
Kaib.) φηςί (om. γ, Herenn.)· πεῖ — ἄςφαλτος (ἁ sequitur fr. 74
[16] Et. Orion. p. 62,31 Cώφρων φηςὶν ἀπὸ τοῦ πυκτεύω πυκταλεύω.

2 εχει·    3 ἁλὸςχὸν  χῆρα    4 ὦας·    5 νῦν
6 ἵςτιανθωκῆτε·, ‘ει· supra τε script.    7 τὤμφᾱκες φερῶ    cκύλακα·
8 πεῖγαρᾱ ἄ :ὅυτᾱ:    9 δάιδιὸν·    10 βὰνωτόν·    11 ταὶ
12 πάςαι·  πᾶςαι Kassel–Austin    ενταυτα, θ supra alt. τ script.
13 ορῆτε·  δᾶελον    14 cβῆτε   ‘ευκᾱμίαν    15 νῦν   ἁς
16 τᾶν : τᾶνδε Norsa–Vitelli    λευω, c supra υ script.    17 ποτνια·
δείπνου Eitrem et Gow    μέν

*MIMOI ΓΥΝΑΙΚΕΙΟΙ*

## 4 (*PSI* 1214)

### Fr. 4A (*lines 1–20*)

A. Put down the table right away. Take a lump of salt in your hand, and laurel by your ear. Now go to the hearth and sit down. Give me the axe, you; bring the puppy here. Now, where is the pitch?

B. Here.

A. Take the taper and the incense. Come, let all the doors be open please. You (pl.) watch over there. Put the torch out right now. Let me have silence now, while in these women's name I do my fighting: 'Lady, rec[eive] your feast and faultless offerings . . .'

18–19   ἀντά[ | ]ῦν . . ν· καὶ κα . μῶν δέπ . [
20            ] . [            ] . [
        − − − − −

col. ii   ῦ[
          [
          α[
24        α[
          − − −
          − − −

Fr. b. 25   πέρρα . [
            μυχοδ[
            μορμολυ[κ
            κογχουαι[
            κυναναιδ[
30          μισητατα[
            − − −

            − − −

Fr. c      . [ . . . . ] . . ιαδες
           θύραν τὰν αὐτος έ . . [
           ἐκ Cτυέλλας
           ῑκῶς . [ . . . . . ]ọ . [
35         ετεθ . [
           − − − − −

[29] Schol. (Ge) Hom Φ 394 d (κυνάμυια) φασὶν ὅτι δεῖ γράφεςθαι (-ειν
Nicole) κυνόμυια. ὅταν γὰρ ἐπιφέρηται ςυμφώνωι (ἄμφω cod., corr.
Hefermehl. Stud. in Apollod. Π. θεῶν fr. Genavensia, diss. Bln. 1905,
p. 24) τὰ παρὰ τὸν κύνα, ο γραπτέον . . . μήποτε οὖν ἐςτιν ἡ κυνάμυια †και
μυῖα† (κυν καὶ ἅμυια Erbse) ὡς παρὰ Cώφρονι κυναναιδές (κυνάπαιδες cod.,
corr. Hefermehl) καὶ κυνάγχη        [30] Eust. in Od. p. 1651,1 (Suet. Π
βλαςφ. 24 p. 49 Taill., sed vid. Slater ad Ar. Byz. fr. 396) ἄλλοι δὲ
(Tryph. fr. 10 Vels.) μιςήτην βαρυτόνως πρὸς διαςτολὴν τῆς ὀξυτονουμένης
τὴν κοινὴν καὶ ῥαιδίαν, λέγοντες καὶ χρῆςιν αὐτῆς εἶναι παρὰ Κρατίνωι (fr.
354) καὶ Cώφρονι

18 ἀντά       ἀντά[ςειν ed. pr., -ςεις Latte Kl. Schr. p. 492, -ςαι Gallavotti
-ςαςαν Festa ap. ed. pr.        19 ῦ]ν . . ν·    χᾶ]ν[δό]ν Latte    μῶνδέ vel
λλῶνδέ    κ' ἀπ' ἅμων Gallavotti, καλαμῶν? Koerte        21 ῦ[
27 marg. sin. ]ειν . ι et ] . κω        29 κυνὰ        30 μιςητάτα [γύναι
Gallavotti    32 ἔκọ[πτε Olivieri²        33 ἐκ        34 ῑκῶς

Fr. 4B

27  Mormolu[ka
28  of a conch [
29  shameful as a dog[
30  disgusting . . .[


Fr. 4C

32  door which he himself . . .[
33  from Styella        [
34  come (?) . . .[

Fr. d    οὐδέ χ᾽ ὕδ[ω]ρ… ειος… ε. [
    δοίη καταρρυφῆcαι·
    τὸ γὰρ | κακὸν γλυκύπικρον ἐὸν | ἐπεπείγει.
    cπατιλοκολύμφευ | μ. ϛδε. . μ. χοδέοντεc·
40 ὁ γὰρ | τῖλοc ἀcτατὶ κοχυδεύων
    ἀποτοcίτουc ἄμ᾽ ἐπεποιήκει.
    τ[. . . . .]. ακος cτ.[. ̇]ν
    . . . .]μεc ἀcκοὶ πεφυcαμ[έ]νοι
    . . . .]δ᾽ ἐπανδὺc βιῆται
    . . . .]αμερον ὅπερ ἧc
    . . . .]υδρηρον ⟦α⟧δρυψον[
    . . . .]. ν ἐκεραύνω[c]εν
    . . . .]. . . . οδεcτε. [
    . . . . .]δε. . νεδυν. . [
————

**36** δέχ᾽ **37** marg. sin. αυτα δοιη· ρυφήcὰι·, alt. ρ supra ρ script. **38** πεπείγει· ἐπείγει ed. pr. **39** τῖλο cπατιλο-κολυμφεῦμ[ε]c Gallavotti [θα]μ[ὰ] Kerényi τεc· χοδιτεύοντεc Pohlenz ap. ed. pr. (PSI) **40** ἀcτατί ἀcτα⟨κ⟩τὶ Gallavotti, Pohlenz, Koerte εύων **41** ποτό ἂμ ἥκει· **42** ἄκοc τ[ὸc θυ]λάκοc ed. pr., qui etiam de ἄκοc cogitant ̇]ν gen. in -ῶ]ν vel -ᾶ]ν suppl. ed. pr. **43** ]μεc· ἀ[μὲc vel εἰ]μὲc ed. pr. ἀcκ cᾶμ **44** δύc· **45** ]αμερον vel ]μαλερον ἐπ]άμερον Kerényi **46** ὑδρηλὸν? Olivieri αδρυψὸν

*5

Argum. Theocr. 2 p. 269,18 W. τὴν δὲ Θεcτυλίδα ὁ Θεόκριτοc ἀπειροκάλωc ἐκ τῶν Cώφρονοc μετήνεγκε μίμων

*6

Schol. (KEA) Theocr. 2 p. 270,5 W. ('scholium quod in libris ad v. 69 vel 70 refertur, argumenti deperditi partem puto' Wendel, praeeunte Bethe, De Theocriti edd. antiquiss., Ind. schol. Rost. 1896 p. 11; ad v. 59 sqq. trahit Herzog p. 226[25]) τὴν δὲ τῶν φαρμάκων ὑπόθεcιν ἐκ τῶν Cώφρονοc (Εὐφορίωνοc KEA, corr. Adert) μίμων μεταφέρει (defic. EA) ὑπό τε τὸν [cτρ]όφιγγα ὀρρο[. .] ποτὲ βληθέν

## Fr. 4D (*lines 36-49*)

. . . (it?) wouldn't let me gulp down any water; for the evil, bittersweet, presses upon me. And we're swimming in the shit . . . we were pouring (it) out. For the diarrhoea had come streaming out and left us without food or drink . . . swollen wine-skins . . . which was . . . watery . . . thunder-bolted . . .

## [Fragments *5–*9]

### *5

(Argument to Theocritus, *Id.* 2) And Theocritus inappropriately took the character Thestylis from Sophron's mimes.

### *6

(Scholion on Theocritus, *Id.* 2) He takes the whole subject of magic from Sophron's mimes . . . [The following words are hopelessly corrupt, and may have nothing to do with Sophron.]

*7

Schol.[1] (EAG) Theocr. 2,12, p. 272,4 W. τὴν Ἑκάτην χθονίαν φαcὶ θεὸν
καί νερτέρων πρύτανιν, καθὰ καὶ Cώφρων. Schol.[2] (KAG) p. 271,23 W.
χθονίαν δὲ τὴν Ἑκάτην φηcί, παρόcον Περcεφόνης τροφόc, ἢ παρόcον ⟨νερτέρ-
ων⟩ πρύτανιν (-εῖον K, -είαν AG, corr. et suppl. Adert e Schol.[1]) αὐτὴν
τέθεικε Cώφρων (κέκληκε AG)

**8

Plut. superst. 10 p. 170 B (post Timoth. fr. 3 Wil.) καὶ μὴν ὅμοια τούτοιc
καὶ χείρω περὶ Ἀρτέμιδοc οἱ δειcιδαίμονεc ὑπολαμβάνουcιν· αἴτε κα (αἴ τε κᾶν
codd.) ἀπ' ἀγχόναc ἀίξαca, αἴτε κα λεχοῦν διακναίcaca (αἴ τε καλεχόνα
κναίcaτε codd., λεχόνα κν- def. Herzog, -όνα μαιώcaca Lobeck, λεχὼ
μαιωcaμένα Bergk), αἴτε κ' ἂν νεκρὸc μολοῦca (αἴ τε κανέκεκροc μαίουca
fere codd., ἀλαίνουca Herzog) πεφυρμένα (ἀνπεφ- sive ἂν πεφ- codd.)
ἐcέλθηιc, αἴτε κα (ἐcῆλθεc, αἴ τε καὶ fere codd.) ἐκ τριόδων (τριπ- codd.)
καθαρμάτεccιν ἐπιcπώμενα τῶι παλαμναίωι cυμπλεχθῇιc (-εῖca codd.)
'aliquando suspicatus sum haec indigitamenta ex Sophronis mimis
esse petita' Bergk PLG⁴ III p. 680. incantationem Doricam restituit et
Sophroni tribuit Wil. Gr. Leseb. I 2 p. 336 et II 2 p. 210 (ἐcέλθηιc iam
Bergk, post Lobeck qui εἰc-), huic mimo Kl. Schr. IV p. 160.

*9

κύων πρὸ μεγαρέων μέγα ὑλακτέων

Epimer. Hom. μ 64 μέγαρον μέγαροc. ζητεῖται τὸ (τῶι cod., corr. Kaibel)
παρὰ τῶι Cώφρονι κύων — ὑλακτέων, οὐ γὰρ ἐπι τῆc πόλεωc τὰ Μέγαρα ὁ
Μεγαρεύc καὶ οἱ Μεγαρεῖc, τῶν Μεγαρέων, ἀλλ' ἀντὶ τοῦ πρὸ τῶν οἴκων· καὶ
γὰρ δῆλον ὅτι πρὸ τῶν οἴκων ὑλακτοῦcιν οἱ κύνεc. ἔcτιν οὖν ἀπὸ τοῦ μέγαροc
μεγάρεοc κτλ.

### Ταὶ θάμεναι τὰ Ἴcθμια

Argum. Theocr. 15 (Cυρακόcιαι ἢ Ἀδωνιάζουcαι) p. 305,7 W. παρέπλαcε δὲ
τὸ ποιημάτιον ἐκ τῶν παρὰ Cώφρονι Ἴcθμια θεωμένων (θεμ- codd., corr.
Valck. p. 189 A et 195 A, θαμ- Blomfield).

**10

φέρ' ὦ τὸν δρίφον

Et. gen. AB (Et. magn. p. 287,50) δρίφοc Cυρακοccίων· φέρ — δρίφον.
δίφροc γὰρ καὶ δρίφοc. Hesych. δ 2390 δρίφον (δίφρον cod., corr. Salm)· τὸν

*7

### prytanis of those below

(Scholion[1] on Theocritus, *Id.* 2) He calls Hecate a chthonic goddess, and prytanis of those below, just like Sophron. (Scholion[2] on Theocritus, *Id.* 2) He calls Hecate 'chthonic', because she was Persephone's nurse, or because Sophron made her the 'prytanis — below'.

**8

Whether you come hastening from a hanging, or from grinding to death a woman giving birth, or coming from ranging among corpses, or whether you have been engaged with a murderer, or drawing him to you from the crossroads by means of the blood he has cleansed from himself.

(Plutarch, *On Superstition*) And indeed superstitious people make assumptions like that and even worse, about Artemis: 'whether — himself'.

*9

### a dog barking loudly before the house

(*Homeric Parsings*) μέγαρον μέγαρος. The line in Sophron, 'a dog — house', is the subject of special consideration, for he does not mean 'before the city of Megara' . . . but rather 'before the house'. And clearly dogs do bark in front of houses etc.

### [Women watching the Isthmia]

(Argument to Theocritus, *Id.* 15) He copied the poem from the women watching the Isthmia in Sophron, though it is different in poetic character.

**10

### bring the stool here

(*Etymologicum genuinum* and *magnum*) δρίφος ('stool') is Syracusan: 'bring — here'. For δίφρος and δρίφος are both forms.

δίφρον. Δωριεῖc † καὶ Εὐcτόχιοc (κατὰ cυcτολὴν ὡc ⟨θάρcοc, θράcοc⟩ Latte
Kl. Schr. p. 677)
φέρ' ὦ Latte (coll. fr. 4,7): φέρ' ὦ Et. magn.: φέρω AB
Sophronis esse et huic mimo tribuendum Valck. p. 211 B

### Νυμφοπόνοc

11

κἤπειτα λαβὼν προῆχε, τοὶ δ' ἐβάλλιζον
βαλλίζοντεc τὸν θάλαμον cκάτουc ἐνέπληcαν

Athen. 8. 362 c (βαλλίζειν, post Epich. fr. 68) καὶ Cώφρων δ' ἐν τῆι ἐπιγραφομένηι Νυμφοπόνωι φηcίν· κἤπειτα — ἐβάλλιζον. καὶ πάλιν· βάλλιζοντεc
— ἐνέπληcαν.
2 cκάτουc A: cκατὸc Ahrens p. 468

12

Poll. X 107 (codd. F, CL) καὶ πατάνη δὲ καὶ πατάνιον τὸ ἐκπέταλον
λοπάδιον . . . ἡ μέν πατάνη Cώφρονοc εἰπόντοc ἐν Νυμφοπόνωι πατάνα
αὐτοποίητοc (πάντα αὐτοπ- L), τὸ δὲ πατάνιον Εὐβούλου ἐν Κατακολλῶντι·
(fr. 46). Id. VI 90 (codd. FL, A, BC) πατάνιον ἢ (πάτανον BC, cf. Hesych.
π 1094 πάτανα· τρύβλια) πατάνα (defic. BC)· οὕτω γὰρ Cώφρων εἴρηκεν,
πατάνα αὐτοποίητοc

### Πενθερά

13

cυμβουλεύω τ' ἐμφαγεῖν· ἄρτον γάρ τιc τυρῶντα τοῖc παιδίοιc ἴαλε

Athen. 3. 110 c (post fr. 27. 28) καὶ τυρῶντοc δ' ἄρτου μνημονεύει ὁ Cώφρων
ἐν τῆι ἐπιγραφομένηι Πενθερᾶι οὕτωc· cυμβ. — ἴαλε
τ' ἐνφαγεῖν A: τιν ἐμφαγεῖν Cobet ms. (teste Peppink Obs. p. 25) et
Wil. ap. Kaibel in ed. Athen. (qui δ' vel 'γὼν ἐμφ., in CGF γ' ἐμφ.): τιν
φαγεῖν Desrousseaux     τυρῶντα A: -όεντα Ahrens

### [Κοικόα]

14

πάρφερε, Κοικόα, τὸν cκύφον μεcτόν

Athen. 9. 380 e (παραφέρειν, post Ar. fr. 482) Cώφρων δ' ἐν γυναικείοιc
κατὰ ⟨τὸ add. Kaibel⟩ κοινότερον κέχρηται λέγων· περίφερε — μεcτόν.
πάρφερε Ahrens: περίφ- A (παράφ- Dalec.)

## Busied about the Bride

### 11

taking it he held it up (*sc.* as a shield), and they started to throw
by throwing they filled the bed-chamber with shit

(Athenaeus, on βαλλίζειν) And Sophron in the mime entitled *Busied
about the Bride* says: 'taking — throw'. And again 'by throwing — shit'.

### 12

(Pollux) Both πατάνη and πατάνιον mean a flat dish . . . The πατάνη is
mentioned by Sophron, who says in *Busied about the Bride* 'home-made
plate'. The πατάνιον is mentioned by Eubulus (fr. 46). (Poll. 6. 90)
πατάνιον or πάτανα; Sophron says this: 'home-made plate' (πατάνη).

## Mother-in-Law

### 13

and I recommend (you?) take a bite; since someone sent
cheese-bread for the children

(Athenaeus) Sophron also mentions cheese-bread in the mime entitled
*Mother-in-Law* as follows: 'I recommend — children'.

## [Koikoa: Fragments 14–*17]

### 14

bring the cup full, Koikoa

(Athenaeus, on παραφέρειν) And Sophron uses it in the more common
form in his Women's mimes, saying: 'bring — Koikoa'.

15

τάλαινα Κοικόα, κατὰ χειρὸς δοῦcα ἀπόδος ποχ' ἁμὶν τὰν τράπεζαν

Athen. 9. 408 F Ἀριστοφάνης δὲ ὁ γραμματικὸς ἐν τοῖς πρὸς τοὺς Καλλιμάχου πίνακας (fr. 368 Sl.) χλευάζει τοὺς οὐκ εἰδότας τὴν διαφορὰν τοῦ τε κατὰ χειρός καὶ τοῦ ἀπονίψαςθαι. παρὰ γὰρ τοῖς παλαιοῖς τὸ μὲν πρὸ ἀρίcτου καὶ δείπνου λέγεcθαι κατὰ χειρός, τὸ δὲ μετὰ ταῦτα ἀπονίψαcθαι. ἔοικε δ' ὁ γραμματικὸς τοῦτο πεφυλαχέναι παρὰ τοῖς Ἀττικοῖς, ἐπεί τοι Ὅμηρος πῆι μέν φηcι· (a 138) . . . πῆι δέ· (a 146) . . . καὶ Cώφρων ἐν γυναικείοις· τάλ. — τράπ.

Κοικόα Dindorf: καὶ κοα A    ποχ A: τάχ' Kaibel tacite (non in ed.
Athen.)    ἁμὶν τᾶν A

16

Demetr. Lac. De poem. lib. II = P. Herc. 1014, cols. lv–lx (pp. 120 ff.
Romeo + Hordern (2002c))

(55) ωανιν ται [ ] .. δ[ο|κ]ιμαζειν †ινους κα[ι τὴν]| ἀλήθηαν τ[ο]υ λεχθε[ντος] | ὑφ' ἡμῶν ρά⟨ι⟩διον ἐcτ[ιν] |⁵ cυνιδεῖν ἐπι[βάλ]λ̣[ον] | τας τοῖς προεκκει-μέ[νοιc] | ὑπὸ τῆς εἰcαγομένη[c] | γυναικόc· Κοικόαν μὲν | γὰρ ὠνοματο-πόηcεν |¹⁰ [τὴ]ν δούλην ξενίζ[ου|caν] ἤ, φηcι, καλεῖ[ν | ]α .θ .. ηc φηcι[ν Εὐ|ρε]ιπ[ι]δου . α . τι [ ]ωτρα |
　　　　　 ]. [ . . . ]ει[ . ]ι[
15　　　 ]ητ[ . ]ω[
　　　　　 ]. [
　　　　　 ]τ . [
　　　　　 ]. α[
　　　　　 ] . επ λε
20　　　 ]ιν[
　　　　　 ]δι
　　　　　 ]ο[ . . . ]. [
　　　　　 ]. [

(56) . ργο . [– – – | .. ] . ν[ . . . ]η τῆc περ[ὶ | – – –]ω[ .. κ]οινότητό[c | φηcιν [καὶ] δίδωcι[ν αἰ] |⁵ cχροῦ [ ] ἔργοῦ· [τοῦ] | τῳ [δ' ἱc]χ[υ]ρῶc βλέπ[ων], | cυνάπτει δ' ἀκολού|θωc †κεινει πᾶν οἱο[cο]ῦν | θᾶccον ὃ πάλιν [cυνεκ] |¹⁰ δοχικῶc ἀφέ[cτηκε | τ]ῶν π[ροε]ιπομέν[ων .. ]η |

(55) 1–3 suppl. De Falco    3 τ[ο]ῦ λεχθέ[ντος Romeo    5
suppl. De Falco    6 προεκκειμ[ένοιc Lucignano    10–11
Romeo : ξενίζ[ειν De Falco    12 καλει[ Hordern : καλὸ[ν Romeo :
καλ[ὰ De Falco    12–13 Romeo

15

wretched Koikoa, quick, pour water for our hands and
  give us our food

(Athenaeus) The grammarian Aristophanes in his books on
Callimachus' *Pinakes* (fr. 368 Sl.) mocks those who don't know the
difference between κατὰ χειρὸς and ἀπονύψαςθαι. For among the ancients
κατὰ χειρός was used for washing before breakfast and dinner, and
ἀπονύψαςθαι for washing after. The grammarian apparently observed
this in Attic, since Homer says somewhere . . . (*Od.* 1. 138), and somewhere else . . . (*Od.* 1. 146); and Sophron in his Women's mimes:
'wretched — food'.

16

(Demetrius Lacon, *On Poems* 2) **(55)** . . . to test . . . and it is easy
to see the truth of what we have said if we consider what was said
before about the woman he brought in. For he (*sc.* Sophron)
called the slave-girl Koikoa, because she was foreign, who ('or'?),
he says, . . . to call (?) . . . Euripides . . . (*at least 10 lines missing*)
**(56)** action (*2 lines missing*) of the common feature concerning
. . . he says and provides . . . of a shameful act. Considering this
in detail, he immediately links by way of analogy everything
which is in turn separated from the preceding words because of
synecdoche . . . (*at least 9 lines missing*) **(57)** (*3½ lines missing*) and
to use the noun according to antonomasia, saying **(fr. 16A)** 'fried
in a pan' . . . instead of 'garlic' (μῶλυ); this is derived from μωλύω,
which means 'cook slowly'; the women's words, as for an intel-
lect which is also sluggish (?), are the same thing as if she says **(fr.
16B)** 'Nothing for you . . .' (*at least 3 lines missing*) **(58)** (*6 lines
missing*) agreeing with these is the line: **(fr. 16C)** 'I made a single
piece of garlic because you (?) . . . and I made (*sc.* another?)'.
('These words?) are clear(ly) . . . action . . . slowly . . . the (?) . . .
together with the covert meaning . . . Aeschylus . . . (*3 lines missing*) **(59)** (*3 lines missing*) articles (?), altering the styles in the
mimes from the blunt (*1 word missing*) altering the articles (?).
After this there is both antonomasia and metalepsis. Since 'for
the sheep' is the same thing as **(fr. 16D)** 'I tend the [women?] . . .
(*sc.* like goats)', and the phrase **(fr. 16E** = fr. 74) 'dust-reduced' is
said instead of '. . .'; for instead of '. . .' . . . it seems (*5 lines missing*) **(60)** (*1½ lines missing*) instead of 'for people' . . . making . . .

.ος ν[- - -]. . [- - -]δ. . νφ[
. . [ 　　　　]π[
　　　　　　　　](vac.)
15 　　　　　](το[
　　　　　　　　](vac.)
　　　　　　　　](vac.)
　　　　　　　　]τ. [
　　　　　　　　]. . [
20 　　　　　　　]ε. [
**(57)** 　　]τ[. . .]ν[
　　　　　]τον κει. . την[
　　　　　]αι[- - -]ω. [
　　　　　]αται. .

καὶ κατὰ |⁵ [ἀντο]νομασίαν ὀνόμα|[τι χ]ρῆϲθαι **(fr. 16A)** "τη[γανιϲτ]|ὸν"
λεγόμενον. . [.]. [ πα|ρ]ειμένον ἀντὶ τοῦ μῶ|λυ ὃ παρῆκται ἀπὸ τῶν |¹⁰
μωλυομένων· ταῦτα | δ' ἐϲτὶν τὰ βραδέωϲ ἑ|ψόμ[ε]να· τὰ γυναικῶν | ὡϲ
[π]αρὰ καὶ τὴν νω|θρὰν [ϲ]ύνεϲιν τἀτὸ λε|¹⁵γοῦ[ϲ]α τῶι **(fr. 16B)** "μη[δ]ὲν
ϲοι ἁ | α[. . .] οιτ[. . .]η εντ |
　　　　　τ. [ 　　　]ρα[
　　　　　π[ 　　　]. [
**(58)** 　　κει[ 　　　].
　　　　　ϲ. [
　　　　　. [
　　　　　μεν[
5 　　　　. . ω[ 　　].[
　　　　　α[ 　　　]τ[
| ϲυμφώνωϲ τα[ύταιϲ] ἐπί|κεῖτα[ι] τό **(fr. 16C)**· "ἔν μῶλυ 'ποήϲα ὅτι |
καζεο κἀποή[ϲα]". ἐμ|¹⁰φαίνονται [ 　|
　　　　　αρεπει. εργον. κ. [
　　　　　βραδέ[ω]ϲ κα. . . [

**(56)** 3 κ]οινοτητ[όϲ Romeo : κο]ινότητ[α De Falco 　　4–5 suppl.
Romeo 　　6 [ἰϲ]χ[υ]ρῶϲ Gigante 　βλέπων Romeo : ὡϲ βλέπ[εται
De Falco : ὡϲ βλέπ[ειϲ Lucignano 　　8 κεινεῖ De Falco ('κεινεῖ?'),
Romeo : κειν' εἰ Lucignano : fort. ⟨ἐ⟩κεινῆι vel ⟨ἐ⟩κεῖνο Hordern 　9
οἱο[ϲο]ῦν Romeo 　　10 ϲυνεκ]δοχικῶϲ Crönert 　ἀφέ[ϲτηκε Romeo
11 Romeo
**(57)** 5 ἀντο]νομαϲίαν Lucignano: μετο]- Romeo 　　5–7 suppl.
Romeo 　　12 Romeo : γυναικ[ικ]ῶϲ παρὰ κτλ. De Falco
14–15 τἀτὸ λεγοῦ[ϲ]α τῶι Janko (per litt.) 　　15 ἁ Hordern
**(58)** 7 suppl. Romeo 　　8 'ποήϲα ὅτι Janko (per litt.)
9 καζεο Hordern : καζεϲ Romeo 　κἀποή[ϲα] Janko

anyone of those who examine what is in accordance with the passage concerning poems (?). For one should understand that in this way **(fr. 16F)** 'gape vacantly' (is used) for those who are slow learners in the expressions ('reproaches'?) taken from Sophron's mimes . . . the subjects (?) (*at least 9 lines missing*) . . .

56 SOPHRON

..ϲ[– – –]τοδ[
τὸ παρ’ ὑπο.[         ]ν
15      ].αιρ.[
ατη..ο Αἰϲχύλο[-
.ι.ϲ.εν ην[
.ε..[ ]δ̣[ ]εϲτ[
.]εθρ[
(59)      ].[   ].τ.[
.λαγ..νη[ ]α
η..αζα απ.[...] αρθα
| ϟινῶν δὲ τῶν μ[ε]ίμων |⁵ εἴδη ἀπὸ αὐθε[κάϲτω]ν |.]‥ †αρθα κινῶν [ |
μετὰ τοῦτο δὲ ⸌καὶ⸍ ἀντονο|μαϲίαν ἔχει καὶ μετά̣|ληψιν· τὸ μὲν γὰρ
"[ὁ]ι̣|¹⁰εϲϲι" τατὸν ἐϲτιν τῶι (fr. 16D) "αἰ|πολῶ τὰϲ †α[.]δηϲει[.]". | τὸ
δὲ (fr. 16E) "[λε]ι̣[ο]κό[νε]ιτε" πα|ρεί̣λη[κ]ται ἀ̣[ν]τὶ τοῦ | "ϲπ[..]ῳ[.]".
ἀντὶ γὰρ τοῦ |¹⁵ ὡϲ α̣..ον..[.] ἔοικεν |
δ..[..]τοδ[..].μη.[
νι[.]ε.[..]αι[
..[– – –].[
..[..].λουπ[
20      τ.[..].λε[
(60)      .[
..[...]ω. ἀντὶ τοῦ "ἀν-
θρώποιϲ [.].α[
μενοϲ..[         ]τιϲ
|⁵ ζητού[ντω]ν ἃ κατὰ τὸν | τόπον τὸν περὶ [π]οη|μάτων· τοιαῦτ[α (fr. 16F)
κοι|]κύλ[λ]ειν γὰρ ἐν προφ[οραῖϲ | ταῖϲ ἐκ τῶν Ϲώ[φρ]ονοϲ |¹⁰ μείμων τοῖϲ
ὀψι[μ]αθέϲιν | [... αἰ]ρείϲθω· τὰ δὲ πράγ|[ματα..] κα[ὶ      ].|
]νδ[      ].ϲ
]ιη[      ]ιδ
15      ]μεν̣[      ].α
]ϲθαι[
εϲ[      ]ρ.[
υπαν̣[
                  ].
20                  .]

14 ὑπό[νοιαν Crönert : ὑπο[θέϲιν Lucignano      16 Romeo
(59) 3, 6 ἄρθ⟨ρ⟩α Romeo, De Falco (6 ἔναρθ⟨ρ⟩α) : fort. ὀρθὰ      5 εἴδη
Hordern : ει δη Π      α[ὐ]θε[κάϲτω]ν Romeo      9–10 [ὁ]ϊεϲϲι Romeo
11 α[.]ηϲειϲ Romeo
(60) 2 ἀ[ν]θρώποιϲ Romeo : ἀ[ν]θρώπου Crönert, De Falco      3–4
τιϲ | ζ. Hordern      6–7 κοι]κύ[λλ]ειν De Falco      9 ὀψι[μ]αθέϲιν
Romeo      10 αἰ]ρείϲθω Romeo

*17

πίμπλη δέ, Κοικόα

Et. gen. AB (Et. magn. p. 478,13, Et. Gud. p. 288,23 Sturz) οἱ . . .
Δωριεῖϲ λέγουϲι πίμπλη, οἷον (πίπλη οἷον A, om. Et. magn., Et. Gud.) π. δ.
κ.· καὶ γὰρ τὸ ὅρα ὅρη λέγουϲιν, οὕτωϲ πίμπλα πίμπλη (deficit B). Ἡρωδιανὸϲ
(deficit Et. magn.) Περὶ παθῶν (II p. 209,18 L.)
δέ B: om. A, Et. magn., Et. Gud.    Κοικόα Et. magn.: καὶ κόα Et.
Gud.: κυκεῶ AB    Sophroni tribuit Valck. p. 305 B

## Mimorum muliebrium incertorum fragmenta

18

αἱ δὲ μὴ ἐγὼν ἔμαϲϲον ταῖϲ αὐταυτᾶϲ χερϲίν

Apoll. Dysc. pron., GrGr II 1,1 p. 62,23 Schn. μόνη διπλαϲιάζεται παρὰ
Δωριεῦϲιν ἡ αὐτόϲ ἐν τῶι αὐταυτόϲ· αἱ — χερϲίν. Ϲώφρων
ἔματτον Valck. p. 207, -ϲϲον Kaibel: μαθον cod.    αὐταύταϲ Porson
ms. ap. Blomfield 1826, p. 569, -ᾶϲ Ahrens: αυταυταιϲ cod.

19

ἔτι μεθὲν ἁ καρδία παδῆι

Apoll. Dysc. pron., GrGr II 1,1 p. 66,3 ἐμέθεν. πυκνῶϲ αἱ χρήϲειϲ παρὰ
Αἰολεῦϲιν . . . ἀλλὰ καὶ παρὰ Ϲυρακουϲίοιϲ· ἔτι — παδῆι, Ϲώφρων γυναικείοιϲ.
p. 76,29 τὸ ἔτι — παδῆι ἐγκέκλιται

20

ἁ δ' ἄρ' ἄμ' ἐλωβῆτο

Apoll. Dysc. pron., GrGr II, 1,1 p. 100,4 ἁμὲ Δωριεῖϲ· ἁ — λωβῆτο.
Ϲώφρων γυναικείοιϲ ἄμ' ἐλωβῆτο Ahrens p. 472 (praeeunte Bekker): ἁμὲ
λ- cod.

*21

ἦ ῥα καλὼϲ ἀποκαθάραϲα ἐξελεπύρωϲεν

Apoll. Dysc. adv., GrGr II 1,1 p. 169,22 (εἰϲ ωϲ λήγοντα ἐπιρρήματα)
παρὰ Δωριεῦϲιν ἔνια ὀξύνεται, ὥϲτε ('num ὅτε?' Ahrens) κατ' ἔγκλιϲιν
ἀνεγνώϲθη· ἦ — ἐξελ.
    Sophroni tribuit Bast apud Schaef. Greg. Cor. p. 313

## *17

### fill, Koikoa

(*Etymologica*) The Dorians says πίμπλη ('fill'), thus 'fill — Koikoa'; and they also say ὄρη not ὄρα ('see'), and so πίμπλη not πίμπλα. Herodian, *On Modification of Words*.

## Unplaced Women's Fragments

### 18

### If I didn't knead them with my very own hands

(Apollonius Dyscolus, *On Pronouns*) αὐτός is doubled into αὐταυτός only in Doric: 'If — hands'. Sophron.

### 19

### my heart still leaps within me

(Apollonius Dyscolus, *On Pronouns*) ἐμέθεν. The usage is common in Aeolic . . . but also in Syracusan: 'my heart — me'. Sophron in his Women's mimes. (The same) In the phrase 'my heart — me' the accent is enclitic.

### 20

### and indeed she mistreated us

(Apollonius Dyscolus, *On Pronouns*) ἀμέ is Doric: 'and — us'. Sophron in his Women's mimes.

## *21

### cleaning it off nicely she peeled back the skin

(Apollonius Dyscolus, *On Adverbs*, on words in -ως) Again, in Doric some are oxytone, so that we read with loss of accent when enclitic: 'cleaning — skin'.

*22

αὐτῶ ὁρῇς, Φύϲκα;

Apoll. Dysc. adv., GrGr II 1,1 p. 190,17 τὰ τῶι ο παρεδρευόμενα παρὰ Δωριεῦϲι τῶν ἐπιρρημάτων ἀπειράκιϲ ἐν ἀποκοπῆι γίνεται τοῦ θεν καὶ ἐν μεταθέϲει τοῦ ο εἰϲ ω, καθὼϲ προείπομεν (p. 185,14 sq. cum corr. p. 258) αὐτόθεν αὐτῶ — Φύϲκα, τουτόθεν τουτῶ· (fr. 81) . . . τῆιδε εἶχε καὶ τὸ πόθεν λεγόμενον οὕτωϲ, πῶ· (fr. 121).
Sophroni trib. Valck. p. 305 C.

23

τίνεϲ δ' ἐντί ποκα, φίλα, τοίδε τοὶ μακροὶ κόγχοι; :: ϲωλῆνέϲ θην τοῦτοί γα, γλυκύκρεον κογχύλιον, χηρᾶν γυναικῶν λίχνευμα

Athen. 3. 86 ε Ϲώφρων δ' ἐν μίμοιϲ· τίνεϲ — λίχνευμα. Athen. epit. (CE) 1.1. Ϲώφρων δὲ τὸν ϲωλῆνα γλυκύκρεών φηϲι κογχύλιον — λίχνευμα. Demetr. eloc. 151 (post fr. 52) ὅϲα τε ἐπι τῶν γυναικῶν ἀλληγορεῖ, οἷον ἐπ' ἰχθύων ϲωλῆνεϲ — ἰχνεύμαϲι. καὶ μιμικώτερα (μιμητικ- cod., in marg. γρ. καὶ μικρότερα, corr. Victorius) τὰ τοιαῦτά ἐϲτι καὶ αἰϲχρά

δὲ ἔντι Α      τοίδε τοὶ μακροὶ κόγχοι Maas: τοίδε τοι -αὶ -αι Α: ταίδε ταὶ -αὶ -αι Blomfield: τοίδε τοὶ μακρογόγγυλοι Kaibel (coll. Epich. fr. 40,7) ϲωληνϲθην Athen. Α (de CE vid. supra): ϲωλῆνεϲ Demetr.      τοῦτοί γα Athen. Α: om. CE, Demetr.      γλυκύκρεον Athen. Α, Demetr.: -εων Athen. CE      κογχύλιον Athen. CE. Demetr.: -εον Athen. Α      λίχνευμα Athen.: ἰχνεύμαϲι Demetr.

24

ταί γα μὰν κόγχαι, ὥϲπερ αἴ κ' ἐξ ἑνὸς κελεύματοϲ κεχάναντι ἁμὶν πᾶϲαι, τὸ δὲ κρῆϲ ἑκάϲταϲ ἐξέχει

Athen. 3.87 α (κόγχαι λεγόμεναι θηλυκῶϲ, post Ar. fr. 67 et Telecl. fr. 20) καὶ Ϲώφρων γυναικείοιϲ (γυν. om. CE)· αἴ — ἐξέχει. ἀρϲενικῶϲ δέ . . . (Aesch. fr. 34 R., Aristonym. fr. 1, Phryn. fr. 51). Et gen. Α (Et. magn. p. 502,19) κέλευμα . . . Ϲώφρων· οἴ — κελεύματοϲ. Φιλ(όξενοϲ) ῥη(ματικῶι, fr. 378 Theod., Φιλ. ῥ. om. Et. magn.)

ταὶ γα . . . κόγχαι Ahrens: αἴ γα . . . κόγχαι Athen.: οἴ γε . . . -οι Et. (prob. Maas, contra Athenaei testimonium)      αἴ κ' Athen.: om. Et.: αἰκ Kaibel      κελεύματοϲ Athen. Α, Et.: κελεύϲμ- Athen. CE      ἁμὶν Ahrens: ἀμὶν ACE      πᾶϲαι . . . ἑκάϲταϲ CE: πᾶϲαι . . . ἔκαϲτοϲ Α: πάντεϲ . . . ἔκαϲτοϲ Maas

*22

can you see from there, Physka?

(Apollonius Dyscolus, *On Adverbs*) Among the Dorians those adverbs with *o* in the penultimate syllable frequently appear with apocope of θεν and lengthening of *o* into ω, just as we said before αὐτόθεν becomes αὐτῶ, 'can — Physka', and τουτόθεν becomes τουτῶ: (fr. 81) . . . In this manner he also has πῶ instead of πόθεν: (fr. 121). (Cf. also p. 208,1 & fr. 121.)

23

A. Whatever are these, dear, these long shellfish?
B. Why, they're razor-fish, a sweet-meated shell-fish, a delicacy for widow-women.

(Athenaeus) Sophron in his mimes: 'whatever — widow-women'. (Demetrius, *On Style*) Some periphrases are rather wordy, as when . . . and all the metaphors he uses in connection with the women, as if they were fish: 'razor-fish — widow-women'. And this sort of periphrasis is both typical of the mime and indecent.

24

Indeed, the conches, just as if at one command, gape open for us, all of them, and the flesh of each one sticks out

(Athenaeus, on κόγχαι as a feminine noun) And Sophron in his Women's mimes: 'indeed — out'. But as a masculine . . .; (*Etymologicum genuinum* A and *magnum*) κέλευμα: . . . and Sophron 'indeed — command'. Philoxenus, *On Verbs* (fr. 378 Theod.).

## 25

ἴδε καλᾶν κουρίδων, ἴδε καμμάρων, ἴδε φίλα·
θᾶσαι μὰν ὡς ἐρυθραί τ᾿ ἐντὶ καὶ λειοτριχιῶσαι

Athen. ¹3. 106 D κουρίδας δὲ τὰς καρῖδας εἴρηκε Cώφρων ἐν γυναικείοις
οὕτως· ἴδε — λειοτριχιῶσαι. ²7. 306 C (κάμμοροι, post Epich. fr.
53) καὶ Cώφρων δ᾿ ἐν γυναικείοις μίμοις αὐτῶν μέμνηται
ἴδε καλᾶν Mus.: -εν -ὰν A¹   ἴδε καμμάρων (-όρων ACE²), ἴδε φίλα A¹:
'conieceram [in ed. Athen.] ἴδε καμμαρίδων φῦλα, sed pulchrum illud ἴδε
φίλα tenendum (cf. fr. 23), nec improbandus fortasse genetivus' Kaibel
λειοτριχιῶσαι A: λειοστρακιώσαι Ahrens

## 26

δεῖπνον ταῖς θείαις κριβανίτας καὶ ὁμώρους καὶ ἡμιάρτιον Ἑκάται

Athen. 3. 110 BC ὧν καὶ Cώφρων ἐν γυναικείοις μίμοις μνημονεύει λέγων
οὕτως· δεῖπνον — ἑκάται
θείαις A: θεαῖς Wil. ap. Kaib.      ἑκάται A: ἑκάσται Ahrens

## 27

τίς σταιτίτας ἢ κλιβανίτας ἢ ἡμιάρτια πέσσει;

Athen. 3. 110 C (vid. fr. 26) οἶδα δὲ . . . ὅτι Ἀττικοὶ μὲν διὰ τοῦ ρ στοιχείου
λέγουσι καὶ κρίβανον καὶ κριβανίτην, Ἡρόδοτος δ᾿ ἐν δευτέραι τῶν ἱστοριῶν
ἔφη (92,5)· κλιβάνωι διαφανεῖ. καὶ ὁ Cώφρων δὲ ἔφη (καὶ Cώφρων CE)· τίς
— πέσσει.
τίς A: om. CE      ἢ ἡμιάρτια CE: ἢ om. A

## 28

εἰς νύκτα με † αἰτιᾶι σὺν ἄρτωι πλακίται

Athen. 3. 110 C (vid. fr. 26) ὁ δ᾿ αὐτὸς μνημονεύει καὶ πλακίτα τινὸς ἄρτου
ἐν γυναικείοις· εἰς — πλακίται
με αἰτιᾶι σὺν A: duce Casaubono μ᾿ ἐστιάσειν Meineke μ᾿ ἰστ- Botzon μ᾿
ἐσίτισεν Blomfield μ᾿ ἰστίασεν Hauler 'nisi fuit potius μελίτειον vel
μελιτίταν σὺν' Kaibel

## 29

τῶν δὲ χαλκωμάτων καὶ τῶν ἀργυρωμάτων ἐγάργαιρεν ἁ οἰκία

Athen. 6. 230 A (π. τῆς τῶν ἀργυρωμάτων χρήσεως) Cώφρων δ᾿ ἐν
γυναικείοις μίμοις φησί· τῶν — δοκια. Schol. (Γ, Sud. ψ 22) Ar. Ach. 3a. i
καὶ παρὰ τῶι Cώφρονι δέ· ἁ δὲ οἰκία τῶν ἀργ. γάργαιρε
τῶν δὲ χαλκ. καὶ Athen.: om. Schol. Γ, Sud.      τῶν ἀργ. ἐγάργαιρεν ἁ

## 25

Look at the beautiful shrimps, look at the lobsters,
  look, my dear!
See how red and smooth they are!

(Athenaeus) Instead of καρίδας Sophron says κουρίδας ('shrimps') in his Women's mimes, thus: 'see — are'. (The same). And Sophron mentions them (κάμμοροι 'lobsters') in his Women's mimes.

## 26

A dinner for the aunts, oven-bread and neighbour-bread
  and a half-loaf for Hecate

(Athenaeus) Sophron mentions these (breads) in his Women's mimes, saying: 'a dinner — Hecate'.

## 27

Who is baking sweet-bread or oven-bread or half-loaves?

(Athenaeus) I know . . . that Attic has both κρίβανον ('oven') and κριβανίτην ('oven-bread') with ρ, but Herodotus in the second book of his *Histories* (2. 92. 5) says κλιβάνωι διαφανεῖ ('red-hot oven'). Sophron also has 'who — loaves'.

## 28

At night she entertained me (?) with a flat cake

(Athenaeus) The same writer also mentions a bread called πλακίτα in his Women's mimes: 'at night — cake'

## 29

the house was teeming with objects of bronze and silver

(Athenaeus) (on the use of ἀργυρώματα) Sophron in his Women's mimes says: 'the house was gleaming with objects of bronze and silver'. (Scholion on Aristophanes, *Acharnians*, *Suda*) And in Sophron: 'the house was teeming with objects of silver'.

οἰκία Blomfield: τῶν ἀργ. ἐμάρμαιρε δοκια Athen.: ἁ δὲ οἰκία τῶν ἀργ. γάργαιρε Sud.: οἰκιῶν τῶν ἀργύρων μετὰ γαργάρου Schol. Γ

## 30

Athen. 7. 324 F (post fr. 49) κἀν τοῖc γυναικείοιc δὲ ἔφη· τρίγλαν γενεᾶτιν
... p. 325 C γενεᾶτιν δ᾽ ἔφη τὴν τρίγλην Cώφρων, ἐπεὶ αἱ τὸ γένειον ἔχουcαι ἡδίονέc εἰcι μᾶλλον τῶν ἄλλων.

## 30A

(Athen. 9. 394 D) οἱ δὲ Δωριεῖc τὴν πελειάδα ἀντὶ περιcτερᾶc τίθεαcιν, ὡc Cώφρων ἐν γυναικείοιc.

## 31

θᾶcαι ὅcα φύλλα καὶ κάρφεα τοὶ παῖδεc τοὺc ἄνδραc βαλλίζοντι·
οἷόνπερ φαντί, φίλα, τοὺc Τρῶαc τὸν Αἴαντα τῶι παλῶι

Demetr. eloc. 147 (παραβολή) Cώφρων δὲ καὶ αὐτὸc ἐπὶ τοῦ ὁμοίου εἴδουc φηcί θᾶcαι — παλῶι. καὶ γὰρ ἐνταῦθα ἐπίχαριc ἡ παραβολή ἐcτι καὶ (ἐcτι, {καὶ} Kaibel) τοὺc Τρῶαc διαπαίζουcα ὥcπερ παῖδαc. Epimer. Hom. ε 182 τὸ βάλλω κοινόν, τὸ βαλλίζω παρὰ Cώφρονι (cf. fr. 11)
⟨εἰc⟩ τοὺc Ahrens     πλω cod., superscr. ά

## 32

πρὶν αὐτὰν τὰν νόcον εἰc τὸν μυελὸν cκιρωθῆναι

Et. magn. p. 718,1 cκιρωθῆναί φαμεν ἐπὶ τοῦ ῥύπου τοῦ cφόδρα ἐμμένοντοc καὶ δυcεκπλύτου. Cώφρων ἐν τοῖc γυναικείοιc τροπικῶc· πρὶν — cκιρωθῆναι.
cκιρωθῆμεν Ahrens

## 33

ὑγιώτερον κολοκύνταc

Et. magn. p. 774,41 = Et. Sym. V ζητεῖται τὸ παρὰ Cώφρονι ὑγ. κολ. πῶc οὐ λέγει (-εται Et. Sym.) ὑγιέcτερον; ῥητέον (ῥητορικῶc Et. Sym.) οὖν ὅτι ἑκοντὶ ἥμαρτε τὸ ἄκακον τῆc γυναικείαc ἑρμηνείαc μιμούμενοc (μιμ. ἑρμ. Et. Sym.) ὃν τρόπον κἀκεῖ ἐcολοίκιcε· ... (fr. 34). Φιλόξενοc (fr. 351 Theod.)

## 30

(Athenaeus) And in his Women's mimes too he says 'the bearded red mullet'. (The same) Sophron calls the red mullet 'bearded', since those with a beard are sweeter than other sorts.

## 30A

(Athenaeus) The Dorians use πελείας ('rock-pigeon') instead of περιστερά ('pigeon'); so Sophron in his Women's mimes.

## 31

See with how many leaves and dry sticks the boys
   are pelting the men!
Just like they say, my dear, the Trojans pelted
   Aias with mud.

(Demetrius, *On Style*) Sophron says in the same way: 'see — mud'. The charm of the comparison is that it makes fun of the Trojans as if they were children.

## 32

before the illness itself becomes engrained to the marrow

(*Etymologicum magnum*) We say 'become engrained' (cκιρωθῆναι) of dirt which is set fast and difficult to wash out. Sophron uses it figuratively in his Women's mimes: 'before — marrow'.

## 33

healthier than a gourd

(*Etymologica*) There is discussion of Sophron: 'healthier — gourd'. Why doesn't he say ὑγιέcτερον? We must say it was simply because he deliberately made an error to imitate the simplicity of the women's speech. Similarly, he also committed an error when he says . . . (fr. 34).

## 34

τατωμένα τοῦ κιτῶνος, ὁ τόκοc νιν ἀλιφθερώκει

Et. magn. p. 774,45 = Et. Sym. V (vid. fr. 33) ὃν τρόπον κἀκεῖ (-εῖνο Kaibel) ἐϲολοίκιϲε· τατ. — κιτ., ἀντὶ (τὸν codd. corr. Valck. p. 201A) τοῦ ἐνέχυρα θεῖϲα (καὶ θείϲ codd., corr. Valck.), ὁ — ἀλιφθερώκει. Φιλόξενοϲ (fr. 351 Theod.) ἀλιφθερώκει Et. magn. DP: ἀλιφερ- Et. magn. M, Et. Sym.

## 35

ἅμα τέκνων θην δευμένα

Plut. De E apud Delph. 5 p. 386 D (codd. Γ[X¹FD]Π[a AE]x[X³g B]) τοῦ εἴθε τὴν δευτέραν ϲυλλαβὴν * * * (ὥϲπερ καὶ τὸ θην add. Bernardakis [ed. a. 1891, p. 6], plura excidisse censet Paton [ed. a. 1893, p. 5]) παρέλκεϲθαί φαϲιν (φηϲιν FΠ), οἷον τὸ Cώφρονοϲ· ἅμα — δ. ἅμα codd.: ὁμᾶι Ahrens p. 475 (cf. p. 370): ἄλλα Wil. apud Sieveking [ed. a. 1929 p. 6]: ἁ μάτηρ Paton   δευμένα Γ: δεύ- X³: δευομένα ΠΒ

## 36

ὁ μιϲθὸϲ δεκάλιτρον

Poll. IV 173 (codd. FS, A, BC) καὶ μὴν οἵ γε Δωριεῖϲ ποιηταὶ (vid. test. 19) τὴν λίτραν ποτὲ μὲν νόμιϲμά τι (-ματοϲ FS) λεπτὸν (om. B) λέγουϲιν, οἷον ὅταν Cώφρων ἐν τοῖϲ γυναικείοιϲ μίμοιϲ λέγηι (ὅτι add. A)· ὁ — δεκάλ. (sequitur fr. 71)

## 37

Poll. X 175 (codd. FS, BCL) καὶ βαίταϲ δὲ τὰϲ τῶν ἀγροίκων (ἀργύρων FS) διφθέραϲ ἐν τοῖϲ γυναικείοιϲ μίμοιϲ ὁ Cώφρων ἐκάλεϲεν.

## 38

ἁ δ' ἀμφ' ἄλητα κυπτάζει

Schol. vet. (EΓ) et Tricl. (Lh) Ar. Ach. 263b περιϲπωμένωϲ δὲ τὸ Φαλῆϲ ἀναγνωϲτέον (τὸ Φ. π. ἀναγν. Lh), ὡϲ Ἑρμῆϲ (deficit Γ, succedit Γ³). οὕτωϲ δὲ Ἀττικοί. παρὰ Δωριεῦϲι δὲ βαρυτόνωϲ· ἡ δ' — κυπτάζει. Cyrill. An. Par. IV p. 179,16 ἄλειαρ· τὰ ἀπὸ πυρῶν (πυλῶν cod.) ἄλευρα, τὰ δὲ ἀπὸ κριθῆϲ ἄλφιτα (cf. Schol. Hom. υ 108) . . . † ἡ ἀλέα γὰρ καὶ ἄλετα † (leg. τὰ ἀλείατα sive ἀλήατα καὶ ἄλητα), ἔνθεν ὁ μιμογράφοϲ ἔπαιξεν (ἔπεξεν cod.)· ἀλλ' — κυπτάζει. Et. gen. (AB) α 457 Lass.-Liv. ἄλητα. Cώφρων (-ονα B)· ἀμφ' ἄλητα. ἀλήατα κατὰ ϲυγκοπὴν ⟨ἄλητα add. Kaibel⟩. (deficit B) οὕτωϲ Ἡρωδιανὸϲ ἐν τοῖϲ Περὶ παθῶν.

## 34

### deprived of her chiton, the interest on it has ruined her

(continues from fr. 33) Similarly, he also committed an error when he says 'deprived — chiton' (instead of 'putting down a security') 'the interest — her'. Philoxenus (fr. 351 Theod.).

## 35

### together desiring children (?)

(Plutarch, *On the E at Delphi*) [Plutarch's text is clearly lacunose, and the sense required here is unclear.]

## 36

### the pay ten *litra*s

(Pollux) Moreover, the Doric poets sometimes call a certain small coin a λίτρα, as when Sophron in his Women's mimes says 'the pay ten *litra*s'.

## 37

(Pollux) Sophron in his Women's mimes also calls the skins worn by rustics βαίτας.

## 38

### and she bends over the barley-meal

(Scholia on Aristophanes, *Acharnians*) 'Phales' is to be read perispomenon, like 'Hermes'. That is how it is in Attic. But in Doric it is barytone: 'she bends ἀμ φάλητα ('over the phallus')'. (Cyrillus, *Lexicon*) ἄλειαρ: the meal from wheat is called ἄλευρα, and that from barley ἄλφιτα . . . whence the mimographer puns: 'but she bends ἀμφάλιτα'. (*Etymologicum genuinum*) ἄλητα: Sophron 'ἀμφ' ἄλητα ('over the barley-meal')'. ἀλήατα with syncope, so Herodian in *On Modifications of Words*.

ἁ δ' Nauck Phil. 4 (1849) 265: ἡ δ' Schol. Ar. ΕΓ³: ὁ δ' Schol. Ar. Lh:
ἀλλ' Cyrill.    ἀμφ' ἄλητα Et. gen. A: ἀμφάλητα Schol. Ar., Et. gen. B
ἀμφάλιτα Cyrill.: αὖ φαλῆς κατα- Ar. Schol. Lh

39

Schol. (V) Ar. Pac. 28 d (27 sq. ἢν μὴ παραθῶ τρίψας δι' ἡμέρας ὅλης |
ὥσπερ γυναικὶ γογγύλην μεμαγμένην) ὡς τῶν γυναικῶν ἑαυταῖς (τὸ σταῖς
Meineke Call. hymn. et epigr. [1861] p. 147) ἐπιμελέστερον τριβουσῶν,
ὥστε μὴ διακεχύσθαι τὴν μᾶζαν διὰ τὸ ἄτριπτον εἶναι, ἀλλὰ συνεστράφθαι.
παρατετήρηκε δὲ ταῦτα καὶ Cώφρων

40

ἐνθάδε κυπτάζοντι πλεῖσται γυναῖκες

Schol. (RΓ) Ar. Lys. 17 (ἡ μὲν γὰρ ἡμῶν περὶ τόν ἄνδρ' ἐκύπτασεν)
κυπτάζειν ἐστὶ τὸ περί τι πονεῖσθαι (-εῖν Γ, -εῖσθαι etiam Sud. κ 2740) καὶ
διατρίβειν. κομψῶς δὲ τῆι ἀμφιβολίαι καὶ χαριέντως (χάριτες Γ) ⟨ἐχρήσατο
add. Kuster⟩, καθὰ καὶ Cώφρων· ἐνθ. — γυναῖκες. Schol. Bar. (cf. Schol.
Ar. II 4 p. xiii) κυπτάζειν ἐστὶ τὸ περί τι διατρίβειν. Cώφρων· ἐνθ. —
γυναῖκες. σημαίνει δὲ ἡ λέξις καὶ τὸ ἐπικύπτειν καὶ στραγγεύειν
κυπτάζοντι Ahrens -ουσι codd.

*MIMOI ANΔPEIOI*

**Ἄγγελος**

41

ἐξ Ἑστίας ἀρχόμενος καλέω Δία πάντων ἀρχαγέταν

Schol. (S) Arat. 1 p. 44,9 Mart. ζητεῖται διὰ τί ἐκ τοῦ Διὸς ἤρξατο καὶ οὐκ
ἀπὸ τῶν Μουσῶν, ὡς Ὅμηρος. οἰκειότερον ἡγήσατο ἀρχὴν τῶν Φαινομένων
ποιήσασθαι, ἀπὸ τοῦ Διός, ἐπειδὴ καὶ τῶν Μουσῶν ἀρχηγέτης αὐτός ἐστιν. οὐ
φαίνεται δὲ Ἄρατος μόνος οὕτως ἦρχθαι, ἀλλὰ καὶ Κράτης ὁ κωμικὸς εἰπών
(fr. 44)· ἐξ Ἑστίας ἀρχόμενος εὔχομαι θεοῖς, καὶ Cώφρων· ἐξ — ἀρχηγέτην.
Schol. German. (AP, ΠSV) p. 55,5 et 109,15 Br. (p. 45,6 Mart.)
*non solus autem ita coepisse videtur Aratus, sed et Crates comicus a Vesta
incipiens † et profari carmina et Sophron in mimo qui Nuntius inscribitur*
(var. lect. scr-): *a Vesta incipiens omnes* (omnis A) *invoco* (deos add. P)
*Iovem omnium principem*
καλέω . . . ἀρχαγέταν Kaibel: καλῶ . . . ἀρχηγέτην cod.

## 39

(Scholion on Aristophanes, *Peace* (27-8: 'unless I work the stuff over all day long and serve it up kneaded into a ball, as if to a lady') ) Because women knead the dough attentively, to make sure that the bread does not fail to rise because it hasn't been sufficiently pounded, but is kept firm. Sophron has also observed this.

## 40

### here most of the women bend over

(Scholion on Aristophanes, *Lysistrata*) κυπτάζειν means to be busied over and to spend time at something . It can be used cleverly and wittily, in an ambiguous manner, as in Sophron: 'here — bend over'. (The same) κυπτάζειν means to spend time over something. Sophron: 'here — bend over'. The expression means to bend over and be busy.

## II. MEN'S MIMES

### Messenger

## 41

### Starting from Hestia I call Zeus, the founder of all

(Scholion on Aratus, *Phaenomena*) Why did he begin from Zeus, and not from the Muses, like Homer? He intended to make the opening of the *Phaenomena* more appropriate, beginning from Zeus, since Zeus is himself the leader of the Muses. And it seems Aratus was not the only one to begin in this way, but also the comic poet Crates, who says 'starting from Hestia I pray to the gods' (fr. 44) . . . and Sophron: 'starting — all'. (The same) But Aratus seems not to be the only one who began in this way, but also Crates the comic poet, who begins from Vesta . . . and Sophron in the mime entitled Messenger: 'starting from Vesta . . . all'.

## Ὡλιεὺς τὸν ἀγροιώταν

### 42

βλέννωι θηλαμόνι

Athen. 7. 288 A βλέννος τούτου μέμνηται Cώφρων ἐν τῶι ἐπιγραφομένωι Ὡλιεὺς τὸν ἀγρ⟨ο⟩ιώταν· βλ. θηλ. ἔcτι δὲ κωβιῶι τὴν ἰδέαν παραπλήcιος

### 43

Athen. 3. 86 A παρὰ Cώφρονι δ᾽ οἱ κόγχοι μελαινίδες λέγονται· (fr. 96) . . . ἐν (δὲ add. Schweigh., ἃc ante ἐν Desrousseaux τῶι ἐπιγραφομένωι Ὡλιεὺς τὸν ἀγροιώταν χηράμβας ὀνομάζει

### 44

Athen. 7. 309 C (κωβιοί) καὶ Cώφρων ἐν τῶι Ἀγροιώτηι κωθωνοπλύται φηcὶ καὶ τὸν τοῦ θυννοθήρα δὲ υἱὸν ἴcωc ἀπὸ τούτου Κωθωνίαν προcηγόρευcεν (fr. 46). Cικελιῶται δ᾽ εἰcὶν οἱ τὸν κωβιὸν κώθωνα καλοῦντεc, ὡc Νίκανδρόc φηcιν ὁ Κολοφώνιοc ἐν ταῖc Γλώτταιc (fr. 141 Schn.) καὶ Ἀπολλόδωροc ἐν τοῖc περὶ Cώφρονος (244 F 217 Jac.).
Ἀγροιώτηι· κωθωνοπλύται (vel κωθολινοπλ-) Casaub.: -ωτικῶι θωλινοπλ- A

## Θυννοθήρας

### 45

ἁ δὲ γαστὴρ ὑμέων καρχαρίαc, ὅκκα τινὸc δῆcθε

Athen. 7. 306 D Cώφρων Θυννοθήραι· ἁ — δῆcθε
ὅκκα τινὸc Ahrens, Botzon: ὁκαττινοc A: ὅκα τινὸc Schweigh.

### 46

Athen. 7. 309 C (vid. fr. 44) τὸν τοῦ θυννοθήρα δὲ υἱὸν . . . Κωθωνίαν προcηγόρευcεν

### 47

ἐγκίκρα, ὡc εἴω

Et magn.[1] p. 423,23 (brevius Et. gen.[1] AB s.v. ἤϊε, om. nomine auctoris et mimi) ἔcτιν εἴω τὸ πορεύομαι, διὰ διφθόγγου, ὥc φηcι Cώφρων ἐν Θυννοθήραι· ἐγκ. — εἴω. Choerob. in Theod. can., GrGr IV 2 p. 104,34 Hilg. ≅ Epimer. Hom. [1]A 47[A] (~ 176[B] p. 178,21 Dyck) ≅ Et. magn.[2]

## The Fisherman against the Countryman

### 42

### with the sucking blenny

(Athenaeus, on βλέννος). Sophron mentions this in the mime entitled *The Fisherman against the Countryman*: 'with — blenny'. It is of similar appearance to the goby.

### 43

(Athenaeus) In Sophron κόγχοι ('conches') are called μελαινίδες (fr. 96). . . in the mime entitled *The Fisherman against the Countryman* he calls them χηράμβας.

### 44

(Athenaeus, on gobies) Furthermore, Sophron in the *Countryman* says κωθωνοπλύται, and perhaps it is from this word that he called the tunafisher's son Cothonias (= fr. 46). It is Siceliotes who say κώθων for κωβιός ('goby'), according to Nicander of Colophon in his *Glosses* (fr. 141 Schn.), and Apollodorus in his commentaries on Sophron (*FGrH* 244 F 217).

## Tunafisher

### 45

### your (pl.) belly's a shark when you (pl.) want something

(Athenaeus) Sophron in *Tunafisher*: 'your — something'.

### 46 = fr. 44

### 47

### mix it so I can set off

(*Etymologica*) εἴω means πορεύομαι ('go'), with a diphthong, as Sophron says in *Tunafisher*: 'mix — set off'. (Choeroboscus on Theodosius, *Canons*; *Homeric Parsings*; and *Etymologicum magnum*) εἴω means πορεύομαι, as in Sophron 'ἐγκ. — εἴω', i.e. 'mix so that I can set off'.

p. 121,29 (brevius Et. gen.[2] A s.v. ἀπῆιμεν, om. nom. auctoris) εἴω . . . τὸ
πορεύομαι, ὡς παρὰ Cώφρονι· ἐγκ. — εἴω, τουτέcτι κέραcον ἵνα πορευθῶ (~
sine nom. auctoris Eust.[1] in Il. p. 933,41, brevius Epimer. Hom.[2] ι 29 et
Et. gen.[3] B s.v. ἔνθ' εἴην = Philox. fr. 397 Theod., cf. etiam fr. 619).
Epimer. Hom.[3] ε 183 (p. 326,16 Dyck) κιγκρῶ, ἀφ' οὗ τὸ παρὰ Cώφρονι
ἐγκ. — εἴω. Eust.[2] in Il. p. 234,39 κιγκρῶ, οὗ χρῆcιc τὸ ἐγκ. — εἴω, ἤγουν
κίρνα ὡς ὀδεύω (Philox. fr. **667 Theod.)
    ἐγκίκρα Et. gen.[1] et [3], Et. magn.[1], Epimer.[2] et [3], Eust.: ἐγκί(η)ρα
Choerob.: ἐγκίγκρα Et. magn.[2]: κίγκρα Et. gen.[2], Epimer.[1]

## 48

λοξῶν τὰc λογάδαc

Et. magn. p. 572,36 (om. Et. gen. AB, λ 158 Alp.) λογάδεc· ἐπὶ τῶν
ὀφθαλμῶν τὰ λευκά . . . εἴρηται δὲ οἷον λοχάδεc, ἐν αἷc αἱ κόραι λοχῶcι καὶ
οἷον λέχοc εἰcὶν αὐταῖc (hucusque Et. Orion. p. 92,6–9). ἢ οἷον λευκάδεc
. . . ἢ ὅτι λοξοῦνται ἐν τῶι βλέπειν κατὰ τὰc ἐπιcτροφάc. Cώφρων ἐν
Θυννοθήραιc (-θη DM, -θηραι Kaibel)· λοξ. — λογάδαc. οὕτωc Cωρανόc.

## Παιδικὰ ποιφυξεῖc

Schol. Nicandr. ther. 180 ποιφύζειν . . . λέγεται . . . ἐπὶ τοῦ ἐκφοβεῖν, ὡc
Cώφρων ἐν μίμοιc (-ωι Hauler) παιδικὰ (-ὰc codd., corr. Ald.) ποιφυξεῖc
(-ύξειc GVRvp, -ίξειc CK, -ύζειc L, corr. Kaibel praeeunte Haulero).

## 49

τρίγλαc μὲν γένηον, τριγόλα δ' ὀπιcθίδια

Athen. 7[1]. 324 F (post fr. 66) ἐν δὲ τῶι ἐπιγραφομένωι Παιδικὰ ποιφυξεῖc
(παιδὶ καcποιφυξὶc A, corr. Casaub. qui -φύξειc, -φυξεῖc Kaibel praeeunte
Haulero) φηcί· τρίγλ. — ὀπιcθίδια (sequitur fr. 30). paullo post[2] Τρύφων
φηcὶν ἐν τοῖc περὶ ζώιων (fr. 121 Vels.) τὸν τριγόλαν (τρυγ- A) τινὰc οἴεcθαι
κόκκυγα εἶναι διά τε τὸ ἐμφερὲc καὶ τὴν τῶν ὀπιcθίων ξηρότητα, ἣν
cεcημείωται ὁ Cώφρων λέγων· τρίγλαc — ὀπ.
    μὲν [2]ACE: om. [1]A    γένηον Meineke, duce Ahrensio qui -ειον: τ'
ενηον [1]A: γε πίοναc [2]ACE    τριγόλα δ' ὀπιcθίδια Schweigh.: -λα δ'
ὀπιcθίαν [2]A: -λα δ' ὀπίcθια [2]CE: λαπιcθίδια [1]A    cf. Epich. fr. 79,2 et vid.
W. Schulze Kl. Schr. p. 73°

(Eustathius, commentary on Homer, *Iliad*) κιγκρῶ, whence 'ἐγκ. — εἴω', or 'mix it so I can go'. (Much the same is reported in various other sources.)

## 48

### casting sideways the whites of their eyes

(*Etymologicum magnum*) λογάδες: the whites of the eyes . . . that is as it were the λοχάδες, where the pupils as it were lie in ambush (λοχῶcι) and have their bed (λέχος). Or perhaps λευκάδες ('whites') . . . or because they are cast sideways (λοξοῦνται) when one looks around. Sophron in *Tunafisher*: 'casting — eyes'. Thus Soranus.

## You'll frighten off boys

## 49

### the chin of a mullet, but a *trigolas'* hinder-parts

(Athenaeus, following fr. 66) In the mime entitled *You'll frighten off boys* he says 'the chin — hinder-parts'. . . (The same) Tryphon says in *On Animals* (fr. 121) that some think the τριγόλας the same as the piper because of the general similarity and the extreme dryness of its anus. Sophron mentions this, saying: 'the chin — hinder-parts'.

*Προμύθιον*

50

κοντῶι μηλαφῶν αὐτὸ τυφεῖς

Prov. cod. Par. suppl. 676 apud Cohn CPG Suppl. I p. 82 nr. 94 κοντ[ῶι
μηλαφᾶις]· κατὰ τῶν τὰ ἄδηλα τελέως τεκμαιρομένων (cf. Phot. κ 305 =
Sud. κ 652). ὥσπερεὶ λέγοι τις· κοντὸν κ[α]θ[εὶς] δι᾽ α[ὐτοῦ] ψηλαφᾶις.
Cώφρων ἐν Προμυθίωι· κοντῶι — τύψηις. ἔοικε δὲ διαφ[έρειν] τὸ ψηλαφᾶν τοῦ
μηλαφᾶν, ἤτοι ὅτι τὸ μὲν τὸ δι᾽ ἑτέρου ἅπτεςθαι, τὸ δὲ ψηλαφᾶν [ ] ἐςτὶ ταῖς
χερςὶ θιγεῖν
    κοντ[ῶι μηλαφᾶις] suppl. Cohn    κ[α]θ[εὶς] δι᾽ α[ὐτοῦ] suppl. Crusius
διαφ[έρειν] suppl. Cohn    τυφεῖς Wil. Kl. Schr. IV p. 51 (a. 1899):
τύψηις cod.

51

Antiatt. p. 85,24 βλεν⟨ν⟩όν· τὸν νωθῆ καὶ μωρόν (Hesych. β 695). Cώφρων
Προμυθίωι (-μηθεῖ cod., corr. Jernstedt). Phot. β 157 βλεννόν· τὸν μωρόν.
οὕτως Cώφρων. cημαίνει δὲ καὶ τὸν νωθῆ

## Mimorum virilium incertorum fragmenta

52

ἐνθάδε ὧν κἠγὼ παρ᾽ ὑμὲ τοὺς ὁμότριχας ἐξορμίζομαι πλόον
δοκάζων· †ποντίναι† γὰρ ἤδη τοῖς ταλικοῖςδε ταὶ ἄγκυραι

Demetr. eloc. 151 ἔχουςι δέ τι ςτωμύλον καὶ ἀλληγορίαι τινές, ὥσπερ τό
† δελφοῖ παιδίον ὑμῶν ἁ κύων φέρει. καὶ τὰ Cώφρονος δὲ τὰ ἐπὶ τῶν γερόντων·
ἐνθάδε — ἄγκυραι. sequitur fr. 23
    ἐνθάδε ὧν J. G. Schneider in editione (1779) p. 158: ενθαδεον (accentu
super α deleto) cod.    ὑμὲ Ahrens: ὕμμε cod.    ὁμότριχας cod.: ὅτρ.
Schneider    ποντίναι γὰρ cod.: πόντιαι γὰρ Gale: πόντιον· ἀρτέαι γὰρ
Kaibel    ταλικοῖςδε ταὶ edd.: ταλίκοις δέται cod.: -οις ἀρτέαι ταὶ Raderm.

53

κνυζοῦμαι δὲ οὐδὲν ἰςχύων· ἁ δὲ ξυςμὰ ἐκ ποδῶν εἰς κεφαλὰν
ἱππάζεται

Epimer. Hom. κ 125 (O, Et. Gud.) εἴρηται δὲ κνυζοῦν καὶ τὸ ξύειν παρὰ
Δωριεῦςι . . . ὡς Cώφρων· κνυζ. — ἰςχύων (deficit O)· ἁ δὲ — ἱππάζεται. Et.
gen. AB (Et. magn. p. 523,3) τὸ δὲ κνυζῶ cημαίνει πολλάκις τὸ ξύειν, ὡς
παρὰ Cώφρονι ἐν μίμοις, οἷον· κνυζ — ἰςχύων . . . οὕτως Ἡρωδιανός (I

## Promythion

### 50

prodding with the pole you'll strike it

(Proverb collection) [you prod with a p]ole: of those who arrive at a final conclusion on the basis of unknown facts. Just as one might say: 'pushing the pole right through it you're feeling about'. Sophron in *Promythion*: 'prodding — strike it'. Apparently ψηλαφάω is different from μηλαφάω; the first means to reach through another thing, but ψηλαφάω [     ] means to touch with the hands.

### 51

(The Antiatticist) βλεν⟨ν⟩όν: someone sluggish and stupid. Sophron in *Promythion*. (Phot. β 157) βλεννόν: an idiot. Thus Sophron. It also means a sluggard.

## Unplaced men's fragments

### 52

Since I'm here with you old fellows like me, I'll watch the tide
    and put out to sea; for men of our age have . . . 'anchors'!

(Demetrius, *On Style*) Some periphrases are rather wordy, like [a corrupt quotation] and the one relating to the old men in Sophron: 'since — "anchors" '.

### 53

I'm scratching myself even though I've no strength left;
    and the itch is galloping from my feet to my head.

(*Homeric Parsings*) In Doric κνυζοῦν is found for ξύειν . . . as Sophron: 'I'm — head'. (*Etymologicum genuinum*) κνυζῶ often means ξύειν, as Sophron in his mimes, thus: 'I'm — left' . . . So Herodian.

76 SOPHRON

p. 445,5 L., cf. Philox. fr. 120 Theod.). Eust. in Od. p. 1766,33 ὁ δ᾽ αὐτός
(Herodianus ) . . . διασκευάζων . . . ὡς ταὐτόν ἐςτι τό τε ξύειν καὶ τὸ κνεῖν
('l. κνῆν᾽ Kaibel) . . . παράγει χρήςεις τοιαύτας· ξύομαι — ἰςχύων, τουτέςτι
κνῶμαι, καὶ Cώφρων· βαιὰ δ᾽ ἔξυςμαι (κνῶμαι. Cώφρων. καί· ἁ δὲ ξυςμὰ
Kaibel) ἐκ — κεφαλήν, ἤγουν κέκνηςμαι.
κνυζοῦμαι Kaibel: κνύζομαι Epim., Et. gen.: ξύομαι Eust.     δε¹ Epim.:
δ᾽ Eust.: om. Et. gen.     ποδῶν Et. Gud.: ποδὸς Eust.     κεφαλάν
Ahrens: -ήν Et. Gud., Eust.

54

τὸ γὰρ ἀπεχθόμενον γῆρας ἁμὲ μαραῖνον ταριχεύει

Stob. IV 50ᵇ,65 (ψόγος γήρως) vol. V p. 1044 H. (codd. MA) Cώφρονος τὸ
— ταριχεύει. Schol. (M) Aesch. Cho. 296 (ταριχευθέντα) καὶ ὁ Cώφρων· τὸ
— ταριχεύει
γὰρ ἀπεχθόμενον om. Schol. Aesch.     ἁμὲ Ahrens: ἅμμε Schol.
Aesch.: ἅμα Stob.

55

τί μὰν ξύcιλος; :: τί γάρ; cύφαρ ἀντ᾽ ἀνδρός

Et. gen. AB (Et. magn. p. 736,57) cύφαρ· οὐχ ἁπλῶς τὸ γῆρας ἀλλ᾽ ὡς
ἐπιγέννημα γήρως . . . τὸ κατερρυςωμένον, τουτέςτι τὸ δέρμα (deficit B). καὶ
Cώφρων ἐν τοῖς ἀνδρείοις δεδήλωκε μίμοις (δεδ. μ. om. A) εἰπών· τί μὰν —
ἀνδρός. τὸν ἀνακρινόμενον γέροντα ξύcιλον παίζων εἴρηκεν ἀπὸ τοῦ κνᾶcθαι
(detritum in A, vid. ἠνάcθαι fuisse) καὶ ξύειν τὸ δέρμα, κἄπειτα
ἀποκρινόμενον (-όμαιμον A, -αμένου Kaibel) cύφαρ ἀ ἀ., δέρμα ψιλόν, ὡς
τῶν ἄλλων ἤδη δεδαπανημένων (brevius Et. Orion. p. 144,15, in sede
Sorani et Eust. ex Herodiano, post fr. 53).

56

καθαιρημένος θην καὶ τῆνος ὑπὸ τῶ χρόνω

Apoll. Dysc. pron., GrGr II 1,1 p. 59,12 Schn. Δωριεῖς τῆνος· καθ. —
χρόνω. Cώφρων
καθαιρημένος Ahrens: καθηιρ- cod.     τῶ χρόνω cod.: τῶι -ωι Ahrens

57

ὦ οὗτος, ἦ οἴηι cτρατείαν ἐccεῖcθαι;

Apoll. Dysc. pron., GrGr II 1,1 ¹p. 57,18 (οὗτος κατὰ τὸ δεύτερον
πρόσωπον) ὦ — ἐccεῖcθαι; Cώφρων ἀνδρείοις. ²p. 21,11 (οὗτος ἐπὶ κλήςεως)
ὦ — ἐccεῖcθαι; Cώφρων
οἴηι Ahrens: οιη ²cod.: οιη ¹cod.     cτρατείαν Bekker: -ηαν ²cod.: -ιαν
¹cod.

### 54

For hateful, withering old age is pickling us.

(Stobaeus) Sophron: 'for — us'. (Scholion on Aeschylus, *Libation-Bearers*) And Sophron: 'for — us'.

### 55

A.  Why ξύcιλοc ?
B.  What else? (I'm a [?]) piece of wrinkled skin instead of a man!

(*Etymologica*) cῦφαρ refers not simply to old age, but to the result of old age . . . what has become wrinkled (i.e. the skin). And Sophron in his Men's mimes makes this clear when he says: 'why — man'. The old man asking the question jokingly says ξύcιλοc instead of being scraped and scratching the skin, and the one who answers 'piece of wrinkled skin — man' (that is, with plucked skin) as if the rest had been destroyed.

### 56

and he too worn out by time

(Apollonius Dyscolus, *On Pronouns*) τῆνοc ('that') is Doric. 'and — time'. Sophron.

### 57

hey you, do you think there's going to be an expedition?

(Apollonius Dyscolus, *On Pronouns*, on οὗτοc in the second person) 'hey you — expedition?' Sophron in his Men's mimes.

58

οὐχ ὁ δεῖν τυ †ἐπικαζε†

Apoll. Dysc. pron., GrGr II 1,1 p. 59,21 ὁ δεῖνα . . . παρὰ δὲ Cυρακουcίοιc
δίχα τοῦ α· οὐχ — ἐπικαζε. Cώφρων ἀνδρείοιc
οδιν cod.  τυ cod.: τι Guttentag ap. Schn.  ἐπικαζε cod.: ἐπείκαζε
Guttentag: ἐπίαζε Botzon p. 15: 'possis ἐπείραζε Kaibel: ἐπύγιζε vel
ἐπύγαζε Blomfield

59

Ἡρακλῆς τεοῦς κάρρων ἧς

Apoll. Dysc. pron., GrGr II 1,1 p. 74,21 τῆι μὲν οὖν ἐμοῦ cύζυγος ἡ cοῦ
. . . καὶ τῆι ἐμοῦς Δωρίωι (vid. Epich. fr. 140) ἡ τεοῦς· Ἡρ. — ἧς Cώφρων
κάρρων Valck. p. 303 C: καρων cod.  ἧς Ahrens p. 467: ἦν cod.

60

ὑμὲς δὲ ἐπεγγυάμενοι θωκεῖτε

Apoll. Dysc. pron., GrGr II 1,1 p. 93,22 ὑμεῖς. Δωριεῖς ὑμές (ὕμμες
cod.)· ὑμὲς — θωκεῖτε. Cώφρων

61

ἐμὲ δ᾽ Ἀρχωνίδας ἴαλλε παρ᾽ ὑμέ

Apoll. Dysc. pron., GrGr II 1,1 p. 100,10 ὑμᾶς . . . Δωριεῖς ὑμέ· ἐμὲ —
ὑμέ. ἀνδρείοιc Cώφρων

62

λιχνοτέρα τᾶν πορφυρᾶν

Athen. 3. 89A Ἀπολλόδωρος δ᾽ ὁ Ἀθηναῖος ἐν τοῖς περὶ Cώφρονος (244 F 216
Jac.) προθεὶς τὸ (τὰ A, corr. Mus., cf. fr. 63) λ. τ. π. (accedunt CE) φησιν
ὅτι παροιμία ἐστὶν (ἡ δὲ παρ. ἡ λέγουσα λιχνότερος πορφύρας CE) καὶ λέγεται
(καὶ λέγει A, om. CE, corr. Kaibel), ὡς μέν τινες, ἀπὸ τοῦ βάμματος
(εἴρηται add. CE, ἀκούουσιν add. Cobet ms. teste Peppink Obs. p. 23)· οὗ
γὰρ ἂν προσψαύσηι (οὗ γὰρ ψαύσει CE) ἕλκει ἐφ᾽ ἑαυτὸ καὶ τοῖς παρατε-
θειμένοις (προσπαρατ- A) ἐμποιεῖ (ἔμποι A) χρώματος αὐγήν. ἄλλοι δ᾽ ἀπὸ
(ἐπὶ A) τοῦ ζώιου

63

καταπυγοτέραν τ᾽ ἀλφηστᾶν

Athen. 7. 281 E (inde Et. gen. AB = Et. Magn. p. 72,51 = An. Par. IV
p. 6,27, Eust. in Il. p. 1166,45) Ἀπολλόδωρος ὁ Ἀθηναῖος ἐν τῶι τρίτωι περὶ

58

(Apollonius Dyscolus, *On Pronouns*) The fragment is too corrupt to translate. Apollonius is illustrating the Syracusan use of ὁ δεῖνα without the final α (ὁ δεῖν).

59

### Heracles was stronger than you

(Apollonius Dyscolus, *On Pronouns*) So ϲοῦ corresponds with ἐμοῦ . . . and τεοῦϲ with Doric ἐμοῦϲ: 'Heracles — you'. Sophron.

60

### you (pl.) sit pledged

(Apollonius Dyscolus, *On Pronouns*) ὑμεῖϲ. Doric ὑμέϲ. 'you — pledged'. Sophron.

61

### Archonidas sends me to you (pl.)

(Apollonius Dyscolus, *On Pronouns*) ὑμᾶϲ . . . Doric has ὑμέ. 'Archonidas — you'. Sophron in his Men's mimes.

62

### greedier than purple-shells

(Athenaeus) Apollodorus of Athens in his books on Sophron says (*FGrH* 244 F 216), after the lemma 'greedier — shells', that it is a proverb and states that according to some it derives from the dye; this draws to itself whatever it touches, and so produces in whatever is placed next to it its own tinge; but others say the proverb relates to the animal itself.

63

### and more lecherous than the wrasse

(Athenaeus) Apollodorus of Athens, in the third book on Sophron, the one on the Men's mimes, says (*FGrH* 244 F 214), after the lemma

Cώφρονος τῶι εἰς τοὺς ἀνδρείους μίμους (244 F 214 Jac., nulla Sophronis mentio in Athen. CE et Eust.) προθεὶς τὸ κ. τ᾽ ἁ. φησίν· "ἰχθῦς τινες οἱ ἀλφησταὶ τὸ μὲν ὅλον κιρροειδεῖς (κηρο- A), πορφυρίζοντες δὲ κατά τινα μέρη. φασὶ δ᾽ αὐτοὺς ἁλίσκεσθαι σύνδυο καὶ φαίνεσθαι τὸν ἕτερον ἐπὶ τοῦ ἑτέρου κατ᾽ οὐρὰν ἑπόμενον. ἀπὸ τοῦ οὖν κατὰ τὴν πυγὴν θατέρωι τὸν ἕτερον ἀκολουθεῖν τῶν ἀρχαίων τινὲς τοὺς ἀκρατεῖς καὶ καταφερεῖς οὕτω καλοῦσιν"
τ᾽ Athen. A: om. CE, Eust., Et.   ἀλφηστᾶν A, Et.: -ῶν CE, Eust.

## 64

κέστραι βότιν κάπτουσαι

Athen. 7. 286 D Cώφρων δ᾽ ἐν μίμοις ἀνδρείοις βότιν καλεῖ τινα ἰχθὺν ἐν τούτοις· κέστραι — κάπτουσαι. καὶ μήποτε βοτάνην τινὰ λέγει. p. 323A καὶ Cώφρων ἐν ἀνδρείοις· κέστραι — κάπτουσαι

## 65

Athen. 7. 287 C (βεμβράδες) καὶ Cώφρων ἐν ἀνδρείοις· βαμβραδόνι †ραφεια† ραφεια A: ῥαφίδι Casaub.: 'latet aliud velut τραφερᾶι' Kaibel.

## 66

τριγόλαι ὀμφαλοτόμωι
τριγόλαν τὸν εὐδιαῖον

Athen. 7. 324 E Cώφρων δ᾽ ἐν τοῖς ἀνδρείοις τριγόλας τινὰς ἐν τούτοις ὀνομάζει· τρ. ὀμφ., καί· τρ. τ. εὐδ.
2 τριγόλαν Mus.: -αι A

## 67

Ἠπιάλης ὁ τὸν πατέρα πνίγων

Demetr. eloc. 156 ἐν δὲ τοῖς πράγμασι λαμβάνονται χάριτες ἐκ παροιμίας. φύσει γὰρ χαρίεν πρᾶγμά ἐστιν παροιμία, ὡς ὁ Cώφρων μὲν ἐπίης, ἔφη ὁ — πνίγων. καὶ ἀλλαχόθι πού φησιν· (fr. 105)
Ἠπιάλης ex fr. 68: ἐπίης cod.: Ἐπιάλης Gale: Ἠπιόλης Kaibel

## 68

Ἡρακλῆς Ἠπιάλητα πνίγων

Eust. in Il. p. 561,17 ἐν δὲ ῥητορικῶι λεξικῶι (Ael. Dion. η 12) φέρεται ὅτι Ἐπιάλτην Ἀττικοί φασι δαίμονά τινα (vid. ad Phrynichi fabulam, VII p. 395) . . . ἑτέρωθι δέ, ὅτι ἐπιάλτης ὁ πνιγαλίων ὑπό τινων (cf. Phot. s.v. Ἠπιάλης, p. 72,16 = η 214), ὁ δ᾽ αὐτὸς καὶ ἠπίαλος. ἐν δὲ τοῖς Ἡρωδιανοῦ (I p. 69,13 L.) κεῖται καὶ ἠπιάλης ἠπιάλητος. οὗ χρῆσις, φησί, παρὰ Cώφρονι, οἷον· Ἡρ. — πν.

'more lecherous — wrasse': 'Some fish, the alphestae, are generally of yellowish appearance, but have purple in certain spots. It is said they are caught in pairs, and one appears after the other, following at the tail. From this, that one follows at the behind of the other, some of the old poets call incontinent and lascivious men by their name.'

## 64
### sharks gulping down *botis*

(Athenaeus) Sophron in his Men's mimes calls a certain fish βότιϲ in these words 'sharks — *botis*', And perhaps he means a plant (βοτάνη). (The same) And Sophron in his Men's mimes: 'sharks — *botis*'.

## 65
### with a well-fed (?) sprat

(Athenaeus) And Sophron in his Men's mimes: 'with — sprat'

## 66
### with the navel-cutting *trigola*
### the *trigola* that brings fair weather

(Athenaeus) Sophron in his Men's mimes calls certain fish *trigolas* with these words: 'with — *trigola*', and 'the *trigola* — weather' (fr. 49 follows).

## 67
### Epiales who throttles his father

(Demetrius, *On Style*) Charm in content derives from the use of proverbs, because a proverb is naturally something charming, as Sophron said 'Epiales — father'. And somewhere else he says (fr. 105).

## 68
### Heracles throttling Epiales

(Eustathius, commentary on Homer, *Iliad*) In the *Lexicon of Rhetoric* it is reported that in Attic Epialtes is a sort of monster . . . and elsewhere that nightmares are called *epialtes* by some, but also ἠπίαλοϲ. In the works of Herodian (I p. 69,13 L.) are found the forms ἠπιάλης, genitive ἠπιάλητοϲ. Of which, he says, this is an example in Sophron: 'Heracles — Epiales (Ἠπιάλητα)'.

## 69

Et. Gud. z (Par. suppl. 172) ap. Theod. Gl. 50 (1972) 30 μαcτροπόc· παρὰ τὸ μαίεcθαι τοὺc τρόπουc τῶν πορνευουcῶν γυναικῶν (hucusque = Et. Orion. p. 101,30). οὕτωc ἐν ὑπομνήματι (Apollodori, om. Jacoby) τῶν Cώφρονοc ἀνδρείων.

## 70

Harp. p. 267,19 Dind. (π 180 K.) πωλάc· ἀντὶ τοῦ πράcειc Ὑπερείδηc ἐν τῶι πρὸc Ἀπελλαῖον (fr. 12 J.). ἔcτι τοὔνομα καὶ ἐν τοῖc Cώφρονοc ἀνδρείοιc.

## 71

cῶcαι δ᾽ οὐδὲ τὰc δύο λίτραc δύναμαι

Poll. IV 174 (codd. FS, A, BC; vid. fr. 36) καὶ πάλιν ἐν τοῖc ἀνδρείοιc· cῶcαι — δύν.
δύναμαι FSA: om. BC

## 72

Ἡράκλειc, πνίγειc γύλιόν τι

Schol. (RV, Sud. γ 476) Ar. Pac. 527 b. a (γύλιοc) ἔcτι δὲ καὶ (καὶ om. V) ζῶιον, οὗ μέμνηται Cώφρων (οὗ μ. C. om. Sud.)· Ἡρ. — τί (om. R, Sud.). ἔcτι δὲ (om. R, Sud.) ὁ καλούμενοc ὑπό τινων χοιρογρύλλιοc (-γρυλλοc ex -γρυλιοc V)
πνίγειc Kaibel: -οc V    τί V: τύ Kaibel

## *73

μωρότεροc εἶ Μορύχου, ὃc τἄνδον ἀφεὶc ἔξω τὰc οἰκίαc κάθηται

Zenob. vulg. V 13 μωρότεροc εἶ Μορύχου· αὕτη ἡ παροιμία λέγεται παρὰ τοῖc Cικελιώταιc, ἐπὶ εὐηθέc τι διαπραccομένων, ὥc φηcι Πολέμων ἐν τῆι πρὸc Διόφιλον ἐπιcτολῆι (fr. 73 Pr.). λέγεται δὲ οὕτωc· μωρότεροc — κάθηται. Μόρυχοc δὲ Διονύcου ἐπίθετον . . . καταγνωcθῆναι δὲ αὐτοῦ εὐήθειαν παρόcον ἔξω τοῦ νεὼ τὸ ἄγαλμα αὐτοῦ ἐcτι, παρὰ τῆι εἰcόδωι ἐν ὑπαίθρωι. eadem fere Phot. μ 652 = Sud. μ 1343, nulla Polemonis aut Siciliae mentione Zenob. Ath. III 68, brevius Apost. XI 91
εἶ Zen., Sud.: εἰμι Phot.    Μορύχου Zen. vulg., Sud. GM: Μωρ-Phot., Sud. AFV: Μωρ -Διονύcου Zen. Ath.    τἄνδον Phot., Sud., ex corr. Zen. Ath.: τὰ ἔνδον Zen. vulg.    τῆc codd.

### 69

(*Etymologicum Gudianum*) μαcτροπόc ('pimp'): since he brings forth (μαίεcθαι) the characters (τρόποι) of women who are prostitutes. Thus in the commentary on Sophron's Men's mimes.

### 70

(Harpocration, *Lexicon of the Ten Attic Orators*) πωλάc ('sale'): instead of πράceιc. Hyperides in *Against Apellaeus*. The word also appears in Sophron's Men's mimes.

### 71

I can't save even two *litra*s

(Pollux) And again in the Men's mimes: 'I can't — *litra*s'.

### 72

By Heracles, you're strangling a hedgehog

(Scholion on Aristophanes, *Peace*, on γύλιοc) It is also an animal, which Sophron mentions: 'By Heracles — hedgehog'. Some call it a χοιρογρύλλιοc ('hedgehog').

### *73

You're stupider than Morychus, who has abandoned what's inside and sits outside his temple

(Zenobius, *Proverbs*) 'Stupider than Morychus': This is a proverb among the Siceliotes, used of those who do something silly, as Polemon explains in his letter to Diophilus. The full expression is as follows: 'you're — temple'. Morychus is an epithet of Dionysus . . . and it is to condemn his silliness in as much as his statue is outside his temple, in the open air by the entrance. (Much the same is reported in other sources.)

84 SOPHRON

INCERTI GENERIS MIMORUM FRAGMENTA

74

πεῖ ἐccί, λειοκόνιτε;

Ammon. adf. voc. diff. 423 (γπ, Sym.) = Herenn. Phil. 157 (post fr. 4,8)
πεῖ — λειοκόνιτε (εἴτε add. Herenn.), ἀντὶ τοῦ ποῦ εἶ (εἶ om. γπ)
πεῖ ἐccὶ λειοκόνιτε Sym., Herenn.: ποῖος εἰλιcκοπεῖται γπ

75

πῦc ἐc μυχὸν καταδύηι

Ammon. adf. voc. diff. 423 = Herenn. Phil. 157 (post fr. 74) ὅταν δὲ εἰc
τόπον θέληι εἰπεῖν, φηcί· πῦc — καταδύηι; τουτέcτιν ἀντὶ τοῦ εἰc τίνα μυχόν
(εἰc τὴν ἄβυccον Herenn.)
πῦc codd.: ποῖc Ahrens      ἐc Ammon.: εἰc Herenn.      καταδύηι
Ammon.: ει Herenn.

76

Antiatt. p. 93,25 ἐκποιῆcαι· ἀντὶ τοῦ ἐκτελέcαι. Cώφρων.

77

ἐγὼν δέ τοι καὶ πάλαι ὤψεον

Apoll. Dysc. pron., GrGr II 1,1 p. 50,9 Schn. Δωριεῖc ἐγών. Cώφρων·
ἐγὼν — ὤψεον. Choerob. in Theod. can., GrGr IV 2 p. 56,31 Hilg.
(codd. CVO) τὸ δὲ ὀψείω, ὅπερ cημαίνει τὸ ἐπιθυμίαν ἔχω τοῦ θεωρῆcαι,
ὀφεῖλον εἶναι ἐν τῶι παρατατικῶι ὤψειον διὰ τῆc ει διφθόγγου, ἐπειδὴ καὶ ὁ
ἐνεcτὼc τὴν ει δίφθογγον ἔχει κατὰ τὴν παραλήγουcαν, ἐγένετο ὤψεον παρὰ
Cώφρονι κατὰ ἀποβολὴν τοῦ ι, οἷον· ἐγώ — ὤψεον, ἀντὶ τοῦ ἐγὼ καὶ πάλαι
ἐπεθύμουν (ἐπιθυμῶ VO) θεωρῆcαι. περὶ δὲ τούτων . . . ἐν τῶι ῥηματικῶι
Ἀπολλωνίου . . . μαθηcόμεθα
ἐγὼν Apoll. Dysc.: ἐγὼ Choerob. CV, ἔχων O      τοι codd.: τυ Bekker
(τοι pro τυ in cod. Apoll. Dysc. p. 54,11)      πάλαι Apoll. Dysc.,
Choerob. V: πάλιν Choerob. O, μάλα C      ὤψεον codd.: -ειον Bekker

78

τὶ τυ ἐγὼν ποιέω;

Apoll. Dysc. pron., GrGr II 1,1 p. 54,7 ἡ . . . τυ ὀρθῆc τάcεωc οὖcα εὐθεῖαν
cημαίνει παρὰ Δωριεῦcι . . . ἐγκλινομένη δὲ αἰτιατικήν . . . τί — ποιέω;
Cώφρων

### III. UNPLACED FRAGMENTS

### 74

where are you, you dust-reduced wretch?

(Ammonius, *On the Difference between Related Words* = Herennius Philo, *On the Meanings of Different Words*, following a quotation of fr. 4A. 8) 'Where — wretch', instead of ποῦ εἶ.

### 75

Where into the corner are you slinking off?

(following fr. 74) and when he wants to say 'to a place', he says 'where — off?' This is instead of 'into what corner'.

### 76

(The Antiatticist) ἐκποιῆcαι: instead of ἐκτελέcαι ('complete'). Sophron.

### 77

Indeed I've wanted to see for a long time

(Apollonius Dyscolus, *On Pronouns*) ἐγών is Doric. Sophron: 'Indeed — time'. (Choeroboscus on Theodosius, *Canons*) ὀψείω, which means 'I have the desire to see', should be ὤψειον in the imperfect with the diphthong ει, since the present tense also has the diphthong ει in the penultimate syllable; in Sophron it becomes ὤψεον by omitting the ι, thus: 'Indeed — time', instead of 'I've wanted to see for a long time'. We learn about these things in Apollonius' *On Verbs*.

### 78

What will I do to you?

(Apollonius Dyscolus, *On Pronouns*) τύ with the accent in Doric indicates the nominative . . . but when enclitic it marks the accusative . . . 'what — you?' Sophron.

## 79

ἐκπεφάναντί τεος ταὶ δυсθαλίαι

Apoll. Dysc. pron., GrGr II 1,1 p. 74,28 τῆι ἐμέος (cf. Epich. fr. 140) ἡ
τέος κατ᾽ ἔγκλιϲιν εὔζυγος· ἐκπ. — δυϲθαλίαι. Ϲώφρων. τὸ γὰρ ὀρθοτονού-
μενον κτητικὴν ϲημαίνει
ἐκπεφάναντι Ahrens p. 473 (-φήναντι aim Bekker): εκπεφαντι cod.: -ται
Valck. p. 302 C

## 80

οὐχ ἥϲϲων τεοῦ

Apoll. Dysc. pron., GrGr II 1,1 p. 75,16. 22 ἀπὸ τῆϲ ϲοῦ Δώριος ἐγίνετο
ἡ τεοῦ (τεους cod., corr. Bekker) ὁμότονος . . . Ϲώφρων· οὐχ — τεοῦ.

## 81

τουτῶ θάμεθα

Apoll. Dysc. pron., GrGr II 1,1 p. 77,13 τῆϲ ἐκεῖνος καὶ οὗτος αἱ γενικαὶ
παρὰ Δωριεῦϲι διὰ τοῦ ω, τήνω καὶ τούτω, τοῦ τέλους βαρυτονουμένου . . .
πρός οἷς καὶ τὸ τουτῶ περισπώμενον. ἐπιρρήματός ἐστι παραστατικόν, τουτῶ
θάμεθα. Ϲώφρων. Id. adv., ibid. p. 207,27 ἐστι καὶ παρὰ ἀντωνυμίαν παρηγ-
μένα παρὰ Δωριεῦϲι, τουτόθεν, ὃ δὴ ϲυνήθως ἀποκόπτοντες τὴν λοιπὴν
ϲυλλαβὴν ἐκτείνουϲιν εἰς τὸ ω· τ. θ. (sequuntur frs. 22 et 121). p. 190,20
(post fr. 22) τουτόθεν, τουτῶ· τ. θ.

## 82

μόνον ἐμίνγα τὸ τοῦ γόγγρου τέμαχος

Apoll. Dysc. pron., GrGr II 1,1 p. 81,20 Δωριεῖς ἐμίν καὶ ἔτι ἐμίνγα.
Ϲώφρων· μόνον — τέμαχος (sequitur Rhint. fr. 10). Et. gen. AB (Et.
magn. p. 732,36) ἐπ᾽ αὐτοῦ δὲ τοῦ γε τρέπεται (τὸ ε εἰς α apud Dorienses,
non in compositis ut ϲύγα tantum)· τοῦτό γα — τέμαχος
μόνον ἐμίνγα Apoll. Dysc.: τοῦτό γα Et.

## 83

οὐκέτι οἱ δῶ;

Apoll. Dysc. pron., GrGr II 1,1 p. 82,18 (οἱ dat.) καὶ Δωριεῖς ὁμοίως ἡμῖν
λέγουϲιν οὐκέτι οι δω. Ϲώφρων
οἱ δῶ Blomfield (οἶ δῶ Bekker), signum interrogationis add. Kassel: οι
δω cod.: οἱ δωϲῶ Schneider

## 79

### Your misfortunes have come to light

(Apollonius Dyscolus, *On Pronouns*) To ἐμέος corresponds enclitic τέος:
'your — light'. Sophron. The pronounciation with the oxytone accent
indicates the possessive.

## 80

### no weaker than you

(Apollonius Dyscolus, *On Pronouns*) From coῦ came Doric τεοῦ with the
same accent . . . Sophron: 'no — you'.

## 81

### let us see from here

(Apollonius Dyscolus, *On Pronouns*) The genitives of 'that' (ἐκεῖνος)
and 'this' (οὗτος) in Doric are in ω, τήνω and τούτω, the ending being
barytone . . . Furthermore, there is also perispomenon τουτῶ. It marks
the adverb: 'let us — here'. Sophron. (The same, *On Adverbs*) The
inflection also exists in Doric for the pronoun τουτόθεν, which
commonly loses the final syllable and lengthens the residual syllable to
ω: 'let us — here' [frs. 22, 121 follow]. (The same) [after fr. 22] τουτόθεν
becomes τουτῶ 'let us — here' [fr. 121 follows].

## 82

### just the slice of conger-eel for me

(Apollonius Dyscolus, *On Pronouns*) Doric has ἐμίν and ἐμίνγα.
Sophron: 'just — me'.

## 83

### Am I not to give him/her any more?

(Apollonius Dyscolus, *On Pronouns*, on dative οἷ) The Dorians say the
same as us: 'am — more'. Sophron.

## 84

τί οὐ παρ᾽ ἔμ᾽ ἐςτράφθη;

Apoll. Dysc. pron., GrGr II 1,1 p. 82,26 ἡ ἐμέ πρὸς παςῶν διαλέκτων
λέγεται. παρὰ Δωριεῦςι μετὰ τοῦ ι, ἐμεί, ἧι ςυνεχῶς Ἐπίχαρμος χρῆται (fr.
140). κοινῶς μέντοι ὁ Cώφρων· τί — ἐςτρ.

## 85

ὑμέων γὰρ ἀπρὶξ ἔχονται

Apoll. Dysc. pron., GrGr II 1,1 p. 95,25 (ὑμῶν possessivum, ὑμέων
personale) ὑμέων — ἔχονται. Cώφρων

## 86

ὁ δ᾽ ἐκ τῶ ςκότεος τοξεύων αἰὲν ἕνα τινὰ ὧν ζυγαςτροφεῖ

Apoll. Dysc. pron., GrGr II 1,1 p. 96,15 ἐν ἴcωι τῶι αὐτῶν παρὰ
Cυρακουςίοις τίθεται τὸ ὧν. Cώφρων· ὁ — ζυγ.
τω cod.: del. Bekker      ὧν cod.: ὧν (eorum) J. F. Reitz ap. M.
Maittaire Gr. Ling Dial. ed. F. G. Sturz (1807) p. 561¹⁰: ὧν (= οὖν) Wil.
ζυγαςτροφεῖ cod.: ζυγοςτρ- Bekker: ἄζυγα ςτρ- Ludwich: ζυγοςτοιχεῖ (in
fronte aciei incedit) Reitz: -ςτατεῖ vel -μαχεῖ Botzon

## 87

ὅca κα ὗμιν αἰνέcω

Apoll. Dysc. pron., GrGr II 1,1 p. 97,28 ὑμῖν . . . παρ᾽ Ἴωςι
⟨προ⟩περιςπᾶται (corr. Bekker) ἐγκλινομένη, καθὸ ςυςτέλλει τὸ ι. καὶ ἔτι
παρὰ Δωριεῦςιν· ὅcαις — αἰνέcω. Cώφρων. καὶ ἐν ὀρθῆι τάcει· (fr. 88)
ὅca κα Kaibel: ὅcαις cod.

## 88

οὐ μάν τοι δίφρον ἐπημμένον ὑμίν

Apoll. Dysc. pron., GrGr II 1,1 p. 98,1 (ὑμῖν, post fr. 87) καὶ ἐν ὀρθῆι
τάcει· οὐ — ὑμίν

## 89

Apoll. Dysc. pron., GrGr II 1,1 p. 99,15 Cυρακούςιοι ψιν· †αμανι ψιν
γενομενα. Cώφρων
αμανι cod.: ἄμιν ἦ Sturz ap. Maittaire (vid. ad fr. 86) p. 563³: τὰ μὰν
Botzon     'temptari possunt multa, velut ἄμ᾽ ἀνία ψιν γενομένα' Kaibel

## 84

### Why didn't (s)he turn alongside me?

(Apollonius Dyscolus, *On Pronouns*) ἐμέ occurs in all dialects. In Doric
it has an iota, ἐμεί, which is the form constantly used by Epicharmus (fr.
140). However, Sophron uses the common form: 'why — me'.

## 85

### for they hold on to you tight

(Apollonius Dyscolus, *On Pronouns*, on possessive ὑμῶν, personal
ὑμέων) 'for — tight'. Sophron.

## 86

### though (or 'since') he shoots in the dark he always . . . one of them

(Apollonius Dyscolus, *On Pronouns*) Equivalent to αὐτῶν you find ὧν
('of them') in Syracusan. Sophron: 'though — them'.

## 87

### whatever I promise you

(Apollonius Dyscolus, *On Pronouns*) Enclitic ὑμῖν is properispomenon
in Ionic, because the ι is shortened. And also in Doric: 'in all — you'.
Sophron (fr. 88 follows).

## 88

(Apollonius Dyscolus, *On Pronouns*, following fr. 87) And with the
acute accent: [translation uncertain].

## 89

(Apollonius Dyscolus, *On Pronouns*) Syracusan has [dative] ψιν. . . .
Sophron. [The quotation is hopelessly corrupt.]

## 90

πῶς ψε καὶ γινώσκωμες;

Apoll. Dysc. pron., GrGr II 1,1 p. 101,2 ψέ Cυρακούcιοι. Cώφρων· πῶς — γιν.

ψε καὶ Bekker: και ψε και cod. (sed prius και del.): ψέ κα Ahrens γινώcκωμες Ahrens: -μεν cod.

## 91

τίς μοι τὰ λᾶια ἐκτίλλει;

Apoll. Dysc. adv., GrGr II 1,1 p. 157,8 λήϊος, ἀφ᾽ οὗ λάϊος καὶ λάϊον καὶ λάϊα καὶ ἐν cυναιρέcει . . . τοῦ α λᾶια· τίς — ἐκτίλλει; Cώφρων

## *92

οὐδ᾽ ὅπως ἄριστα

Apoll. Dysc. adv., GrGr II 1,1 p. 173,3 (ὥς, πῶς) τὰ ἀπ᾽ αὐτῶν ἀναφορικά, προcλαμβάνοντα τὸ ο, ὡς ἂν τῶν τόνων ἐν τοῖς μονοcυλλάβοις κατηναγκαcμένων, γενόμενα διcύλλαβα δέχεται καὶ προοφειλομένην τάcιν, ἡνίκα γίνεται ὅπου καὶ ὅπηι καὶ ὅπως . . . ὅθεν δοκεῖ μοι καὶ κατὰ τὴν Δωρικὴν διάλεκτον τῶι μὲν προκατειλεγμένωι λόγωι ὅπως (το πως cod., corr. Bekker) ἀναγινώcκειν, οὐδ᾽ — ἄριστα, τῶι μέντοι μᾶλλον αὐτοὺς cυγκαταβιβάζειν τὰ ἐπιρρήματα ὁπῶc, ὥcτε ἀμφοτέρας τὰς ἀναγνώcεις λόγου ἔχεcθαι

ὅπως cod.: ὁπῶc Ahrens

Sophroni tribuit Ahrens

## *93

ταυτᾶι ταὶ θύραι, μᾶτερ

Apoll. Dysc. adv., GrGr II 1,1 p. 180,6 τό . . . οἱ τοί φαcι Δωριεῖc, καὶ τὸ αἱ ταί· ταῦται — μᾶτερ

ταυτᾶι Wil. ap. Kaib.: ταῦται cod.: ταύται Ahrens

Sophroni trib. Bast (ap. Schaefer Greg. Cor. p. 457[70]), Ahrens

## 94

ὕδωρ ἄκρατον εἰς τὰν κύλικα

Athen. epit. 2. 44 B ὅτι καὶ ἐπὶ τοῦ ὕδατος ἔταττον οἱ παλαιοὶ τὸ ἄκρατον. Cώφρων· ὕδωρ — κύλικα. hinc Eust. in Il. p. 916,37

τὰν Blomfield: τὴν CE, Eust.

## 90

### How can we recognize them?

(Apollonius Dyscolus, *On Pronouns*) Syracusan has [accusative] ψε.
Sophron: 'how — them'.

## 91

### who can pluck this crop for me?

(Apollonius Dyscolus, *On Adverbs*) λήϊον ('standing crop'), whence
λάϊος, λάϊον, and λάϊα; and with synaeresis of the α, λᾶια: 'who — me'.
Sophron.

## *92

### nor so that the best

(Apollonius Dyscolus, *On Adverbs*, on ὥς, πῶς) While in the standard
forms the accent falls on the only syllable, the relative forms, which
have an ο prefix, have the accent on the preceding syllable, so they
become ὅπου, ὅπηι, and ὅπως . . . from this it seems to me that also in
Doric one should read ὅπως according to the foregoing argument, 'nor
— best', but from the fact that they had to transfer the accent of adverbs
to the final syllable ὁπῶς; so that both readings have some rational
justification.

## *93

### the doors here, mother

(Apollonius Dyscolus, *On Adverbs*) The Dorians say τοί for οἱ, and ταί
for αἱ: 'the — mother'.

## 94

### unmixed water into the cup

(Athenaeus) The ancients used 'unmixed' of water as well. Sophron:
'unmixed — cup'.

## 95

στρουθωτὰ ἐλίγματα ἐντετιμημένα

Athen. epit. 2. 48 C (στρώματα) Cώφρων δὲ στρ. ἐλ. φησιν ἐντ.
ἐντετιμημένα C: -τετιμένα E: -τετιλημένα Casaub.: -τετμαμένα Meineke

## 96

μελαινίδες γάρ τοι νικοῦνται ἐμὶν ἐκ τοῦ μικροῦ λιμένος

Athen. 3. 86 A παρὰ Cώφρονι δ᾽ οἱ (οἱ del. Kaibel) κόγχοι μελαινίδες
λέγονται· μελ. — λιμένος. sequitur fr. 43
νικοῦνται Meineke Anal. Ath. p. 40 (νιςς- iam Casaub.): νηςοῦντι A

## 97

Athen. 3. 91 B μνημονεύει τῶν σπατάγγων καὶ Cώφρων
σπατάγγων A (-ῶν Kaibel): -άνων CE

## 98

Athen. 7. 312 C Ἐπίχαρμος δ᾽ ἐν Μούςαις χωρὶς τοῦ ς μυραίνας αὐτὰς καλεῖ
οὑτωςὶ λέγων· (fr. 89) . . . ὁμοίως δὲ καὶ Cώφρων.

## 99

βόες δὲ λαρινεύονται

Athen. 9. 387 B λαρινεύεςθαι, ὅπερ ἐςτι ςιτίζεςθαι. Cώφρων· β. δὲ λ.

## 100

κατάστρεψον, τέκνον, τὰν ἡμίναν

Athen. 9. 479 B καὶ Cώφρων· καταστ. — ἡμίναν.

## 101

ἐκρατηρίχθημες

Athen. 11. 504 B (κρατηρίζειν) καὶ ὁ τοὺς μίμους δὲ πεποιηκώς (test. 5) . . .
λέγει που κηκρατηριχημες ἀντὶ τοῦ πεπώκειμεν. Hesych. ε 1663
ἐκρατηρίχθημεν· ἐμεθύςθημεν
'dedimus formam a Wack. Kl. Schr. II p. 860 sq. restitutam prob.
Schwyzer' Kassel–Austin.

## 102

Choric. 32 (or. 8, apol. mim.), 16 οὗτος τοίνυν ὁ Πλάτωνα λαχὼν
ἐραστὴν (test. 7) μιμεῖται μὲν ἄνδρας, μιμεῖται δὲ γύναια. φθέγγεται ⟨δὲ⟩ καὶ

## 95

precious wraps embroidered with birds

(Athenaeus) Sophron says: 'precious — birds'.

## 96

black conches will come to me from the little harbour

(Athenaeus) Sophron mentions black conches: 'black — harbour'.

## 97

(Athenaeus) Sophron also mentions cπατάγγεc.

## 98

(Athenaeus) Epicharmus in *Muses* calls them (moray eels) μυραίναc without the *s*, saying: (fr. 89) . . . Similarly also Sophron.

## 99

and the bogues grow fat

(Athenaeus) λαρινεύεcθαι means 'to feed'. Sophron: 'and — fat'.

## 100

turn the cup over, child

(Athenaeus) And Sophron: 'turn — child'.

## 101

and we were kratered

(Athenaeus) The writer of those mimes which Duris says (*FGrH* 76 F 72) were always in Plato's hands says somewhere: 'and — kratered', instead of 'we were drunk'.

## 102

(Choricius, *Orations*) The writer whom Plato loved (i.e. Sophron) imitated both men and women; and even the little child, who does not know

παιδίον αὐτῶι μήπω γινῶςκον ὀρθῶς οὐ μητέρα καλεῖν, οὐ πατέρα προς-
αγορεύειν

## *103

Demetr. eloc. 127 (cf. 162) τοῦ δὲ αὐτοῦ εἴδουc (τῆc ὑπερβολῆc, vid. fr.
adesp. 144) ἐcτὶ καὶ τὸ φαλακρότεροc εὐδίαc καὶ τὸ κολοκύντηc ὑγιέcτεροc
(cf. fr. 33 et Epich. fr. 152)

## 104

Demetr. eloc. 153 ἤδη μέντοι ἐκ δύο τόπων ἐνταῦθα ἐγένετο ἡ χάριc· οὐ γὰρ
παρὰ προcδοκίαν μόνον ἐπηνέχθη, ἀλλ' οὐδ' ἠκολούθει τοῖc προτέροιc. ἡ δὲ
τοιαύτη ἀνακολουθία καλεῖται γρῖφοc, ὥcπερ ὁ παρὰ Cώφρονι ῥητορεύων
Βουλίαc· οὐδὲν γὰρ ἀκόλουθον αὐτῶι (αὐτὸ P, corr. cod. M) λέγει. καὶ παρὰ
Μενάνδρωι δὲ ὁ πρόλογοc τῆc Μεccηνίαc (test. ii)

## 105

ἐκ τοῦ ὄνυχοc γὰρ τὸν λέοντα ἔγραψεν. τορύναν ἔξεcεν.
κύμινον ἔπριcεν

Demetr. eloc. 156 (post fr. 67) καὶ ἀλλαχόθι πού φηcιν· ἐκ — κύμινον
ἔcπειρεν. καὶ γὰρ δυcὶ παροιμίαιc καὶ τριcὶν ἐπαλλήλοιc χρῆται, ὡc ἐπι-
πληθύωνται (-ονται P, corr. cod. M) αὐτῶι αἱ χάριτεc· cχεδόν τε πάcαc ἐκ
τῶν δραμάτων αὐτοῦ τὰc παροιμίαc ἐκλεξαι ἔcτιν
ἔπριcεν Hemst., Ar. Plut. (1744) p. 193: ἔcπειρεν P: ἔπριεν Cobet Coll.
crit. p. 237 ('scribebatur propter ι longum ἔπρειεν et sic peccatum est')

## *106

λαδρέοντι δὲ τοὶ μυκτῆρεc

Epimer. Hom. δ 78 (δείδω) παρὰ τὸ δείω κατὰ πλεοναcμὸν τοῦ δ . . . καὶ τὸ
παρὰ τῶι Cυρακουcίωι· λαδρ. — μυκτῆρεc. ἔγκειται γὰρ τὸ λ⟨α⟩ (suppl.
Kaibel) ἐπιτατικὸν ⟨καὶ τὸ⟩ ῥέω· ⟨λα⟩ρέοντι (suppl. Dyck) ἀντὶ τοῦ μεγάλωc
ῥέουcι. Et. gen. λ 8 (AB; Et. magn. p. 544,33) λαδρέοντι· παρὰ τὸ λα καὶ τὸ
ῥέω λαρέοντι, μεγάλωc ῥέοντι, πλεοναcμῶι τοῦ δ. Περὶ παθῶν

## 107

Epimer. Hom. μ 66 (μακροτάτη, de forma comparativa, p. 502,44 Dyck)
ἡνίκα δὲ κοινὴ ἡ cυλλαβή, διφορεῖται ἡ γραφή. ἐνταῦθα οὖν κοινὴ ἡ μα·
δύναται καὶ διά τοῦ ω ἐὰν βραχείαι χρήcηται, καὶ διὰ τοῦ ο ἐὰν μακρᾶι . . .
ὁμοίωc τὸ ἐρυθρότατοc παρὰ Cώφρονι μακρᾶι χρηcαμένωι τῆι ρυ

clearly how to call his mother or address his father, cries out [*sc. μᾶ, πᾶ,* or *πάππα, ἄττα?*].

## *103

(Demetrius, *On Style*) Belonging to this type [of exaggeration] is 'balder than a clear sky' and 'healthier than a gourd' (fr. 33).

## 104

(Demetrius, *On Style*) The charm derives from two features; not only does it proceed contrary to expectation, but it does not follow from the earlier parts. This sort of anacolouthon is called a riddle, just like the speaker Boulias in Sophron, for he says nothing that hangs together. And in Menander in the prologue of *Messenia*.

## 105

he drew the lion from its claw, he scraped the ladle,
    he sliced cumin

(Demetrius, *On Style*) Charm in content derives from the use of proverbs, because a proverb is naturally something charming, as Sophron said (fr. 67) . . . And somewhere else he says 'he — cumin'. He uses two or three proverbs in succession, so that he may multiply the charm. Almost every proverb can be extracted from his plays.

## *106

and (his) nostrils are streaming

(*Homeric Parsings*, on δείδω 'I fear') from δείω with pleonastic δ . . . and in the expression used by the Syracusan: 'and — streaming'. For there the λα intensifies ῥέω meaning 'flowing greatly', with pleonastic δ. (*Etymologica*) 'are streaming' (λαδρέοντι): from λα and ῥέω, 'they flow greatly', with pleonastic δ. *On Modifications of Words.*

## 107

(*Homeric Parsings*, on μακροτάτη) Whenever a syllable has a vowel which can be either long or short, the transcription can vary. Here μα- can be either short or long. It is both possible to have ω if μα is short, and o if it is long . . . Similarly, ἐρυθρότατος ('extremely red') in Sophron who treats the ρυ as long.

## *108

Et. magn. p. 134,11 ἀρά· ἡ εὐχή . . . παρὰ τὸ ἀρύειν, ὅπερ ἐπὶ τὸ ἐπικαλεῖσθαι ἔταττον, καὶ μάλιστα Cυρακούcιοι· ἀρύετ' ἂν † φύζην† ἀντὶ τοῦ ἐπικαλεῖcθε καὶ ἐφέλκεcθε

## 109

Et. gen. a 1256 (AB; Et. magn. p. 151,48) ἀcαλὴc ὁ ἀμέριμνοc. οὕτωc Ἡρωδιανὸc (I p. 318,16 L.) καὶ Ἀπολλόδωροc (244 F 238 Jac.). καὶ γὰρ ἀcαλέαν (ἀcελεαν A, ἀcάλε(ι)αν? Kaibel) ὁ (om. A) Cώφρων τὴν ἀμεριμνίαν καὶ ἀλογιcτίαν καλεῖ

## 110

Et. gen. β 122 (AB; Et. magn. p. 197,54, Et. Sym. β 107) βιπτάζω. Cώφρων καὶ Ἐπίχαρμοc (fr. 171) τὸ βαπτίζω βιπτάζω λέγουcιν. οὕτωc (οὐ A) Ἡρωδιανόc (II p. 388,1 L.)

## 111

Et. gen. β 290 (Et. magn. p. 216,55) παρὰ τὸ βῦ βύκτηc· τὸ γὰρ βῦ ἐπὶ τοῦ μεγάλου ἔλεγον. καὶ Cώφρων βυβὰ (βύβα B) ἀντὶ τοῦ μεcτὰ καὶ πλήρη (-ηc A, -ειc B) καὶ μεγάλα

## 112

ἐν ὄccωι δέει δαδύccεcθε

Et. gen. AB (Et. magn. p. 289,7, om. Sophronis memoria) δοῖδυξ . . . παρὰ τὸ δαδύccω, ὃ cημαίνει τὸ ταράccω. Cώφρων ἐν μίμοιc· ἐν — δαδ., ἀντὶ τοῦ (τοῦ om. A) ταράccεcθε (-εcθαι A) κτλ. (Philox. fr. *467 Theod.)
ὄccω A: ὄcω B    δαδύccεcθε Kaibel: -cθαι A: δαδοίccεcθε (-θε ex -θαι) B

## 113

ἔχε τὸ δελήτιον

Et. gen. AB (Et. magn. p. 254,53, Et. Sym. V) δελήτιον· τὸ δέλεαρ. Cοφοκλῆc (fr. spur. 1124 R.)· ἔχε — δελήτιον. ἢ Cώφρων (ἢ Cώφρων om. Et. gen., Et. Sym. Cώφρων om. Et. magn. D). οἱ δὲ τὸ ἄγγοc (οἱ δὲ τὸ ἄ. om. B) ἐν ὧι τὸ δέλεαρ ἔγκειται
ἔχει Et. Sym.

## 114

Et. gen. A¹¹B (Et. magn. p. 334,10) ἐμβραμένα· παρὰ Cώφρωνι ἡ εἱμαρμένη. καὶ Λάκωνεc οὕτωc λέγουcιν (κ. Λ. οὕτω λ. in fine glossae habet

*108

(*Etymologicum magnum*) ἀρά ('prayer'): . . . from ἀρύειν, which the Syracusans particularly use for 'invoke': . . . [the text here is corrupt] instead of 'invoke and compel to come'.

109

(*Etymologica*) ἀcαλής means 'carefree'. So Herodian and Apollodorus. And Sophron calls carelessness and thoughtlessness ἀcαλέα.

110

(*Etymologica*) βιππάζω: Sophron and Epicharmus (fr. 171) say βιππάζω for βαπτίζω ('plunge'). So Herodian

111

(*Etymologica*) βύκτης ('swelling') from βῦ. For they said βῦ of big things. And Sophron has βυβά instead of 'full' and 'filled' and 'large'.

112

you're stirred up by so much fear

(*Etymologica*) δοῖδυξ ('pestle') . . . like δαδύccω, which means 'stir up'. Sophron in his mimes: 'you're — fear', instead of ταράccεcθε ('you are stirred up').

113

take the bait

(*Etymologica*) δελήτιον: bait. Sophocles. 'take — bait'. Or Sophron. Some say it means the container in which the bait is placed.

114

(*Etymologica*) ἐμβραμένα: 'destiny' (εἱμαρμένη) in Sophron. And the Spartans say this also. (The *Etymologicum magnum* adds:) From

Et. magn.). ἀπὸ τοῦ εἱμαρμένη (ἀ. τ. εἰμ. om. Et. magn.) ὑπερθέcει τοῦ ρ,
καὶ διὰ τὴν ἀcυνταξίαν πλεοναcμῶι τοῦ β

115

φέρε τὸ θαύμακτρον κῆπιθυcιῶμεc

Et. gen. AB (Et. magn. p. 443,52) θαύμακτρον παρὰ τὸ θαυμάζω . . .
Cώφρων· φέρε — κἀπιθ.
θαύμακτρον codd.: θυμ- (~ θυμιατήριον) intellegendum esse putavit
Blomfield scribendum esse coni. Kaibel    κῆπιθυcιῶμεc Kaibel: κἀπιθ-
codd. (-ίωμεν B): κἀπ᾽ ἰθὺc ἴωμεc Ahrens

*116

ναὶ κάρρων βῶc

Et. gen. AB (Et. magn. p. 492,38, Et. Gud. An. Par. IV p. 54,22) κάρρων.
οἷον· ν. κ. β.
⟨ὁ⟩ βῶc Kaibel    Sophroni tribuit Valck. p. 303 C

117

Et. gen. AB (Et. magn. p. 256,31) Ἡρωδιανὸc λέγει (II p. 238,5 L.) . . . ὅτι
cυνεξέδραμε τὸ (τῶι Lentz) ἄριcτοc ἀριcτερόc καὶ τὸ δεξιὸc δεξιτερόc. τοῦτο
γὰρ cυνεκδρομὴ καὶ οὐ πλεοναcμόc, ὥcπερ καὶ (ὥcπερ, καθὰ Lentz) παρὰ τὸ
πρόβατον γίνεται προβάτιον (-τερον ⟨καὶ⟩ Sylburg, οὕτω καὶ ἀπὸ τοῦ add.
Reitz. apud Kaib.) οἰὸc (om. B, ὀὶc Kaibel) οὖιοc (οἰὸc AB, Et. magn. D,
om. Et. magn. cett.), οἰότεον (οἰότ- A, οἰότερον Et. magn.), ὡc λέγει
Cώφρων. τοῦτο γὰρ οὐ λέγει (Herodianus) πλεονασμόν, ἀλλὰ cυνεκδρομὴν
(οὐ λέγεται -όc, ἀλλὰ -ὴ Et. magn.) τοῦ προβάτεον (-τερον Ahrens). οὕτωc
δεξιτερὸc ὡc (-ὸc ὁ A) ἀριcτερόc

118

τῶι χόλωι χρέομαι

Et. gen. B (p. 311 Mill.) χρέοc· οὐκ ἀπὸ τοῦ χρῶ, ἀλλ᾽ ἀπὸ τοῦ χρέω καὶ
χρέομαι. Cώφρων· τῶι — χρέομαι. οὕτω Φιλόξενοc (Φίλων cod., corr. Reitz.
Gesch. gr. Et. p. 246; fr. 400 Theod.)

119

Et. Gud. p. 450,18 Sturz = Cyrill. Lex., An. Par. IV p. 187,27
παλλακῖνοc· παρὰ τῶι Cώφρωνι (π. Cωφρονίωι Cyrill.) τὸ ὄνομα. δηλοῖ δὲ τὸν
πάλληκα (-ικα codd.; Hesych. π 244 πάλληξ· βούπαιc) ἢ τὸν τῆc παλλακῆc
υἱόν

εἱμαρμένη by transposing the ρ, and then with addition of β because of the difficulty of pronunciation.

## 115

bring the *thaumaktron* and let's burn the incense

(*Etymologica*) θαύμακτρον from θαυμάζω ('wonder') . . . Sophron: 'bring — incense'.

## *116

Yes, the ox is stronger (?)

(*Etymologica*) stronger: thus: 'yes — stronger'.

## 117

(*Etymologica*) Herodian says that ἀριςτερός is by analogy to ἄριςτος, and δεξιτερός to δεξιός. This is analogy and not pleonasm, just as from πρόβατον ('sheep') comes προβάτιον and from οἰός οἴιος, οἰιότεον, as Sophron has it. This he (Herodian) calls not pleonasm but analogy with προβάτεον. So δεξιτερός is like ἀριςτερός.

## 118

I feel angry

(*Etymologicum genuinum*) χρέος: not from χρῶ, but from χρέω and χρέομαι. Sophron: 'I — angry'. So Philoxenus (fr. 400 Theod.).

## 119

(*Etymologicum Gudianum* = Cyrillus, *Lexicon*) παλλακῖνος: the word appears in Sophron. It means either 'youth' (πάλληξ) or the 'son of a prostitute' (παλλακή).

## 120

ἐγὼ δὲ ϲιτούμενοϲ ἀζαίνομαι

Et. Orion. p. 28,4 (inde Et. gen. AB, Sophrone non nominato) ὡϲ παρὰ τὸ ἄζω ἀζαίνω, Ϲώφρων· ἐγὼ — ἀζαίνομαι {καὶ παρὰ τὸ ἄζω ἀζαίνω}, καὶ Ἰωνικῶϲ παρ᾽ Ὁμήρωι· καταζήναϲκε δὲ δαίμων (λ 587), οὕτω καὶ ϲκύζω ϲκυζαίνω ϲιτούμενοϲ ἀζαίνομαι Kassel: ϲίτου μὲν οὐδὲν ἀζ- Et. Orion.: ὀζαίνομαι ϲιτούμενοϲ Et. gen.

## 121

πῶ τιϲ ὄνον ὠναϲεῖται;

Et. Orion. p. 137,12 (inde Et. gen. [1]AB = Et. magn. p. 698,40, Et. Sym.) τὰ τῶι ο παραληγόμενα ἐπιρρήματα ἀποκοπῆι τοῦ θεν καὶ ἐπεκτάϲει τοῦ ο εἰϲ ω γίνεται παρὰ Δωριεῦϲιν, οἷον (om. Et. Orion., Et. Gen.) αὐτόθεν αὐτῷ (cf. fr. 22), τουτόθεν τουτῶ (cf. fr. 81, om. Et. Orion.), οὕτωϲ καὶ (οὔτ. ὡϲ Et. Sym., om. Et Orion.) πόθεν πῶ. Ϲώφρων (καὶ παρὰ Ϲώφρονι Et. magn., Et. Sym. CV, οἷον F) ἐν τοῖϲ μίμοιϲ (om. Et. gen., Et. magn., Et. Sym.)· πώ (πῶ Et. gen. B, Et. Sym.) — ὀναϲεῖται. Et. gen. [2]B (p. 289 Mill.) πολλὰ γάρ εἰϲιν ἐπιρρήματα εἰϲ θεν λήγοντα, ἅτινα ἀποβάλλουϲι τὴν θεν ϲυλλαβὴν καὶ ἐκτείνουϲι τὸ ο εἰϲ ω, οἷον πόθεν πῶ καὶ παρὰ Ϲώφρονι πῶ — ὠνάϲηται ϲημαίνει καὶ τὸ πόθεν, καὶ πάλιν ἐϲτιν αὐτόθεν αὐτῷ κτλ. Apoll. Dysc. adv., GrGr II 1,1 [1]p. 190,21 Schn. (post frs. 22 et 81) τῆιδε εἶχε καὶ τὸ πόθεν λεγόμενον οὕτωϲ, πῶ· πῶ (ουτωϲ πωπο cod., corr. Ahrens p. 374[12]) — οναϲειται. [2]p. 208,2 (post frs. 81 et 22) οὕτωϲ ἔχει καὶ τὸ πῶ — ωναϲειται. cf. etiam Epimer. Hom. κ 143 πόθεν πώ, αὐτόθεν αὐτώ, τουτόθεν τουτώ παρὰ Ϲυρακουϲίοιϲ οὕτωϲ λεγόμενα, Harp. p. 268,8 Dind. (π 132 K.) τὸ . . . πῶ Δώριον, τιθέμενον ἀντὶ τοῦ πόθεν, Hesych. π 4487 πῶ· ποῦ. ὅθεν, πόθεν (πῶ· πόθεν, ὁπόθεν Ahrens). Δωριεῖϲ et Schol. rec. (V⁵⁷) Ar. Plut. 66 f

ὄνον Et. Orion., Et. magn., Apoll. Dysc.: ὦνον Et. gen.[2]: οἶνον Et. Sym. CV: οὖν οἶνον Et. gen.[1], Et. Sym. F, unde ὦν ὄνον Kaibel ωναϲειται Apoll.[2]: ὀν- Apoll.[1], Et. Orion.: ὠνάϲηται Et. gen.[2], Et. magn., compend. Et. Sym. CV (ὠνάϲ et ται certum): ὀνάϲηται Et. Sym. F: οναϲη ex ονηϲη Et. gen. [1]A: ἀναϲεῖται Et. gen. [1]B

## 122

κινηϲῶ δ᾽ ἤδη καὶ τὸν ἀφ᾽ ἱαρᾶϲ

Eust. in Il. p. 633,59 (e Suet. Π. παιδ., cf. 1,13) παροιμία κινεῖν τὸν ἀφ᾽ ἱερᾶϲ ἐπὶ τῶν ἐν ἀπογνώϲει δεομένων βοηθείαϲ ἐϲχάτηϲ. χρῆϲιϲ δὲ ταύτηϲ καὶ παρὰ Ϲώφρονι ἐν τῶι κινήϲω — ἱερᾶϲ, ἔνθα λείπει τὸ πεϲϲὸν ἢ λίθον. eadem in Od. p. 1397,31

κινηϲῶ Ahrens: -ήϲω Eust.      ἱαρᾶϲ Ahrens: ἱερᾶϲ Eust.

## 120

### though I've eaten, I'm parched

(*Etymologica*) ἄζαινω comes from ἄζω. Sophron: 'though — parched', and in Homer the Ionic form, καταζήνασκε δὲ δαίμων (*Od.* 11. 587: 'the divine power dried it up'). So also σκύζω and σκυζαίνω.

## 121

### where can one buy an ass?

(*Etymologica*) Adverbs with *o* in the penultimate syllable drop the θεν and lengthen the *o* into ω in Doric, as in αὐτόθεν > αὐτῶ, τουτόθεν > τουτῶ, and this also happens with πόθεν > πῶ. Sophron in his mimes: 'where — ass'. (Much the same is reported in various other sources.)

## 122

### Now I'll even move the stone from the sacred line

(Eustathius, commentary on Homer, *Iliad*) 'To move the stone from the sacred line' is a saying used of those who are in despair and need the most desperate help. This use is found in Sophron in the line: 'Now — line'.

### 123

Eust. in Od. p. 1457,19 (de formis ἱππότα, τοξότα, ἱππηλάτα sim.) Εὐδαίμων ὁ Πηλουσιώτης Μακεδόνων γλώσσης εἶναι λέγει . . . παράγει δὲ ἐκεῖνος καὶ Ἰλλυρικὸν ὄνομα ἐν ἐπιγράμματι τὸ (47 Preg.) πατὴρ δέ μ᾽ ἔφυσε Κόπαινα . . . καὶ Cυρακούσιον τὸ ὁ Μύριλλα, οὗ μεμνῆσθαι λέγει τὸν Cώφρονα, ἱστορῶν καὶ ὅτι τοῦ Cυρακούσιου τούτου (τὸ add. Kaibel) κύριον Δημοκόπος ἦν ἀρχιτέκτων. ἐπεὶ δὲ τελεσιουργήσας τὸ θέατρον μύρον τοῖς ἑαυτοῦ πολίταις διένειμε, Μύριλλα ἐπεκλήθη. πάντως δὲ τοῖς εἰρημένοις ὀνόμασι τοῖς ὡς ἄλλοι φασὶν Αἰολικοῖς συντέτακται καὶ τὸ ὁ νεφεληγερέτα κτλ.

### 124

δειπνήσας ὠστίζεται τοῖς τρηματιζόντεσσι

Eust. in Od. p. 1397,22 λέγει δὲ ὁ ταῦτα παραδιδούς (Suet. Π. παιδ., cf. 1,9) καὶ ὡς οἱ τῆι παιδιᾶι ταύτηι (κυβείαι) χρώμενοι ἀπὸ τῶν ἐν τοῖς κύβοις τρημάτων τρηματῖται ἐλέγοντο, παράγων καὶ χρῆσιν Cώφρονος τὸ δειπν. — τρημ.
'dativus suspectus, fort. ⟨ἐν⟩ τοῖς' Kaibel

### 125

Ποτειδᾶ δραστοχαῖτα

Hdn. Π. μον. λέξ., II p. 917,3 L. (post Epich. frs. 186 et 70 (Cώφρων τε τὴν κλητικὴν ἔφη ποτ. δρ.
ποτίδα codd. (Ποτιδᾶ Ahrens, 'incertum Ποτιδᾶ an Ποτειδᾶ' Kaibel δραστοχαῖτα codd.: δροσοχ- Cramer Philol. Mus. 1 (1832) 637: δασυχαῖτα Botzon: πρασοχ- vel πρασιοχ- Ahrens

### 126

Hdn. Π. μον. λέξ., II p. 919,2 L. Τρέλλων· παρὰ Cώφρονι τὸ ὄνομα

### 127

Hdn. Π. μον. λέξ., II p. 938,4 L. (εἰς ωρ λῆγον οὐδέτερον) νίκωρ παρὰ Cώφρονι τῶι μιμογράφωι (παρ᾽ ἀσώτωι μιμ. cod., corr. Dindorf)

### 128

ὁδαῖός γ᾽ ἐσσί

Hdn. Π. μον. λέξ., II p. 950,2 L. (ἐσσί) ἡ δὲ χρῆσις παρὰ τοῖς ποιηταῖς καὶ Cυρακουσίοις. διὸ καὶ Cώφρων (σό- cod.) φησί ὁδ. γε ἐς.
ὁδαῖος cod.: fort. ὁδαγός Ahrens: 'an fuit ἀδαῖός?' Kaibel

## 123

(Eustathius, commentary on Homer, *Odyssey*, on ἱππότα, τοξότα, ἱππηλάτα etc.) Eudaemon of Pelusium says these forms belong to Macedonian . . . and he compares the Illyrian name in the epigram 'my father was Kopaina'. . . and the Syracusan name Myrilla, which he says Sophron mentions. Eudaemon relates that this Syracusan's real name was Democopus; he was an architect, and was called Myrilla because when he finished building the theatre he distributed myrrh to his fellow-citizens.

## 124

after dinner he jostles with the dicers

(Eustathius, commentary on Homer, *Odyssey*) The same source (Suetonius) also says that those who play this game (dice) are called 'dicers' (τρηματῖται) from the pips (τρήματα) on the dice, comparing also the usage in Sophron, 'after — dicers'.

## 125

. . .-haired Poseidon

(Herodian, *On Unusual Words*.) Sophron has the vocative: '. . .-haired Poseidon'.

## 126

(Herodian, *On Unusual Words*) Trellōn: the name appears in Sophron.

## 127

(Herodian, *On Unusual Words*, on neuters ending in -ωρ) νίκωρ appears in the mime-writer Sophron.

## 128

you are indeed by the wayside

(Herodian, *On Unusual Words*, on ἐccί) This usage is found in the poets and in Syracusan. Therefore Sophron also says: 'you — wayside'.

## 129

Hesych. α 837 | Prov. cod. Par. suppl. 676 ap. Cohn CPG Suppl. I p. 67 | Prov. Bodl. 15

ἀγροῦ πυγή· παροιμία
ἐπὶ τῶν λιπαρῶς προσ-
κειμένων. ὁ δὲ Σώφρων
τὰ †πλεῖστα μέρη λέγει
5 μεταφορικῶς ἀπὸ τῶν
ὀρῶν.†


καὶ τὰ πιότερα τοῦ ἀγροῦ
10



15
καὶ
ζάπλουτοι ἀγροῦ πυγαί

ἀγροῦ πυγή· παροιμία
ἐπὶ τῶν λιπαρῶς προσ-
κειμένων. ὁ δὲ Ἴοφρων
τὰ †πλεῖστα μέρη λέγει
ἐπὶ τῶν ὀρῶν.†
ὁ δ᾽ Ἵππαρχος ἐπὶ τῶν
ἀγροίκων τίθησιν, οἷον ἐν
Ἰχθύσιν. τινὲς δὲ τὰ
πιότερα τοῦ ἀγροῦ μέρη, ἢ
διὰ τὸ σαρκῶδες, ὡς
Ὅμηρος οὖθαρ ἀρούρης
{καὶ οἱ ζάπλουτοι ἀγροῦ
πυγαὶ λέγονται},
⟨ἢ⟩ μεταφορικῶς ἀπὸ τῶν
ὀρνέων· μαλακώτερα γὰρ
τὰ πρὸς τῆι πυγῆι τῶν
ὀρνέων {πτῖλα}. ⟨καὶ οἱ
ζάπλουτοι ἀγροῦ πυγαί
λέγονται⟩

ἀγροῦ πυγή· παροιμία
ἐπὶ τῶν λιπαρῶς προσ-
κειμένων.




μεταφορικῶς ἀπὸ τῶν
ὀρνέων· μαλακώτατα γὰρ
τὰ πρὸς τῆι πυγῆι τῶν
ὀρνέων

---

**2** ~ D1 = D3 = Macar. I 3, cf. Phot. α 272 et Eust. in Il. p. 310,3 sq.
(Paus. att. α 21)    **4** πλεῖστα codd.: fort. πιότατα Kaibel
**6** Archipp. fr. 29    **8** π[ιό]τερα Par.: πρότερα Hesych. (corr.
Schneidewin ad Append. prov. I 4)    **10–11** (15–16) transp.
Kassel    **11** (16) ἀγροὶ Par.: corr. Kassel, coll. Hesych.    **12** ἢ
add. Kassel    **15** πτῖλα Par.: secl. Kassel, coll. Bodl.

## 130

Hesych. α 977 ἀδαία· εἰς κόρον ἄγοντα, παρὰ τὸ ἀδεῖν· ὁ δὲ Σώφρων τὸν ἀηδῆ
ἀδανὸν ἔφη (cf. 981ᵇ ⟨ἀδαῖον·⟩ ἀτερπές). Eust. in Od. p. 1394,35 ἐν δὲ
ῥητορικοῖς λεξικοῖς (Ael. Dion. α 33) φέρεται καὶ ταῦτα. ἄδην· Ἀττικοὶ τὸ
δαψιλῶς . . . καὶ ἄδος· κόρος, πλησμονή . . . καὶ ἀδαῖον παρὰ Σώφρονι, τὸ εἰς
κόρον ἔργον (ἄγον Kaibel)

## 131

Hesych. α 3006 Ἁλικαύων· ὁ Ποσειδῶν. Σώφρων
Ἁλικύμων Botzon, 'an Ἁλικλύδων?' Kaibel

## 132

Hesych. α 3284 ἀλύδοιμον· πικρόν. παρὰ Σώφρονι

## 129

(Hesychius) 'rump of the country': a saying referring to those areas which are well-off. And Sophron says the †most parts metaphorically from (ἀπό) the mountains†

and the richer (lit. 'fatter') parts of the country

and very rich rumps of the country.

(Proverb collection) 'rump of the country': a saying referring to those areas which are well-off. Iophron [*sic*] says 'the †most parts for (ἐπί) the mountains'. Hipparchus uses it of rustics, as in *Fishes*. Some use it of the richer parts of land, either because of their fleshiness, as Homer says 'the udder of the land' (οὖθαρ ἀρούρης) {and the richest fields are called the rump}, or metaphorically from birds. For the {feathers} near the rumps of birds are softer. ⟨and the richest fields are called the rump of the country⟩.

(Proverb collection) 'rump of the country': a saying referring to those areas which are well-off

metaphorically from birds. For the (feathers) near the rumps of birds are softer.

## 130

(Hesychius) ἀδαῖα: 'leading to sufficiency beyond one's fill'. Sophron says ἀδανός.

## 131

(Hesychius) Ἀλικαύων: Poseidon. Sophron.

## 132

(Hesychius) ἀλύδοιμος: 'sharp'. In Sophron.

133

Hesych. δ 1404 δι' ἀτέλειαν· ⟨διὰ add. Herw., Versl. en Meded. der Kon. Ak. (Amst.) ³11, 1895, 186⟩ τὸ ἄπρακτον. παρὰ Cώφρονι. τινὲς δὲ γράφουσι δι' ἀγγελίαν

134

Hesych. η 855 (inter gl. ἠρύκακεν et ἤρυκεν) Ἡρύκαλον· τὸν Ἡρακλέα Cώφρων ὑποκοριστικῶς
Ἡρύκαλον cod.: Ἤρυλλον Salm.: Ἡράκυλον Latte     ⟨μὰ τὸν⟩ Ἡρύκαλον apud Sophronem fuisse coni. Crusius

135

Hesych. κ 1437 καταστίζων· . . . καταψηφίζων. παρ' ὅσον τῶν ἀτακτούντων τὰ ὀνόματα παρέστιζον (πάρεστι δὲ cod., corr. Mus.) καὶ ἐζημίουν. καὶ Cώφρων κεντήματά φησι ('scil. pro καταστίγματα' Kaibel, qui verba παρέςτ. — φηςι insequenti glossae 1438 κατάςτικτον· ποικίλον adhaerentia huc transponenda esse vidit; παρέςτ. καὶ ἐζ. iam Mus. transposuerat). π 688 τῶι †ἀνακλυσετῶν† ἀφυστερούντων (τῶν ἀνακληθέντων ἀφ. Jungermann, τῶν ἀτακτούντων ⟨καὶ⟩ ἀφ. Kuster, τῶν {ἀν.} ἀφ. M. Schmidt, τῶν ἀτακτούντων {ἀφ.} Hansen) τὰ ὀνόματα παρέςτικται. Cώφρων δὲ κεντήματά φηςιν.

*136

νῦν τ' ἦνθες εἰς χορόν, νῦν τ' ἔπραδες

Hesych. ν 734 νῦν — ἔπραδες· νῦν εἰς χορὸν ἦλθες, καὶ νῦν ἔπαρδες. Sud. ν 606 νῦν — ἔπαρδες (sine expl.)
τ' ἦνθες Hesych.: ἦλθον Sud.     εἰς χορόν Sud.: δεχωρόν Hesych.: ἐς κόρον Meineke Phil. 13 (1858) 536     ἔπραδες Hesych.: ἔπαρδες Sud.

137

Hesych. c 840 cκανὰς ̣ εντα· ἐπίχαλκ . . παρὰ cωφρωνίω cκανὰς πορεύςῃ ἐν τῆι ἀcπίδι. Καλλίας δὲ cκεῦος (fr. 39)
cκανὰς ἰέντα· ἐπίχαλκα Mus.     Cώφρονι· ἐπὶ Heinsius (εἰς mavult Olivieri² p. 135), -νι· ὡς Schow, -νι· ὦ Hansen     'ad sensum rectissime Ahrensius [p. 475] cκανας ῆι ἐν τᾶι ἐπιχάλκωι, cui tamen interpretis verba adcommodari vix possunt, quae satis violenter idem corrigebat cκηνοποιήςῃ ἐν τῆι ἀcπίδι . . . possunt verba ad iuvenem in bellum profecturum dicta fuisse. hinc Theocritus Lyciscae [14] v. 53, ut vidit Wilamowitzius [cf. Textg. d. gr. Buk. p. 161], Cῖμος ὁ τᾶς ἐπιχάλκω ἐραcθεὶς ἐκπλεύcας ὑγιὴς ἐπανῆνθε' Kaibel

## 133

(Hesychius) δι’ ἀτέλειαν: '⟨through⟩ inaction'. In Sophron. Some write δι’ ἀγγελίαν ('through notification').

## 134

(Hesychius) Ἡρύκαλον: Heracles. Sophron, as the diminutive.

## 135

(Hesychius) καταϲτίζων ('tattooing'): . . . 'condemning'; because they tattooed names onto deserters, and fined them. Sophron also says κεντήματα ('pricks').

## *136

now you went to the dance, and now you frated

(Hesychius) 'now — frated': 'now you came to the dance, and now you farted'. (*Suda*) 'now — frated'.

## 137

(Hesychius) [A corrupt lemma in Hesychius.]

108 SOPHRON

*138

Hesych. ψ 94 ψαφοτριβέων· περὶ τοὺς λόγους (λογιςμοὺς Hemst.) τριβομένων

'incerta coniectura ad Sophronem rettuli' Kaibel

139

πεῖ εἶ; :: εἶ τὰ τῶν χοιραγχᾶν

Ioann. Alex. De accent. p. 32,14 πεῖ — χείραγχαν. Cώφρων (sequitur fr. 4,8). Apoll. Dysc. adv., GrGr II 1,1 p. 132,27 Schn. (ἐπίρρημα εἰс ει λῆγον ἐν περιςπαςμῶι) τὸ παρὰ Δωριεῦςι πεῖ γὰρ ἁ ἄςφαλτος (fr. 4,8) καὶ εἶ — χοιραγχᾶν. p. 210,1 Schn. τὸ . . . εἶ — χοιραγχᾶν ἐν ἴςωι ἐςτὶ τῶι ὅπου, καὶ τὸ πεῖ γὰρ ἁ ἄςφαλτος (fr. 4,8) ἐν ἴςωι τῶι πού. p. 207,16 Δώρια . . . τὰ τοιαῦτα μεταποιούμενα· εἶ — χοιραγχᾶν, πεῖ γὰρ ἁ ἄςφαλτος (fr. 4,8). Id. synt. IV 62, GrGr II 2 p. 484,12 οὐ δὴ οὖν τὸ ἐπεί τόπον παρεμφαίνει, ὥςπερ ἔχει τὸ εἶ τὰ τῶν (ειτατον cod., ει in ras.) χοιραγχον (ον in αν mutavit man. 3)

πεῖ εἶ Dindorf: ποῖ εἶ Ioann.: om. Apoll.     εἶ τὰ Apoll.: εἶτα Ioann.

140

μή που τις καὶ[

P. Oxy. 2429 Fr. 1 (a) col. iii (saec. IIᵖ, comm. in Epich. Ὀδ. αὐτομ. = fr. 98,83) ed. Lobel (vol. XXV 1959) παρ᾽ Ὀμή(ρωι) 'μή που τις καὶ Τρ[ῶας' (K 511) μιμεῖται Cώφρων· μή — καὶ[

141

Phot. (b, z) a 471 = Lex. Bachm. p. 39,4 ἀθάρη καὶ ἀθήρα καὶ ἀθέρα (ἀθέρα καὶ ἀθήρα Lex. Bachm.) καὶ ἀθάρα τὸ αὐτό φαςιν . . . ἔςτι δὲ ἡ χρῆςις τῆς λέξεως πολλὴ παρὰ τοῖς Ἀττικοῖς (-κιςταῖς Phot.), κατὰ μὲν τὸ τέλος διὰ τοῦ η προαγομένη, κατὰ δὲ τὴν μέςην διὰ τοῦ α· κατὰ δὲ πολλοὺς ἄλλους κατὰ μὲν τὸ τέλος διὰ τοῦ α, κατὰ δὲ τὴν μέςην διὰ τοῦ η. οὕτως δὲ καὶ Ἑλλάνικος (4 F 192 Jac.) καὶ Cώφρων ἐχρήςαντο. ἐκτείνουςι δὲ καὶ τὸ α, ὡς ἀπὸ τοῦ ἀθήρα τῆς λέξεως μεταληφθείςης. ἴςως δέ, φαςίν, ἀθέρα ἦν ἡ λέξις διὰ τοῦ ε τὸ πρῶτον (τὸ πρ. om. Lex. Bachm.) . . . ὕςτερον δὲ εἰς τὸ η τὸ ε ἐξετάθη . . . τὸ μέντοι ἀθέρα εἰς τὸ ἀθάρα Δωρικῶς γέγονεν, οἱ δὲ ἀθάρην λέγοντες Ἰακῶς φαςι κτλ.

142

Phot. (z) a 2511 = Sud. a 3349 = Lex. Bachm. p. 125,14 ἀποκηδήςαντες· ἀντὶ τοῦ ἀποκακήςαντες. Ὅμηρος (Ψ 413). παρὰ δὲ Cώφρονι ἀποκαδεῖ (-ηδεῖ Phot.) ἀντὶ τοῦ ἀςθενεῖ κεῖται (παρὰ δὲ C. ἀποκακήςαντες ἀφροντιςτήςαντες, cf. Schol. Hom. 1.1., Hesych. a 6381, Et. magn. p. 131,29)

*138

(Hesychius) ψαφοτριβέων: 'engrossed in accounts' (?).

139

A.  Where are you going?
B.  Where the . . . of the pig-stranglers . . .

(John of Alexandria, *On Accents*) 'where — pig-stranglers'. Sophron (fr. 4. 8 follows). (Apollonius Dyscolus, *On Adverbs*) . . . the Doric phrases 'where — pitch' (fr. 4A. 8) and 'where — pig-stranglers'. (Apollonius reports the same phrase in several other places.)

140

lest some other[

(Oxyrhynchus Papyrus, commentary on Epicharmus, *Odysseus the Deserter*) Sophron imitates the line in Homer 'lest some other [god awake the Trojans]' (*Il.* 10. 511), saying 'lest — other['.

141

(Photius, *Lexicon*) ἀθάρη, ἀθήρα, ἀθέρα, and ἀθάρα all mean the same thing ('gruel') . . . The common use of the word in Attic is with η at the end and α in the middle. According to many others the ending should have α, the middle η. This [i.e. ἀθήρα] is the form used by Hellanicus (*FGrH* 4 F 192) and Sophron. They also lengthen the α, so taking the word to be from ἀθήρα. Perhaps, the word was ἀθέρα with ε . . . and later the ε was lengthened to η . . . However, the word ἀθέρα became in Doric ἀθάρα, and in Ionic they say ἀθάρη. . .

142

(Photius, *Lexicon*) ἀποκηδήcαντεc ('being careless'): instead of ἀποκακήcαντεc. Homer (*Il.* 23. 413). And in Sophron we find ἀποκαδεῖ instead of ἀcθενεῖ ('he is ill').

143

Phot. (z) α 2979 = Sud. α 4186 = Lex. Bachm. p. 152,21 ἄϲμα· τὸ δίαϲμα.
οὕτω (καὶ Sud., Lex. Bachm.) Ϲώφρων. καὶ ἄττεϲθαι ὃ ἡμεῖς διάζεϲθαι

144

Phot. β 158 βλέννα· ἡ μύξα. Ϲώφρων δὲ διὰ τοῦ π φηϲὶ πλέννα

145

Phot. κ 194 κάρκαρον· τὸ δεϲμωτήριον· οὕτως Ϲώφρων

146

Phot. λ 359 = Lex. Bachm. p. 291,18 λίτρα . . . ἐπὶ δὲ τοῦ ϲταθμοῦ
Ἐπίχαρμός τε (fr. 37) καὶ Ϲώφρων ἐχρήϲαντο

147

αἴ τιϲ τὸν ξύοντα ἀντιξύει
ὁ χοραγὸϲ ξύεται

Phot. p. 310,12 = Sud. ξ 91 (III p. 499,2) τὸ κνῆν (κνειν Sud.) οἱ Δωριεῖϲ
ξύειν λέγουϲιν, ὡϲ καὶ Ϲώφρων· αἴ τιϲ (-ων ἄν τιϲ Sud., -ονα τίϲ Phot., corr.
Ahrens p. 475) — ἀντιξύει. καὶ πάλιν· ὁ χ. ξ. (ξ. ὁ χ. Sud.)
1  ἀντιξύει Phot.: -ηι Sud. AFVM: -ειν Sud. G

148

Phot. p. 314,26 ὀγκίαν· τὸν ϲταθμόν. Ϲώφρων καὶ Ἐπίχαρμος

149

Phot. p. 379,20 παμφάλυα (-υγα Botzon p. 25)· τὸν πομφόλυγα. Ϲώφρων

150

Poll. IX 46 (codd. FS, ABCL) τῶν δὲ πόλεων μερῶν καὶ . . . προεξέδραι,
θρόνοι (om. FSABC), θῶκοι (defic. ABCL) καὶ ὡς Ϲώφρων φηϲὶ ϲύνθωκοι

151

Priscian. inst. gramm. VI 70 (GrL II p. 254,17) ἥρως ἥρωος, heros
herois; Μίνως Μίνωος, Minos Minois. Sallustius tamen Minonis protulit
genetivum in II historiarum fr. 7 Maur.) . . . nec tamen hoc sine exemplo

## 143

(Photius, *Lexicon*) ἄϲμα: the 'warp' (δίαϲμα). So Sophron. Also ἄττεϲθαι, which we call διάζεϲθαι ('to set the warp in the loom').

## 144

(Photius, *Lexicon*) βλέννα: 'slime' (μύξα). Sophron says it with a π, πλέννα.

## 145

(Photius, *Lexicon*) κάρκαρον: 'prison'. So Sophron.

## 146

(Photius, *Lexicon*) λίτρα . . . Epicharmus and Sophron use it for a weight.

## 147

if some one scratches the scratcher in return

the chorus-master scratches himself

(Photius, *Lexicon*) For 'scratch' the Dorians say ξύειν, as also Sophron 'if — in return', and again 'the chorus-master — himself'.

## 148

(Photius, *Lexicon*) ὀγκίαν: a coin (or weight). Sophron and Epicharmus (fr. 138).

## 149

(Photius, *Lexicon*) παμφάλυα: 'a bubble' (πομφόλυγα). Sophron.

## 150

(Pollux) Parts of the city include . . . chairs of state, thrones, seats (θῶκοι), and, as Sophron says, cύνθωκοι ('benches')

## 151

(Priscian) ἥρωc, genitive ἥρωοc (*heros herois*); Μίνωc, genitive Μίνωοc (*Minos Minois*). Sallust, however, makes the genitive *Minonis* in book 2 of his histories . . . nor, however, is this without parallel in Greek.

*apud Graecos quoque invento. Syracusii enim ἥρων pro ἥρως dicunt.* sic
*Sophron παρ' ἡρώνεccι non ἥρωcι dixit*
παρ' ἡρώνεccι non ἥρωcι scripsimus: HPPΩNECCI pro HPΩCI R (ΠAP EPOCIN
non herosi superscr. r): ΠΑPHPΩCI*NON HPOCIN D (N supra ΩCI et on supra
CIN scr. d): ΠΑPEPONCINENONHPOCI B: ΠΑPE PONECIN, ONEPOCI G: *parenon*
** *enon* H (pro *enoc* add. h): *pareron* (*eron* in lit. 1) *si non erosi* (*i. nocens*
superscr. l) L: ΠHPEPONECI NΩN PΩC i K: ἡρώνεccι non ἥρωcι P. Bondam,
Var. lect. (1759) p. 311, ex cod. Dorvill.: παρ' ἡρώνεccι *pro* ἥρωcι Hertz
(Kaibel)

## 152

Prov. cod. Par. suppl. 676 ap. Cohn CPG Suppl. I p. 71 τὰc ἐν
Ἅιδου τριακάδαc . . . λεχθείη δ' ἂν ἡ παροιμία ἐπὶ τῶν περιέργων καὶ τὰ
ἀποκεκρυμμένα ζητούντων γινώcκειν (= Prov. Bodl. 905). ταῦτα καὶ παρὰ
Cώφρονι (-νοc cod., corr. Cohn) ἐν μίμοιc

## 153

Quint. inst. orat. I 10,17 *grammatice quondam ac musice iunctae fuerunt*
*. . . eosdem utruisque rei praeceptores fuisse cum Sophron ostendit mimorum*
*quidem scriptor, sed quem Plato adeo probavit ut suppositos capiti libros*
*eius cum moreretur habuisse credator, tum Eupolis* (fr. 17)

## 154

τῆτέ τοι· κορῶναί εἰcιν

Schol. (EΓ; Sud. τ 462) Ar. Ach. 204a (i), p. 36,7 Wils. (τῇ) cημαίνει δέ
ποτε καὶ ῥῆμα προcτακτικόν· Κύκλωψ, τῇ, πίε οἶνον (Hom. ι 347). ἐχρήcατο
δὲ καὶ τῶι πληθυντικῶι ὁ Cώφρων (coφὸc Γ) εἰπών· τῆτε — εἰcιν
τοι· Blomfield    εἰcιν codd.: ἐντι Botzon

## 155

ἀργυρίων δεήcηι

Schol. (E) Ar. Nub. 756a (ἀργύριον δανείζεται) ἡ γραφὴ ἀργυρίων
πληθυντικῶc παρὰ Φρυνίχωι κεῖται (fr. 25 Borr.). ὅτι οἱ κωμικοὶ
πληθυντικῶc φαcιν (vid. Ar. fr. 412 et Plat. fr. 63), οἱ δὲ ῥήτορεc ἑνικῶc. καὶ
Cώφρων πληθυντικῶc ἀ. δ.

## 156

ἰλλοτέρα τᾶν κορωνᾶν

Schol. (R) Ar. Thesm. 846 (ἰλλόc) τυφλόc (suppl. e. Sud. ι 323)
διεcτραμμένοc τὴν ὄψιν. Cώφρων· ἰλλ. — κ. Gal. in Hipp. epid. III (CMG

Indeed, the Syracusans say ἥρων for ἥρωc. So Sophron said παρ' ἠρώνεccι ('among the heroes') not ἥρωcι.

## 152

(Proverb collection) The thirtieths (τριακάδεc) in Hades . . . The proverb would be said of busybodies, and those who want to know secret things. This is also in Sophron in his mimes.

## 153

(Quintilian) Grammar and the arts were once linked . . . and there were those who taught both, as Sophron shows, a writer of mimes indeed, but one of whom Plato so approved that it is believed that when he died he had his works beneath his pillow.

## 154

go on, you lot; they're crows

(Scholion on Aristophanes, *Acharnians*, on τῇ) Sometimes it also indicates an imperative: 'Cyclops, go on, drink the wine' (*Od.* 9. 347). Sophron used it also in the plural: 'go on — crows'.

## 155

you'll want monies

(Scholion on Aristophanes, *Clouds*, on ἀργύριον δανείζεται 'the money is lent out for usury') The plural 'monies' (ἀργυρίων) appears in Phrynichus. (The note is) because the comic poets use the plural, and orators the singular. Sophron also uses the plural: 'you — monies'.

## 156

with a bigger squint than crows

(Scholion on Aristophanes, *Thesmophoriazusae*) ἰλλοc ('squinting'): blind, with distorted sight. Sophron: 'with — crows'. (Galen on

# 114    SOPHRON

V 10,2,1) p. 128,3 Wenk. τὸ ἰλλός, ἀφ' οὗ καὶ ὁ Cώφρων δοκεῖ πεποιηκέναι τὸ cυγκριτικὸν ὀνομαζόμενον παρὰ τῶν γραμματικῶν· ἰλλ. — κ. ἰλλοτερά Schol. Ar.: ἰλλότερον Gal. MQV: ἀλήτ- Gal. L    τὰν κορώναν Schol. Ar.: τἀγκύωνα Gal. L: τὰν κύονα Gal. M: ταν κ- QV

## 157

Schol. (VEΘN Barb, Tzetz.) Ar. Plut. 1050 b Ποντοπόςειδον . . . ἀντὶ τοῦ ὦ μέγιςτε Πόςειδον. καὶ Cώφρων (cῶφρον V) γάρ (om. N) φηcι (om. V) πόντος ἀγαθῶν (καὶ πάντων ἀγ. V, om. N), πλῆθος καὶ μέγεθος θέλων cημᾶναι (cημῆναι V, διὰ τούτου πλ. καὶ μέγ. ἀγαθῶν cημᾶναι βουλ. N)

## *158

ἦρ' ἔcθ' ὕδωρ;

Schol. (V) Dion. Thr., GrGr I 3 p. 290,11 Hilg. ὁ ἄρα ἐρωτηματικὸc ὢν μηκύνει τὸ α, cυλλογιcτικὸc δὲ βραχύνει. τρέπεται δὲ ἑκατέρου τὸ α εἰc η, τὸ μὲν μακρὸν παρ' Αἰολεῦcιν οὕτωc, ἦρ' ἔτι παρθενί{κ}ας ἐπιβάλλομαι; Cαπφώ (fr. 107 V.), ἦρ' ἔcθ' ὕδωρ cῶφρον παρὰ Δωριεῦcι, καὶ παρ'Ἴωcι ἦρά τοι ὧδ' αἰεὶ ταχινοὶ πόδεc; (Call. hy. 4,114), τὸ δὲ βραχὺ οὕτωc κτλ. Apoll. Dysc. coni., GrGr II 1,1 p. 223,24 Schn. ἄρα. οὗτοc κατὰ πᾶcαν διάλεκτον, ὑπεcταλμέ[νη]c τῆc κοινῆc καὶ Ἀττικῆc ἦρα λέγεται· ἦρ' ἔτι π[αρ]θενίαc (-ηc cod.) ἐπιβάλλομαι; Cαπφώ (fr. 107 V.), ἦρ' ἔcτι θ' ὕδωρ c[ ]. ἐπὶ τοῦ τοιούτου οὐκ ἐμποδίζοντόc τινοc cυ[ναλοι]φὴν ἐκδέξαcθαι, Τρύφων (fr. 43 Vels.) φηcὶν ἀποκοπὴν παρηκολουθηκέναι κτλ.

ἔcθ' Schol. Dion. Thr.: ἔcτι θ' Apoll.; si recte, cum Bergkio PLG⁴ III p. 740 θὕδωρ legendum, ut Cratet. fr. 17,5 (vid. ad Amips. fr. 2,2)

## 159

τὸ cάρον ἄνελε

Schol. (MA) Eur. Andr. 166 (cαίρειν) παρὰ τὸ cάρον (π. τὸ -όν M, om. A) ὡc παρὰ (ὥcπερ M) Cώφρονι· τὸ — ἄνελε. Hesych. c 244 cάρον . . . βαρυτονητέον, ὡc παρὰ Cώφρονι
τὸ cάρον M: cαρὼν A

## 160

Schol. (MTAB) Eur. Phoen. 3 ἔθοc δὲ τοῖc ποιηταῖc θηλυκῶc λέγειν τοὺc (τὰc B) ἵππουc. Cώφρων (cῶφρον TAB)· τὰν ἵππον

## 161

Schol. (*B) Hom. Ε 576 (III p. 261,14 Dind., cf. Erbse V p. 410,78 adn.) = Schol. Greg. Naz. or. (18,6) 71 p. 11 [241] Picc. τὸ τάλαντον δὲ τὸ

Hippocrates) ἰλλός, from which Sophron also apparently formed what the grammarians call the comparative: 'with — crows'.


## 157

(Scholion on Aristophanes, *Wealth*) 'Sea-poseidon' (Ποντοπόσειδον) . . . instead of 'o greatest Poseidon'. And Sophron says 'sea of good things', when he wants to indicate a large size and number.


## *158

### is there water?

(Scholion on Dionysius Thrax) ἆρα, when it is interrogative, lengthens the α, but when it is inferential it shortens it. Either α may be turned into η, the long as follows in Aeolic: 'do I still long for virginity' (Sa. fr. 107); in Doric 'is there water'; and in Ionic . . . (Callim. *H.* 4. 114). And the short as follows . . . (Apollonius Dyscolus, *On Connectives*) ἆρα: this has the form ἦρα in every dialect except Koine and Attic: 'do — virginity?'. Sappho. 'is there water?' s[    ].


## 159

### pick up the broom

(Scholion on Euripides, *Andromache*) 'sweep' (σαίρειν) from 'broom' (σάρον). Sophron: 'pick up — broom'.


## 160

(Scholion on Euripides, *Phoenician Women*) The poets habitually make horses feminine. Sophron: τὰν ἵππον ('the mare').

## 161

(Scholion on Homer, *Iliad* = Scholion on Gregory Nazianzus, *Orations*) The talent is now called the Attic talent. Among the Siceliotes (om. Schol. Hom.) νῦν λεγόμενον (λεγ. νῦν Schol. Greg.) Ἀττικόν· παρὰ δὲ Cικελιώταιc τὸ μὲν ἀρχαῖον ἦν νόμων (μνῶν codd., νούμμων Scal., cf. Poll. IX 87 et Gloss. 139) κδ', νῦν (νυνὶ Schol. Greg.) δὲ ιβ' (hucusque Sud. τ 34). δύναται δὲ ὁ νόμοc (δύν. δὲ εἶναι Schol. Hom.) τρία ἡμιωβόλια, ὡc ἐν τοῖc περὶ Cώφρονοc Ἀπολλόδωροc (244 F 218 Jac., Sophr. test. 22). ἐκ τῶν Διογενιανοῦ τῆc ἐπιτομῆc τῶν Οὐ{c}ηcτίνου (τ. Οὐ. om. Schol. Hom.) Ἑλληνικῶν ὀνομάτων

### 162

κορώναc ἀνδούμενοι

Schol. (A) Hom. Λ 385 d (κέραι ἀγλαέ) οὐ τῆι τριχὶ ψιλῶc, ἀλλ' ἐμπλοκῆc τι γένοc· εἰc κέρατοc τρόπον ἀνεπλέκοντο οἱ ἀρχαῖοι. Cώφρων· κορ. ἀν. καὶ οἱ Ἀθηναῖοι τέττιγαc ἐνεπλέκοντο κτλ. Eust. ad loc., p. 851,49 οἱ δὲ περὶ Ἡρόδωρον καὶ Ἀπίωνα καὶ τοιαῦτά φαcιν· ἐμπλοκῆc τι γένοc εἰc κέρατοc τύπον ἀνεπλέκοντο οἱ παλαιοί . . . καὶ ἄλλα δὲ ἦcαν τριχῶν κοcμήματα. ὁ γοῦν Cώφρων φηcί που· κορ. ἀν. καὶ Ἀθηναῖοι τέττιγαc ἀνεπλέκοντο κτλ.
ἀνδούμενοι Schol. Hom.: ἀναδ- Eust.

### 163

Schol. (EVφΩΔ) Luc. Lexiph. 21 p. 202,5 R. cιληπορδεῖν παρὰ Cώφρονι τὸ cτρηνιᾶν καὶ ἀβρύνεcθαι. Hesych. c 632 cιλαπορδῆcαι· ἀβρύνεcθαι, θρύπτεcθαι, χλιδᾶν

### 164

]ων κυμβέων ὄγκον ἔχων

Schol. Nic. ther. 526, [1]Pap. Mil. Vogl. II 45 (saec. I[p]) ed. Cazzaniga pp. 32–39 (1961, cum tab. IV) 2 κύμβα λέγεται καθάπερ καὶ [ ]ων — ἔχων, [2](KGPVR Ald) παρὰ Cώφρονι κύμβον ὅ. ἔ., ἀντὶ τοῦ cκυφοειδοῦc ποτηρίου ξυλίν]ων? Cazzaniga κυμβέων Schol.[1]: κύμβου Schol.[2] ὄγκον ἔχων Schol.[1], Schol.[2] KPVR: ὅ. ἔχειν [2]Ald: ἔχον ὅ. [2]G

### 165

ἀεὶ δὲ πρόcω φύλλα ῥάμνου κραcτιζόμεθα

Schol. Nic. ther. 861 ἀλεξιάρηc δὲ ῥάμνου, ὅτι οὐ μόνον ἀπαλέξειν ἐcτὶν ἀγαθὴ ἡ ῥάμνοc εἰc φάρμακα, ἀλλὰ καὶ εἰc φαντάcματα, ὅθεν καὶ πρὸ τῶν θυρῶν ἐν τοῖc ἐναγίcμαcι κρεμῶcιν αὐτήν. ἔcτι δὲ λευκὴ καὶ μέλαινα. μέμνηται δὲ τῆc βοτάνηc καὶ Εὐφορίων (fr. 137 Pow.)· ἀλεξίκακον φύε ῥάμνον, καὶ Cώφρων ὁμοίωc· ἀεὶ — κρ.
πρόcω codd.: πρὼ Ahrens: πρόc ἀῶ Kaibel κραcτιζόμεθα Bussemaker: κρατιζ- codd.: ἀκρατιζ- vel ἀκρατιcδ- Blomfield

the old talent used to be worth 24 *nomoi*, but it is now worth 12. The *nomos* is worth three half-obols, according to Apollodorus in his commentaries on Sophron (*FGrH* 244 F 218). From Diogenian's epitome of Vestinus' *Greek words*.

## 162

### binding crows into them

(Scholion on Homer, *Iliad*) Not simply hair, but a style of braiding. The ancients braided their hair into the form of a horn. Sophron: 'binding — them'. And the Athenians wove cicadas into theirs . . . etc. (Eustathius, commentary on Homer, *Iliad*) The school of Herodorus and Apion say the following: the ancients braided their hair into a style of braiding in the shape of a horn. . . There were other ornaments for the hair. So Sophron says somewhere: 'binding — them'. And the Athenians wove cicadas into theirs. . . etc.

## 163

(Scholion on Lucian, *The Word-Flaunter*) ειληπορδεῖν in Sophron means 'be wanton' and 'become lascivious'.

## 164

### ]. . . with the weight of the cups

(Papyrus scholion on Nicander, *Theriaca*) 'cup' (κύμβα) is said just as also [   ] . . . with — cups'. (Manuscript scholion on the same) In Sophron: 'with the weight of the cup' (*sc.* κύμβα) stands for a cup shaped like a skyphos.

## 165

### hereafter we shall always champ the leaves of the thorn

(Scholion on Nicander, *Theriaca*) 'the magic thorn', because the thorn is good for warding off not only spells, but even ghosts, which is why they hang it up before the doors as an offering to the dead. It can be white or black. Euphorion also mentions the plant (fr. 137 Pow.) . . . and Sophron 'hereafter — thorn'.

118     SOPHRON

166

Schol. (BDPTU) Pind. Nem. 1, inscr. b (II p. 7,2 Drachm.) ἱερὰν εἶναι τὴν κρήνην (Arethusam) Ἀρτέμιδος, τὴν δὲ θεὸν ἱππικὴν εἶναι, καθὸ Cώφρων μὲν αὐτὴν ἀτρέςτην (-έςην PT, -εςήν D, -εςιν U, -έςταν Kaibel), Ὅμηρος δὲ (Z 205) χρυςήνιον (προςεφώνηςεν) κτλ.

167

Tzetz. ad Ar. Ran. 517 b (IV 3 p. 840,7 Kost.) κἄρτι παρατετιλμέναι: νεοξυρεῖς τὸν δορίαλον, τὸ {ν} μύρτον, τὸν χοῖρον, τὸν κύεθον, καὶ ὅσα τοιαῦτα ὁ Cώφρων καὶ ὁ Ἱππῶναξ (fr. 174 W., 183 Deg.) καὶ ἕτεροι λέγουςι

168

μοῖτον ἀντὶ μοίτου

Varr. De l. l. V 179 si datum quod reddatur, mutuum, quod Siculi moeton: itaque scribit Sophron mocton †antimo† (corr. Huschke). Hesych. μ 1557 †μοιτοὶ ἄντιμοι† (corr. Kaibel)· παροιμία Cικελοῖς. ἡ γὰρ χάρις μοῖτον· οἷον χάριν ⟨ἀντὶ χάριτος⟩ (μοι τὸν οἰνοχαριν cod., corr. et suppl. Wil. ap. Kaib.)

169

Zenob. Ath. I 58 = vulg. II 17 = Prov. Bodl. 148 ἀληθέςτερα τῶν ἐπι Cάγραι· ταύτης (sc. τῆς παροιμίας) μέμνηται Μένανδρος (fr. 32) καὶ Cώφρων (καὶ C. om. Bodl.) καὶ Ἄλεξις (fr. 306)

*170

Zenob. vulg. II 94 (brevius Bodl. 267) = Hesych. γ 908 γραῦς ἔριφος· Ἀπολλόδωρος (244 F 301 Jac.) φηςὶν ἔςτι τις παροιμιώδης (fort. -ὡς, compend. in Zen.) λεγομένη ἐριφία γραῦς, ἡ ἐν παρθενίαι γεγηρακυῖα (εἶναι δὲ αὐτὴν οἷον γραῦν ἔριφον, τὴν ἐν π. καταγεγηρακυῖαν Hesych.). οἱ δὲ ἀπὸ (ἐπὶ Kaibel) τῆς ἀκρίδος· τὴν γὰρ ἀρουραίαν ἀκρίδα ὑπό τινων μάντιν λεγομένην (μάτην λέγομεν omissis quae sequuntur Hesych.) κατὰ Cικελίαν γραῦν ἔριφον καλεῖςθαι ἢ γραῦν ἐρίφην (γραῦν ἔριφον ἢ γραῦν ἐρίφων Bodl.). λέγουςι δὲ ὅτι εἴ τινι ἐμβλέψειε ζώωι, κακόν τι ἐκείνωι γίνεται. Sud. γ 431 (inde c 251) γραῦς cέριφος· ἡ ἐν παρθενίαι γεγηρακυῖα. ἀπὸ μεταφορᾶς τῆς ἀρουραίας ἀκρίδος, ἣν καλοῦςι γραῦν cερίφην καὶ μάντιν. Schol. (K) Theocr. 10,18 a (p. 228,15 W.) ἡ καλαμαία· ταύτην οἱ μὲν γραῦν ἔριθον, οἱ δὲ ἀρουραίαν ὀνομάζουςιν. ἔςτι δὲ ἀκρὶς ⟨ἐν τῆι καλάμηι γινομένη suppl. Wendel e Schol. 18 b et c) καὶ καλεῖται μάντις. 18 e (p. 229,9 W., codd. KUEAGPT) Ἀρίσταρχος (Ἀριστοφάνης K) ἐν ὑπομνήματι Λυκούργου (ἐν ὑπομνήςει Λυκ. UEA, om. K) Αἰςχύλου (om. KGPT) φηςὶ τὴν ἀκρίδα (τ.

### 166

(Scholion on Pindar, *Nemean* 1) The spring (Arethusa) is sacred to Artemis, the goddess of horses, so Sophron calls her ἀτρέϲτην ('fearless'), and Homer 'golden-reined' etc.

### 167

(John Tzetzes on Aristophanes, *Frogs*) 'and just plucked': freshly shaved with respect to the δορίαλοϲ, the μύρτον, the χοῖροϲ, the κύϲθοϲ, and all such expressions in Sophron, Hipponax (fr. 174 W. = 183 Deg.), and the rest.

### 168

#### thanks for thanks

(Varro, *On the Latin Language*) We say *mutuum* for giving something in return, but the Sicilians *moeton*; so Sophron wrote †*moetin antimo*† (corr. Huschke). (Hesychius) †μοιτοὶ ἄντιμοι† (corr. Kaibel): a Sicilian proverb. For μοῖτον means 'thanks', so 'thanks ⟨for thanks⟩' [i.e. 'to return like for like'].

### 169

(Zenobius, *Proverbs*) 'truer than the events at Sagra': this proverb is mentioned by Menander (fr. 32), Sophron, and Alexis (fr. 306).

### *170

(Zenobius, *Proverbs*; Hesychius) γραῦϲ ἔριφοϲ: Apollodorus (*FGrH* 244 F 301) says that there is a proverbial saying ἐριφία γραῦϲ, a woman who has become old in maidenhood. Some say it is from the grasshopper; since the field grasshopper, which is called a 'mantis' (μάντιϲ) by some, is named γραῦϲ ἔριφοϲ or γραῦϲ ἔριφη in Sicily. They say that something bad will happen to any living thing it looks at. (*Suda*) γραῦϲ ϲέριφοϲ: a woman grown old in maidenhood. Metaphorically after the field grasshopper, which they call γραῦϲ ϲέριφη and 'mantis'. (Scholion on Theocritus, *Id.* 10) καλαμαία ('cornstalk grasshopper'): some call this γραῦϲ ἔριθοϲ, others the field grasshopper. The grasshopper is also called 'mantis'. (The same) Aristarchus in his commentary on Aeschylus' *Lycurgus* says that something bad will happen to any living thing if this grasshopper looks at it.

ἀ. φ. GPT, τ. ἀ. Κ) ταύτην, εἴ τινι ἐμβλέψειε ζώιωι, τούτωι κακόν τι γίνεϲθαι
(TrGF III pp. 234 sq.)

*171

‒ ‒ ‒ ‒ ‒ ‒ ‒ ‒
]αϲϲ. ου μεδέων διϱ[
]των ἄνωθε πεδίον ε[
]. εμαν τεθει[.] ν[.]ατρι[
]ηϲτοϲ με καὶ πρϱτε[
]καλὰ μάν ἐϲτιν. [
]πὸτ τῶν θεῶν μ. [

PSI 1387 (saec. IIᵖ) ed. Bartoletti (vol. XIV 1957) p. 29 cum tab. III.
Sophroni trib. Maas ap. ed. pr. p. xvi
1 θαλ]αϲϲίον? Kassel      5 λᾱμᾱν

**172

Plato, *Rep.* 10. 607 BC) ταῦτα δή, ἔφην, ἀπολελογήϲθω (M: -είϲθω F: -ίϲθω
AD) ἡμῖν ἀναμνηϲθεῖϲιν περὶ ποιήϲεωϲ, ὅτι (AM: ὅτε FD) εἰκότωϲ ἄρα τότε
αὐτὴν ἐκ τῆϲ πόλεωϲ ἀπεϲτέλλομεν τοιαύτην οὖϲαν· ὁ γὰρ λόγοϲ ἡμᾶϲ ᾕρει.
προϲείπωμεν δὲ αὐτῆι, μὴ καί τινα ϲκληρότητα ἡμῶν καὶ ἀγροικίαν
καταγνῶι, ὅτι παλαιὰ μέν τιϲ διαφορὰ φιλοϲοφίαι τε καὶ ποιητικῆι (AFDM:
μιμητικῆι A²)· καὶ γὰρ ἡ (**fr. A**) "λακέρυζα πρὸϲ δεϲπόταν (AFM: δέϲποτα
D) κύων" ἐκείνη "κραυγάζουϲα (ADM: κράζουϲα F)" καὶ (**fr. B**) "μέγαϲ ἐν
ἀφρόνων κενεαγορίαιϲι" καὶ ὁ (**fr. C**) "τῶν διαϲόφων (edd.: δία ϲοφῶν A: διὰ
ϲοφῶν D: διαϲοφῶν FM: λίαν ϲοφῶν Herwerden) ὄχλοϲ κρατῶν (codd.:
κράτων Adam)" καὶ οἱ (**fr. D**) "λεπτῶϲ μεριμνῶντεϲ," ὅτι ἄρα "πένονται",
καὶ ἄλλα μυρία ϲημεῖα παλαιᾶϲ ἐναντιώϲεωϲ τούτων.

## *171 (*PSI* 1387)

]ruler of the sea (?) . . . [
] . . . from above the plain . . . [
] . . . put[-(?)    ] . . . [
] . . . me and ear[lier(?)
5          ]fine (things?) indeed it is . . . [
]to the gods . . . [

## **172

(Plato, *Republic*) Let these things then, I said, bring to an end our defence in our reconsideration of poetry, since, given her character, we were right to banish her from the city; the argument convinced us. And let us also say to her, in case she charges us with some harshness and boorishness, that there is a long-standing dispute between philosophy and poetry; for consider (these verses): the

(A) yelping bitch barking at her master,

and

(B) great in the empty-talk of fools

and the

(C) crowd of know-alls (?) ruling

and

(D) even those who meditate subtly

that

they starve,

and a thousand other indications of a long-standing antipathy.

# Commentary on Selected Fragments

## I. WOMEN'S MIMES

### Seamstresses

**Title and Subject:** The title is most naturally taken to refer to seamstresses (cf. Antiphanes' Ἀκέστρια, of which only four insignificant fragments (frs. 21–4) remain). The mime will perhaps have portrayed a conversation between two characters, both belonging to a familiar comic type of carping woman. The thievish shopkeepers of fr. 1 may be those who sell the seamstresses' wares for a significantly higher profit, or perhaps the women are complaining about the high cost of goods.

Olivieri understood the title to be related to ἀκεστήρ 'doctor', and assigned fr. 4D to the mime (following Kerényi, 15, and others, e.g. W. Beare in *OCD*³, s.v. *Sophron*). Foreign doctors are known to Old Comedy (Crates fr. 46), more widely attested in Middle and New (Alexis fr. 146; Men. *Aspis* 374–464 with Gomme–Sandbach), and mentioned as characteristic of the Spartan δεικηλιϲτήϲ (above, Sect. II). But there is little here or in the scatology of fr. 4D that really suggests a medical context.

Decimus Laberius, the Roman mimographer, wrote a *Belonistria*, but its content, and relationship with Sophron's play, are unknown.

### Fragment 1

The subject may be 'Syracuse' (Pinto Colombo). Although not all Sophron's mimes were necessarily set there, or even in Sicily (cf. on Fr. **10, [*Women watching the Isthmia*]), most probably were. (The form used by Sophron is unknown; Epich. fr. 231 has genitive Ϲυρακοῦϲ from an abbreviated nominative Ϲυρακώ.)

**φωρτάτουϲ:** a comic superlative (only here) based on the substantive φώρ 'thief', as if that were an adjective like μάκαρ. The form may be intended to reflect the fluidity of real speech (cf. on frs. 33–4 and pp. 14f.).

καπήλουc: this could mean either shopkeepers generally, or tavern-keepers in particular. Dishonest tavern-keepers, male and female, are mentioned in Attic comedy, and comic women are notoriously fond of wine (see e.g. Sommerstein on Ar. *Thesm.* 347–8, Henderson on Ar. *Lys.* 466), but Ἐκλ. διαφ. λέξεων (ed. J. A. Cramer, *Analecta Graeca e codd. Manuscriptis bibliothecarum Oxoniensum* (Oxford, 1835–7), ii. 456. 2: ἕτερόν ἐcτιν οἰνοπώληc καὶ ἕτερον κάπηλοc· καθόλου γὰρ τοὺc πωλοῦντάc τι καπήλουc ἔλεγον. ἔcτιν καὶ παρὰ Cώφρονι ἐν ταῖc Ἀκεcτρίαιc) suggests the κάπηλοι here may be retail-dealers of a less specific type. These also had a dubious reputation (cf. the adjectival use of κάπηλοc to mean 'knavish' at A. fr. 322 R., com. adesp. *620).

## Fragment *2

Assigned to this mime on the strength of a gloss at Hesychius ρ 386, where Kaibel emended the corrupt words ρογία· ἀκέcτρια to Ῥόγκα· ⟨Cώφρων⟩ Ἀκεcτρίαιc. Various ancient names, such as Ῥεγκίαc, Ῥόγκων, and Ῥόγκοc, are connected with the word ρέγκοc 'snore' (cf. Bechtel, *Personennamen*, 497, 599; and note also Epich. fr. 195 ρογκιήν· ρέγκειν). Punning names appear elsewhere in Sophron (frs. 14–17, 46) and in Epicharmus (cf. the teacher Colaphus, 'buffet', of fr. 1), and are of course also a common feature of wider Greek comedy. This one would be more apt for a servant than a seamstress. Snoring is a trait commonly imagined of lazy servants; cf. Strepsiades' insomnia-fuelled complaints about the snoring of his servants at Ar. *Nub.* 5, and esp. the opening to Herodas 8 (1–2: ἄcτηθι, δούλη Ψύλλα· μέχρι τέο κείcηι | ρέγχουcα;). But the name could simply be meant to denote coarseness.

### The women who say they are expelling the goddess

**Title and Subject:** τὰν θεόν is most naturally taken as the object of ἐξελᾶν. The verb itself is equivalent to ἐξελαύνω, and must refer to the expulsion of harmful forces or influences (cf. Plu. *Symp.* 693 F τῶν οἰκετῶν ἕνα τύπτοντεc ἁγνίαιc ράβδοιc διὰ θυρῶν ἐξελαύνουcιν ἐπιλέγοντεc "ἔξω βούλιμον, ἔcω δὲ πλοῦτον καὶ ὑγίειαν"). The mime will have depicted a group of women performing a purificatory rite to counteract the malign influence of a particular goddess.

Less convincing are alternative explanations: Wünsch and Latte compare the expression ϲτρατὸν ἐξελαύνειν, and think the phrase means 'the goddess sets forth (with her retinue)'; Arena (1975), comparing Ἴακχον ἐξελαύνειν, used of the procession of initiates from Athens to Eleusis (e.g. Plu. *Alcib.* 34. 210 c), suggested that a female mystery rite involving a πομπή is meant; Kaibel thought that the goddess is Selene in her character as the moon itself. But none of these suggestions readily accounts for the use of apotropaic drugs.

Significantly, the women only claim they are doing (or will do) it. Parker (223 f.) suggests an element of satire here: '[t]heir haste in assuming bewitchment, their folly in attempting to constrain the gods by magical means, the impiety of supposing that gods pollute men: one of these, perhaps more than one, may have been the target of Sophron's irony'. But such irony seems far from Sophron's purpose in other mimes. A good deal of his humour derives rather from bawdiness and horseplay. Perhaps the ritual was botched, or the goddess's possession took a lewd or comically indecent form (e.g. excessive flatulence, diarrhoea, etc.).

The connection between fragment 3 and others concerned with magic is unclear. Five magical fragments (frs. *5–*9) clearly belong together and represent the mime on which Theocritus' *Pharmakeutria* was based, while fr. 4A depicts a purification ritual. A connection between fr. 4A and *The women who say they are expelling the goddess* is possible, if unproved. The title would at least be apt for a mime depicting a purification rite, though there is no clear evidence for the main speaker of fr. 4A, or even the majority of those involved, being female. However, the relationship with frs. *5–*9 is much less certain. It seems fair to infer that that mime depicted a rite involving love-magic. While purification could be a preliminary procedure for such rituals (see on fr. 4A), a connection between fr. 3 and erotic magic is harder to sustain. While magic drinks can inspire erotic passion—apart from the examples in the magical papyri given below, cf. e.g. Ach. Tat. 4. 15 (Leucippe given a love draught by Gorgias), 5. 22 (Leucippe, pretending to be a Thessalian woman, and therefore by implication skilled in witchcraft, ordered to collect drugs for a potion to make Cleitophon fall in love with Melite)—here, however, the drink explicitly contains *protective* drugs. Furthermore, the invocation of Hecate which appears as fr. **8 (if correctly ascribed to Sophron and then to this mime) is hard to square with the invocation in fr. 4A, at the end of which Hecate is already imagined to be present. Of course, fr. **8, even if by Sophron, does not necessarily belong with the other 'Theocritean' fragments. It is at least tempting to identify the speaker of fr. 4A. 8 with the assistant mentioned at fr. *5.

The title is also given as an example of Doric ταί, but relative αἵ, at Apoll. Dysc. *adv.*, GrGr II 1,1 p. 180,6 Schn. But note relative τάν at fr. 4C. 32.

## Fragment 3

**ὑποκατώρυκται:** a surprising verb, hapax here, though (κατ-)ὀρύccω is common enough. Used of drugs it may imply 'thoroughly dissolved', so as not to be noticeable; cf. the potions administered without the recipient's knowledge at e.g. Ach. Tat. 2. 23. 2 (a sleeping draught), 4. 15 (love potion). Perhaps part of the humour in this mime derived from the affected person's unwillingness to be treated (especially comic if love is indeed at issue, and the purpose of the exorcism was to banish a previous romantic attachment).

**κυαθίδι:** only here; Athenaeus describes it as a vessel shaped like a *kotylos*, a one-handled drinking cup.

**τρικτὺc:** a triad, usually of sacrificial victims (cf. Hesych. τ 1391 τρικτύα· τριάδα. ἔνιοι θυcία κάπρου, κριοῦ, ταύρου). Here the word is an incongruous (and intentionally incorrect?) intrusion from the language of official cult, and so perhaps deliberately high-falutin; cf. on fr. 4A. 4. At Epicharmus fr. 182 the codd. have τριττύαν for a trio of sacrificial animals, but read rather τρικτύαν.

**ἀλεξιφαρμάκων:** i.e. antidotes to φάρμακα, and here 'protective drugs', though at Men. fr. 274 (Ἐφέcια τοῖc γαμοῦcιν οὗτοc περιπατεῖ | λέγων ἀλεξιφάρμακα) the same word evidently refers to spoken charms. Helen mixes a soporific φάρμακον with wine at *Od.* 4. 220 ff. (see S. West ad loc. for further relevant examples), but Simaetha's φάρμακα (Theocr. 2. 15) are probably her incantations rather than anything else. In the magical papyri we occasionally find written spells added to drinks. In *PGM* 1. 232–47, a charm to aid the memory, various *voces magicae* are written on hieratic papyrus before being washed off into spring water from seven springs; the mixture is then drunk over seven days. The formula for a love potion at *PGM* 7. 969–72 requires more *voces magicae* to be written on papyrus; a spoken request is then made that a particular woman fall in love with the speaker, after she has drunk an unspecified draught. It is likely that the words on the papyrus were here also to be washed off into a cup of wine or water.[1]

## [Fragments 4A–D]

These four papyrus fragments represent at least two different mimes. Fr. 4A depicts a magical ritual, fr. 4D a comically exaggerated attack of diarrhoea. The other two fragments are too insubstantial for their subjects to be firmly identified or to establish whether they represent different works.

## Fragment 4A

A ritual is in progress. It takes place in the inner room of a house. Material for a purification is collected; a sacrifice is made; the doors of the room open, a goddess (Hecate) arrives, and is ritually addressed.

In the fifth century magical attack by Hecate is often referred to: cf. e.g. E. *Hipp.* 142 (with Barrett), where the chorus expresses the fear that Phaedra's illness is caused by Hecate, and *Morb. Sacr.* 1, which attacks at length the view that the gods, including Hecate, were responsible for sickness. Theophrastus' Superstitious Man fears magical assault on his house by Hecate, and purifies it against it (*Char.* 16. 7). The mime could have described such an exorcism (so Parker, 223), though purification of an individual is also a possibility (cf. fr. 3). The slightly garbled invocation of Hecate (fr. **8) could perhaps belongs here (but see on that fragment, also on fr. 4A. 17 and the general introduction to *The Women who say they are expelling the goddess*).

This looks very like the beginning of the mime; there is no left margin, so we cannot tell whether there was a title or not. One person gives orders to a number of assistants, some at least of whom are men. This does not preclude the mime being one of the γυναικεῖοι (see above, Sect. II). The sex of the speaker is not

---

[1] But contrast *PGM* 7. 385–9, another spell to inspire love, in which a charm involving *voces magicae* and an invocation of Aphrodite is simply spoken over a cup seven times.

indicated, but πὸτ τᾰνδε, if correct at line 16, implies the presence of women. The sequence of commands and questions somewhat recalls the opening of Theocritus, *Id.* 2, and the details of the exorcism, as far as we have them, are typical of literary depictions. The magical papyri contain very different material: cf. e.g. the exorcism at *PGM* 4. 1227–64, in which the possessed person is struck with an olive branch, and the daimon abjured with (partly Coptic) *voces magicae* (with this we may compare early scapegoat rituals, and especially the potency magic at Hippon. fr. 92).

Whether it is the same mime as *The women who say they are expelling the goddess* remains doubtful. That piece, like this one, must have dealt with purification against a malignant goddess, but the only fragment certainly ascribed provides no obvious connection with the details in the papyrus.

Equally uncertain is the connection between this piece and frs. *5–*9 (on which Theocr. 2 was based). The usual view now is that that mime must have been different from this one (Sophron may have dealt with the subject of magic more than once); or that Theocritus borrowed no more than the general subject of magic, since there is no connection between the papyrus purification and love magic. See e.g. Parker, 223–4; Hutchinson, 154 (with n.19); Dover on Theocritus, p. 97; Page, 330–1. This may be right, but purifications are sometimes associated with erotic magic: Tibullus undergoes nocturnal purification to free him from his love for Delia (Tib. 1. 2. 63–4), and in Lucian (*D. Meretr.* 4. 5) a Syrian witch performs a purification involving sulphur, salt, and fumigation, as part of a rite to make Bacchis' lover Phanias return to her. A similar situation may have formed the background to Sophron's mime (cf. Hordern (2002*a*)); however, without more evidence we cannot be sure.

Deceitful female soothsayers were satirized in Epicharmus' *Robberies* (Ἁρπαγαί), and seers mocked by Archilochus (frs. 182–3). Related genres sometimes parody religious prayer or ritual. Sacrificial preparations were described by a cook in Semonides (fr. 24; see on Sophr. fr. 18), perhaps with comic overtones. The fragments of Hipponax abound with mock-prayers, mostly occurring within a wider narrative (frs. 3–3a, 32, 25, 38, 40), and Ananias parodies traditional cletic invocations (fr. 1). Particularly interesting is the potency ritual described at

Hippon. fr. 92, which ends with a scene reminiscent of that in the other large papyrus fragment of Sophron (fr. 4D). Herodas 4, a poem which may have affinities with Sophron's [*Women watching the Isthmia*], begins with Cynno praying and sacrificing a cock to Asclepius in gratitude for a cure from illness (1–20).

Fumigation also features in fr. 115, but seems to have nothing to do with the rite described here.

**1.** The absence of an initial connecting particle suggests this is the beginning of the mime; cf. e.g. the opening of Semon. fr. 7, almost certainly the start of the poem. Here the beginning is deliberately dramatic; we find ourselves immediately *in mediis rebus.*

**τράπεζαν:** the table will have been used as the altar; a simple piece of household furniture would do for private ceremonies such as this.

**κάτθετε:** for the apocope, see p. 22. Sophron may in fact have written καθθ-, the form, e.g., in an official inscription from Selinus (*c.*450 BC: Dubois, no. 78. 9–10 καθθέμεν = καταθεῖναι).

**2. ὥσπερ ἔχει:** 'just there' or even 'straightaway', both here and at line 14 (cf. S. *Ant.* 1234–5 εἶθ' ὁ δύςμορος | αὑτῶι χολωθείς, ὥσπερ εἶχ', and 1108 ὧδε ὡς ἔχω: Jebb and Kamerbeek both translate 'forthwith'), rather than 'just as it is' (Page). The table is set down right on the spot where the assistants are standing.

**λάζεςθε:** in Homer λάζομαι happily coexists with its semantic doublet λαμβάνω (which we find at Sophr. fr. 11, and frequently in Epicharmus). Cf. Chantraine, *Grammaire*, i. 335–6. Theocritus uses λάζομαι three times, though once in a form based on Ep.-Ionic λάζυμαι (15. 21 λάζεν, in the mouth of the Syracusan Gorgo; 18. 46 λαζύμεναι; λάςδεο at 8. 84[2]), which is probably in fact a secondary form created by analogy with αἴνυμαι (see Frisk, Chantraine, s.v.). λάζομαι is common elsewhere in Hellenistic literature (e.g. A. R. 1. 911; 3. 1365, 1394; Nic. *Th.* 108, 610, etc.).

**3. ἁλὸς χονδρὸν:** salt is used in purifications, perhaps because of its preservative qualities; cf. Lucian, *D. Meretr.* 4. 5 (salt sprinkled on a fire); Men. *Phasma* 50–6 (a mock purification is performed with salt, lentils, and water); Theophr. *Char.* 16. 12 (the Superstitious Man avidly partakes of lustration by salt-

---

[2] For the variation between cδ and ζ in the MSS of Theocr., see Hunter, 24.

water); Theocr. 24. 96 ff. (Alcmene is told first to fumigate her house with sulphur, and then sprinkle it with water mixed with salt). The three latter cases involve salt mixed with water. Here it appears in solid form, and is held in the hands of those at the hearth (a traditional place of supplication; see n.) either to be sprinkled on later (as in Lucian) or held as a phylakterion (so Eitrem). See further Parker, 226–7; Ussher on Theophr. *Char.* 16. 12; Gow on Theocr. 24. 97. At Ov. *Fasti* 2. 537 salt is said to be offered to ghosts, again probably as an apotropaic. Lumps of salt also appear as a purificatory substance in Akkadian and Sumerian texts; in particular, a Sumerian incantation against bile, dating to the Old Babylonian period, requires that a lump of salt be taken in the hand, the incantation recited, and the salt placed in the sick person's mouth (cf. G. Cunningham, *'Deliver me from Evil'. Mesopotamian Incantations 2500–1500* (Rome, 1997), 123 ff. (text 103); P. Michalowski, *Zeitschrift für Assyrologie*, 71 (1981), 1 ff.). In later Mesopotamian incantations dissolving salt is imagined as symbolic of dissolving illness or disease.

For the papyrus accent, see p. 25.

χῆρα: see p. 19.

**4. δάφναν:** another material commonly connected with purification. Simaetha burns it at Theocr. 2. 1, 23, apparently for apotropaic reasons (see Gow ad loc.). Theophrastus' Superstitious Man is said to put laurel leaves in his mouth each morning (to chew them?) in order to ward off malign influences (*Char.* 16. 2; cf. Sophr. fr. 165); spirits were thought to avoid the plant and laurel branches were placed for protective purposes before (city-?)gates (*Geopon.* 11. 2. 5; Hesych. κώμυθα (κ 4841)· δάφνην, ἣν ἱcτῶcι ⟨πρὸ⟩ τῶν πυλῶν). In the magical papyri, laurel, inscribed with magical formulae, is worn as a protective at *PGM* 7. 842, and laurel garlands are used in ritual invocations to Selene, Helios, and Apollo (*PGM* 2. 1–64; 64 ff. (Selene, Helios); *PGM* 1. 262–347 (Apollo)). Cf. also Branchus' purification by laurel at Callim. fr. 194. 28–31 Pf. (iambus 4) with S. Eitrem, *Gnomon*, 4 (1928), 194 ff. and Kerkhecker, 91 ff.; Plu. *Symp.* 693 F; V. *Ecl.* 8. 82, and see Parker (1983), 228–9; L. Deubner, *Kl. Schr.* (Königstein, 1982), 401–3.

**πὰρ τὸ ὦαc:** salt is held in one hand, and laurel 'by the ear'; Sophron probably means a sprig of laurel tucked behind the ear like the flowers at Cratin. fr. 257. 1–2 ἁπαλὸν δὲ cιcύμβριον ⟨ἢ⟩ ῥόδον ἢ κρίνον παρ' οὖc ἐθάκει | μετὰ χερcὶ δὲ μῆλον ἕκαcτοc ἔχων cκίπωπα τ' ἠγόραζον (which Athenaeus, quoting the lines at 12. 553 E, takes to describe the luxury of former times). For the form of the noun, cf. Herodian ii. 921, 14 L: οὖαc καὶ ἡ γενικὴ οὔατοc, καὶ ὅαc ἔνθεν ὄατοc, καὶ ὦαc ἔνθεν ὤατοc, καὶ ⟨ὦc ἔνθεν⟩ ὠτόc. Alcm. *PMGF* 80. 1 has ὤατα; Epich. fr. 18 οὔατοc, where we expect ὤατοc. ὦτ[α is possible in a *defixio* (4th/3rd cent. BC; Dubois, no. 122) from Camerina (a Syracusan foundation resettled from Gela in the early fifth century: Thuc. 6. 5. 3).

Apocope of free-standing παρά is not otherwise attested in Sophron, and Epich. fr. 145 has παρὰ τήνοιc (which Ahrens emended to πὰρ), but for apocope of the verbal affix, cf. fr. 14 πάρφερε. Note also apocope of free-standing ποτί in line 16.

**5. ποτιβάντεc**: equivalent to Att.-Ion. προc-. ποτί is the usual West Greek form of the preposition (cf. Myc. *po-si-*, Argive ποι; OPers. *patiy*, Avestan *paiti*).

**6. ἱcτίαν**: the hearth was a sacred place, and so sometimes the word can refer to an altar. It is thus a suitable location for suppliants and those afflicted by the gods generally (cf. the start of S. *O.T.* where the Thebans, whose city is in the grip of divinely inspired disease, sit (wreathed? See Dawe on *O.T.* 3) by the altars and in the public places of the city).

The form is ἱcτία in most dialects where the word is attested outside Attic (Buck, 23, considers the possibility of influence from ἵcτημι). At Sophr. fr. 41 the MS has Ἐcτίαc, and Epich. fr. 76. 1 has ἑcτιῶν; in both places we should restore ἱ- (the correct form occurs in the MSS at Epich. fr. 32. 4 ἱcτιῶντ'). A late Syracusan inscription (207/6 BC: Dubois, no. 97. 42), recognizing the sanctuary of Artemis at Magnesia on the Meander, also has ἱcτία.

**θωκεῖτε**: Doric (and Ionic) = Att. θακέω. For the verb in this context, cf. e.g. S. *O.T.* 19–20 τὸ δ' ἄλλο φῦλον ἐξεcτεμμένον | ἀγοραῖcι θακεῖ (of the Theban people supplicating the gods at the city's altars).

**7. τὤμφακεc**: a two-edged axe rather than a sword (as Page has it); cf. Hesych. (α 3893) ἄμφακεc (corrected from ἄμφακληc)· ἀξίνη. Here no doubt a small hatchet is meant. Both swords and axes were used in more formal sacrifices; an axe is used to disable the heifer in the sacrifice at *Od.* 3. 430 ff.; the actual killing appears to be done with a different weapon, probably a knife (see S. West on 450, 453). In the detailed description of Aegisthus' sacrifice at E. *El.* 810 ff., the killing is done with a knife, but the corpse dismembered with a Phthian κοπίϲ (836).

The scribe makes the crasis, just as he tacitly makes the elision at line 7 φερῶ, 15 κεγων, and at fr. 4D. 41 ἁμεπ- (rather than φερεῶ, καεγων, ἁμεεπ-). This doubtless reflects not a continuous tradition of spoken performance, but the usages of everyday speech. Sophron himself must have written φερεω: before the invention of written breathings, it is unlikely that φερω would have been analysed as anything other than φέρω.

**ὧ:** this must be an equivalent for ὧδε (attested for literary Doric at e.g. Epich. fr. 34. 1, Theocr. 1. 151), though there is little evidence for the form. The rough breathing is marked in the papyrus, and the same sense is appropriate at fr. 10, where the MS, however, has ὦ. ὧ appears to have been read by some at Theocr. 8. 49, where the MSS read ὧ τράγε . . . ὧ (or ὦ) βάθοϲ ὕλαϲ (the rough breathing also in schol. Theocr. 8. 49b p. 209 W.), but Wilamowitz conjectures ἐϲ, probably rightly.

**ϲκύλακα:** a young dog or puppy. This is certainly the source for schol. Lycophr. 77 (p. 45 Scheer), which states that according to Sophron ἐν μίμοιϲ dogs were sacrificed to Hecate (cf. Ar. frs. 209, 608; E. fr. 958 N²; Plu. *Aet. Rom.* 280 C; Paus. 3. 14. 9, etc.).

The sacrificial animal at E. *El.* 813 is specifically a calf (μόϲχον, 813); young animals will have made better eating (they also have been worth more, and therefore considered a more valuable sacrifice; contrast the jokes in comedy about the poor quality of sacrificial animals, implying stinginess on the sacrificer's part; see Gomme–Sandbach on Men. *Dysc.* 438, *Sicyon.* 184; but of course cost is not a likely concern in the case of puppies). Purificatory sacrifices were usually deemed uneatable (Parker, 283 n. 11), though dogs were occasionally eaten in the ancient world. Ritual sacrifice and consumption of dogs is attested in Sardis (cf. C. H. Greenewaldt, *Ritual Dinners in Early Historic Sardis* (Berkeley, 1976)); and the Hippocratic dietary regimens advise eating roasted dog and puppy meat for certain diets (*Vict.* 79, 82). Porphyry states as a fact (*Abst.* 1. 14. 3) that the Greeks avoided eating dogs, horses, and donkeys, because they were domesticated; but he is arguing a case for radical vegetarianism (cf. P. Garnsey, *Food and Society in Classical*

*Antiquity* (Cambridge, 1999), 83–4). We are not necessarily to think only of a simple sacrifice here: Theophrastus mentions purification by dog (*Char.* 16. 13), and according to Plutarch this involved killing them and rubbing the corpse around the body of the afflicted person (*Quaest. Rom.* 280 BC, 290 D).

Of some interest is the frequency with which dogs (and boars) are mentioned in Akkadian love magic; G. Leick, *Sex and Eroticism in Mesopotamian Literature* (London and New York, 1994), 199, suggests that this is because their behaviour was thought arousing; more probably they were simply considered examples of uncontrolled sexual desire (cf. Leick, op. cit. 210).

**8. γάρ:** can imply assent in dialogue (Denniston, 73 ff., 86 ff.), but that is not needed here. There is no obvious logical connection with what has gone before. Ideally the sense required is something like 'now then', but good parallels are lacking. There are a further eight instances of γάρ in Sophron, five of which seem to mark a causal connection (frs. 4D. 39; 13; 52; 54; 105?); in the remaining three cases the force is unclear because of the lack of context (frs. 4D. 37; 85; 96). There are eight cases in Epicharmus, of which one is most probably causal (fr. 134), and the rest in doubt (frs. 10, 34, 42, 113. 362 and 387, 144, 167 (the last two passages are corrupt)).

Alternatively, read γα (= Att. γε). Denniston (124–5) doubts γε after interrogatives in classical Greek, though he notes that many alleged instances come from Aristophanes, where 'we would expect a lively idiom of this type'. No example occurs in Sophron or Epicharmus, but the fragments preserve relatively few questions.

**ἄςφαλτος:** another purificatory material (because of its preservative qualities?), though Latte calls attention to Pliny's assertion that it was burned in lamps in Sicily (*N.H.* 35. 179). It is used together with sulphur and water by Melampus in the comic purification of the Proetids at Diphil. fr. 125. Pitch (*kupru*) is also a purifying substance in Akkadian texts (W. Burkert, *The Orientalizing Revolution* (Cambridge, Mass., 1992), 61–2).

**οὖτα:** this is the only word in the extant passage spoken by anyone other than the main character. The punctuation given by the papyrus, which will not date to Sophron, cannot be certain (the speaker could be answering his or her own question). But dialogue occurs in other fragments (e.g. 23, 55), and there were presumably subsequent sections of the mime which demanded two speakers; punctuating thus might otherwise seem an odd decision.

**9. δάιδιον:** the torch, since it is mentioned together with incense, is probably to be used for fumigation (cf. Diphil. fr. 126; Tib. 1. 2. 63–4; Lucian, *D. Meretr.* 4. 288). By contrast, the δαελός at line 13 seems to be there solely for illumination. For the accent, see p. 25.

**10. λιβανωτόν:** frankincense was widely used for burning at sacrifices; cf. Ar. *Nub.* 426, *Vesp.* 96, *Ra.* 888. Hecate was honoured together with Hermes by the burning of frankincense at the new moon (Porph. *Abst.* 2. 16), but we should not therefore think that this ceremony is a simple celebration of that sort.

**11. πεπτάϲθων:** the action takes place inside; by contrast, Attic drama always places events in the open air. In the papyri and other literary texts the roof or a courtyard are the more usual places for sun and moon magic. Usually πετάννυμι is used especially of opening large double doors, and so may here be comically grandiose.

Although the preceding ἄγετε looks like a command to the speaker's assistants, the third person plural here is a little surprising, and may be intended to suggest divine agency. Doors often open magically in the presence of a god; so at *Il.* 5. 749 the gates of Olympus open of their own volition (αὐτόμαται) before Hera (cf. 8. 393), and at a further remove Dionysus magically releases his devotees from prison at E. *Ba.* 448. At Callim. *H.* 2. 6–7 Apollo's epiphany is marked by the magical opening of his temple's doors (see further Williams ad loc., with the references collected there).

**μοι:** perhaps an ethic dative ('please'), here comically incongruous; or the sense could simply be 'let me have . . .'.

**12. πάϲαι:** for the accent (Kassel–Austin print πᾶϲαι), see p. 25.

**ὑμὲϲ:** (= Att. ὑμεῖϲ) the form is again attested for Sophron at fr. 60, and is treated by Aristophanes as Megarian (*Ach.* 760 f.) and Boeotian (*Ach.* 862), though the epigraphic evidence is lacunose for both dialects (Colvin, 194). Apollonius (*pron.* 119b) claims that the Boeotian form was οὐμέϲ, citing Corinna (*PMG* 659), though this may be a later development.

**13. ὁρῆτε:** the focus of the mime is now on the speaker's invocation rather than on the activities of the assistants (whether imaginary or otherwise). Almost as soon as the helpers are told to go to the hearth, there is a call for ritual silence and the beginning of the prayer to Hecate; the latter perhaps occupied the central part of the mime (as does Simaetha's incantation in Theocr. 2).

The form (= Att. ὁρᾶτε) shows the expected Doric result of the contraction of -ά-ετε.

**δαελὸν:** cf. Et. gen. (Et. Mag. 246, 23) δαλός . . . λαμπάς . . . λέγεται δὲ καὶ δαελὸς παρὰ Cώφρονι. In the Hesychian glosses δαβῆι· καίηται and δαβελός· δαλός (δ 2, 3), said to be Laconian, β must represent an original Ϝ (cf. O. Masson, in H. Eichner and H. Rix (eds.), *Sprachwissenschaft und Philologie: Jacob Wackernagel und die Indogermanistik heute* (Wiesbaden, 1990), 202–12).

**14. ὥσπερ ἔχει:** see 4A. 2 n.

**εὐκαμίαν:** Hesychius uses εὐκᾱμία (⟨ κημός 'muzzle') and ἡςυχία as glosses for εὐκαλεία (ε 6911; cf. ε 6291, εὐκηλία· ἡςυχία); ritual silence must be meant, though silence is also an appropriate response to a divine epiphany (Dodds on E. *Ba.* 1084; Bulloch on Callim. *H.* 5. 72).

In Athens and elsewhere a ritual cry, εὐφημεῖτε, usually preceded a public prayer, sacrifice, or other ceremony (cf. Ar. *Ach.* 237, 241, *Nub.* 263, 297, etc.). The intention was to avoid all inauspicious speech which might affect the performance of the ceremony. Dover on *Nub.* 263 notes that 'in comic verse, [the cry] may be represented by εὐφημεῖν χρή, cf. *Eq.* 1316 (just before the entry of the rejuvenated Demos), *Pax* 1316 (the beginning of the wedding procession), *Ra.* 354'. In Sophron the circumlocution is more developed, perhaps marking the difference between public and private ritual.

**15. ᾶc:** 'while'. Earlier *ἇ(Ϝ)ος produces ᾶc in Doric, psilotic ᾶc in Aeolic, and ἕωc by metathesis of length in Att.-Ion.; cf. Epich. fr. 35. 15 (there with the subjunctive), Theocr. 14. 70, and the Laconian of Ar. *Lys.* (e.g. 173; see Colvin, 233).

**16. πὸτ τᾶνδε:** = Att. πρὸς τῶνδε. Chantraine (1935) defends the papyrus accentuation, citing πρός + genitive at e.g. *Il.* 1. 238–9 οἵ τε θέμιcτας | πρὸς Διὸς εἰρύαται, *Od.* 11. 67 πρός τ' ἀλόχου καὶ πατρός ('in the name of . . .'). But it is tempting to emend to πὸτ τάνδε (Norsa–Vitelli) = Att. πρὸς τήνδε 'against this (goddess)'; cf. e.g. Anacr. *PMG* 396 ὡς δὴ πρὸς Ἔρωτα πυκταλίζω, Cor. *PMG* 666 περὶ τεοῦς Ἑρμᾶς πὸτ Ἄρεα | πουκτεύει. If the papyrus accentuation is correct it would provide useful support for taking the mime to be one of the γυναικεῖοι.[3]

πότ is apocopated from ποτί; cf. fr. 4A. 5 n.

**πυκταλεύcω**: properly used of striking with the fist, or boxing. Anacreon's fight with Eros (loc. cit.) is also metaphorical, but the boxing imagery is fully active. Here the force of the verb is less clear, particularly so if we read τᾶνδε; with τάνδε it is the goddess who must be forcefully magicked away.

**17. πότνια**: Hecate is now imagined to be present; this may cast doubt on any connection between this mime and fr. **8, where the invocation of Hecate clearly imagines her to be still absent. Divinities are usually formally welcomed or 'received' at epiphanies; most firm examples are Hellenistic, but there was probably earlier sanction for the idea (Dunbar on Ar. *Av.* 1708–9; Bulloch on Callim. *H.* 5. 137).

**δείπνου**: perhaps this should recall the δεῖπνα Ἑκάτηc which at least in Athens were placed at crossroads in order to placate the goddess and keep her away from the town (schol. Ar. *Pl.* 594; Plu. *Quaest. Conviv.* 708 F–709 A; Lucian, *D. Mort.* 1. 1; see Parker, 224). But cf. schol. Theocr. 2. 11d, explaining Theocritus' reference to puppies: διὰ τὸ cκύλακαc ἐκφέρεcθαι δεῖπνα τῆι Ἑκάτηι, citing Ar. fr. 209. The δεῖπνον for Hecate (if the goddess is meant; see ad loc.) in fr. 26 is a flat loaf of bread, just as cakes are offered to Asclepius at Herod. 4. 92.

**18. [ξ]ενίων**: the gods could be imagined as present at a sacrifice, and so as partaking in the offering. In Homer this idea is reflected in expressions such as θεῶν ἐν δαιτὶ θαλείηι, and then in later Greek in the term θεοξένια (see West's comprehensive note on Hes. *Th.* 507–616). ξένια can thus refer to the food consumed in a ritual context. In folk-tale and myth, in both Greece and the Near East (cf. West, *East Face*, 123–4), the idea can take concrete form, when gods receive hospitality from mortal hosts. The concept is also important in the magical papyri; cf. e.g. *PGM* 1. 1–2 [πρᾶξιc] παρεδρικῶc προc[γίνεται δαί]μων, ὃc τὰ πάντα μηνύcει cοι | ῥητῶc κα[ὶ cυνόμιλοc καὶ c]υναριcτῶν ἔcται cοι, 1. 86–7 καὶ ἑτοι[μάcαc] παντοῖα φαγήματα οἶνόν τε Με|δήcιον, προανά[φερε εἴ]c τὸν θεόν, and numerous other passages.

---

[3] M.L.W. notes that 'τᾶνδε might equal τάνδε as Herodian accented ἥδε, τῆνδε [cf. M. L. West, *Homerus. Ilias I* (Stuttgart and Leipzig, 1998), xviii], but this would go against the Dorianizing principle as seen in πάcαι etc.'.

**ἀμεμφέων:** the ξένια are 'blameless' because they have been prepared according to strict ritual and thus the goddess cannot fault them (cf. West, *East Face*, 41, on the comparable term ἄμωμος).

**ἀντά[:** a form of ἀντάω is indicated; the idiom ('meet with offerings') again suggests the real presence of the divinity, as in Homeric ἀντιάω, used of gods taking part in a sacrifice at *Od.* 1. 25, 3. 436, and of a god accepting a sacrifice at *Il.* 1. 67. Matters are complicated by the acute accent in the papyrus. We want the sense to be either imperative or indicative; but the aorist imperative ἄντασον, while semantically attractive, should be proparoxytone (at least in Attic; *ἀντάσον could be meant to represent Doric paroxytonesis, though this is not attested as a feature of the imperative). Infinitives with imperatival force are suggested by Norsa–Vitelli and Gallavotti (respectively ἀντά[ϲειν, ἀντά[ϲαι); for this usage see S. Pulleyn, *Prayer in Greek Religion* (Oxford, 1997), 150 ff. Kerényi proposes the future ἀντά[ϲειϲ, which looks less likely. The aorist indicative ἄντα[ϲαϲ, while appealing for the sense, not only has the wrong accent, but would require the first α, which the papyrus explicitly marks as short, to be long.

**19.** ] ˘ν . . ν: the short mark is quite clear, but the traces of the two missing letters are inconclusive. Norsa–Vitelli print [χα]νδόν 'eagerly' with Latte, which fits the sense.

**καὶ κα.:** I read καικαι, though the second iota survives only as the trace of a downstroke. Gallavotti suggests π, but it is doubtful whether the space is large enough. A. Koerte suggested λ (*APF* 11 [1935], 267 n.3: καλαμων), though the stroke does not seem to be at an angle, and 'reeds' are not really in the right company here. Probably this is simply dittography, and we should read καὶ ἁμῶν δέπ[- (or, if the acute accent in the papyrus is an error, δὲ π[-).

**Fragment 4B**

Little can be made of this scrap. According to Apollodorus (*On Gods: FGrH* 244 F 102a), Sophron made Mormoluka (line 27) Acheron's nurse in the underworld: Γοργύραν δὲ τοῦ Ἀχέροντος γυναῖκα προϲανέπλαϲαν ἀπὸ τοῦ γοργὰ φαίνεϲθαι τοῖϲ πολλοῖϲ τὰ ἐν Ἅιδου· καθὸ δὴ καὶ αὐτοῦ τούτου τιθήνην ὁ Ϲώφρων Μορμολύκαν ὠνόμαϲεν. The name is based on that of Mormo, who was, like Lamia, a well-known child-killing demon (schol. Theocr. 15. 40;

schol. Ael. Arist. *Panath.* p. 42 Dindorf; see S. I. Johnston in J. J. Clauss and S. I. Johnston (eds.), *Medea. Essays on Medea in Myth, Literature, Philosophy and Archaeology* (Princeton, 1997), 58). That Mormoluka figured as a nurse in Sophron is therefore probably humorous. The second term is doubtless connected with λύκος. At Ar. *Thesm.* 417 dogs kept to deter lovers are described as μορμολυκεῖα; cf. also the verb μορμολύττομαι 'scare, frighten'. It may therefore be significant that it is probably she who is referred to as κυναναι[δές in line 29. The latter word is almost certain here; cf. schol. Genav. *Il.* 21. 394 μήποτε οὖν ἐστιν ἡ κυνάμυια καὶ μυῖα ὡς παρὰ Cώφρονι κυναναιδὲς (cod. κυναπαιδές : corr. Hefermehl) καὶ κυνάγχη, rightly adduced by R. Pfeiffer (ap. Norsa–Vitelli, 248).

The last line should be divided μιϲητὰ τα[. For the word and accent in Sophron, cf. Eustath. in *Od.* p. 1651. 1 ἄλλοι δὲ μιϲήτην βαρυτόνωϲ πρὸϲ διαϲτολὴν ὀξυτονουμένηϲ τὴν κοινὴν καὶ ῥαιδίαν, λέγοντεϲ καὶ χρῆϲιν αὐτῆϲ εἶναι παρὰ Κρατίνωι (fr. 354) καὶ Cώφρονι. But why Mormoluka should be described as disgusting or even lewd (for the sense, see E. Dettori, *ZPE* 119 (1997), 132–4) is beyond meaningful conjecture, though clearly it fits with the adjective in line 29. For the form of the word, see Dettori, loc. cit.; Kassel–Austin on Cratin. fr. 354; West, *Studies*, 135 (on Archil. fr. 206). In the margin opposite Mormoluka's name appears a fragmentary, and sadly illegible, scholion.

## Fragment 4C

Another pitiful scrap. A door is mentioned in line 31, followed by a subordinate clause (τάν after the noun must be a relative pronoun = Att. ἥν). The epsilon, followed by two inconclusive traces, could perhaps be the syllabic augment (whence Olivieri's attractive ἔκο[πτε). In line 33 there is a blank after ἐκ Cτυέλλαϲ: spaces usually act as punctuation in papyrus texts, but this does not look like the end of a mime. Styella was allegedly the name of the citadel of Megara Hyblaea (Steph. Byz. p. 588. 7), though Megara was destroyed by Gelon and its citizens largely assimilated to Syracuse in 483 (Dunbabin, 416 f.). According to Thucydides (6. 49. 4) the site was deserted in the later fifth century. How it could have featured in one of Sophron's mimes is thus unclear.

In the next line it is tempting to take ἵκωϲ as a form of the verb ἴκω, though the circumflex is surprising; for the diaeresis on initial iota, cf. fr. 4A. 6, and often in papyri of Doric and other poetry (e.g. Alcm. *PMGF* 3 fr. 3. 72, 79; 4 frs. 2. 4, 3. 4, etc.).

## Fragment 4D

A piece of scatological comedy recalling fr. 11. A group of people suffer from a bout of uncontrollable diarrhoea, and by typical comic hyperbole almost drown in the resulting watery emissions. The speaker's sex cannot be determined, but at least some of those involved are men. This does not, of course, mean that it cannot be one of the γυναικεῖοι (Sect. II). Only the first eight lines of the papyrus provide much sense, and there are no clear indications of what happened in the preceding passages. The scatological comedy of fr. 11 belongs in a festive context, and perhaps we could imagine a symposium or feast as the venue for the events here. Inflated wine-skins are referred to in line 43, and drinking is a recurrent theme.

Several iambi contained first-person scatological narratives, the Greeks finding the whole subject of defecation amusing. The most extended surviving example is the potency ritual resulting in accidental and overwhelming diarrhoea described at Hippon. fr. 92. In Hippon. fr. 73 the speaker's opponent ὤμειξε δ' αἷμα καὶ χολὴν ἐτίλησεν following earlier violence. Fr. 78, from the same papyrus, appears to contain another description of a potency ritual, and refers, though obscurely, to dung-beetles. Defecation in the context of eating features at fr. 114c. The dung-beetle is also mentioned by Semonides at fr. 13 (τὸ δ᾽ ἥμιν ἑρπετὸν παρέπτατο | τὸ ζωΐων κάκιστον ἔκτηται βίον), and though the precise content is unknown, these lines may come, not from a fable as is often supposed, but from another scatological narrative (M. L. West, in *La Fable. Entretiens sur l'antiquité classique* 30 (Vandœuvres and Geneva, 1984), 112; *Studies*, 28); cf. also Semon. frs. 8 and 17. Excrement and defecation of course also feature as subjects for humour in numerous passages of Attic comedy (see Henderson, 187–92).

**37. δοίη:** the subject is not clear, but -ειος in the preceding line suggests it was masculine. It need not, however, actually be a person. The speaker's own incontinence, his physical weakness, or any number of other circumstances, may be preventing him from drinking.

**καταρρυφῆϲαι:** ῥυφάνω is Ionic for ῥοφάνω; here it appears to be also Doric. Hipponax (fr. 165) used ῥυφεῖν = ῥοφέω (from which the forms in -ανω are derived; see Chantraine, s.v.), but we do not know in what context.

**γὰρ:** see fr. 4A. 8.

**38. γλυκύπικρον:** before Sophron only at Sa. fr. 130 Ἔροϲ δηῦτέ μ᾽ ὁ λυϲιμέληϲ δόνει, | γλυκύπικρον ἀμάχανον ὄρπετον, of which this may be a deliberate reminiscence. There is obvious comic value in the contrast between the nouns to which the epithet is applied.

Allusions to other authors in Sophron are not always certain. Phrases shared by Sophron and Alcaeus (e.g. fr. 86) are largely proverbial; and while fr. 140 appears to have been a play on a line from the *Iliad*, the original line itself became proverbial and it is thus unclear whether Sophron was thinking directly of Homer's text or simply had the proverb in mind. There may be a joke on a phrase used by Epicharmus at fr. 4D. 43 (see ad loc.).

**39. ἐπεπε[ί]γει:** they have not yet lost all control over their bowels, but the intensifying prefix ἐπι-, here added to the basic verb ἐπείγω, indicates additional pressure and urgency. For urgency as a comic element in defecation on the Attic stage, cf. e.g. Ar. *Nub.* 1386 ff. and see Henderson, 188–9. For the pluperfect ending in -ει, cf. line 41 and see on fr. 34.

The internal alliteration of π may have humorous overtones; cf. the use of παππάξ and παπαπαππάξ to represent the sound of farting at Ar. *Nub.* 390f.

**ϲπατιλοκολύμφευ|μ.ϲ:** Gallavotti's -μεϲ, 468 n. is hard to avoid, though we would expect the accent to be -εῦμεϲ. However, this does not justify taking -κολύμφευ as a second pers. sg. imperative; the start of the next line becomes an incoherent mess if μεϲ is not taken with the verb. The scribe does not usually break words across the line in this way, but may have been motivated to do so here because of the inordinate length of the word. The characters lose control, and begin to defecate, the event marked by a comically grandiose compound. Kassel–Austin retain the papyrus accentuation.

**40. δε . . μ.:** probably δέ, since we need a connective for the new clause (with sentence-end after ἐπεπείγει). The next word could be θαμά (Kerényi), but the traces are inconclusive.

**χοδέοντεϲ:** Hesychius (χ 584) has χοδιτεύειν as an equivalent to ἀποπαπτεῖν, and so Pohlenz (ap. Norsa–Vitelli) writes χοδ⟨ιτ⟩ε⟨ύ⟩οντες here. But so many scribal omissions look odd, and it is probable that χοδέω was simply another variant form (cf. κέχοδα from χέζω).

**γὰρ**: see fr. 4A. 8 n.

**41. τῖλος**: the speaker's excrement is so thin that it streams out like water. For the word, cf. Pollux 5. 91 (τὰ εἰς ἀπόπατον) λέγουσι δὲ καὶ τῖλον καὶ πέθελον καὶ σπατίλην.

**ἀστατὶ**: so the papyrus; though the adverb (formed from the adj. ἄστᾰτος) only appears here, it could readily have the meaning 'without stopping, endlessly' or 'irregularly' (M.L.W.). An attractive alternative is to write, with Gallavotti, Pohlenz (ap. Norsa–Vitelli), and Körte (*APF* 11 (1935), 267 n. 8), ἀστα⟨κ⟩τί ('in floods').

**κοχυδεύων**: a variant for κοχυδέω (Hsch. κ 3885 = ὑπερχέειν).

**ἀποτοσίτους**: only here, but the sense should clearly be not 'unable to drink or eat' (LSJ), but 'without drink or food', a comic calque of two simpler and more familiar words, ἄσιτος and ἄποτος. (Ajax, having slaughtered the cattle, sits ἄσιτος . . . ἄποτος at S. *Ai*. 324, not 'unable to eat . . . unable to drink' with grief, but 'without food . . . without drink'.) Those affected have now defecated so much that they no longer have anything left in their bowels.

**ἐπεποιήκει**: for the ending, cf. line 39 ἐπεπείγει and see on fr. 34.

**42–9.** The text here becomes too fragmentary to recover any clear sequence of ideas. In line 42 Norsa–Vitelli (p. 250) think of θυ]λάκος (though sacks are not particularly required by the context), but prefer ἄκος ('remedy'); there seems no reference to a cure for the diarrhoea in what follows, though I suppose the speaker may be hoping or praying for one. Line 43 seems to continue the theme of drinking with ἀσκοί (the start of a new sentence) which are πεφυσαμ[έ]νοι, i.e. inflated. The same phrase is reported for Epicharmus, in the (metrically problematic) phrase αὖτα φύσις ἀνθρώπων, ἀσκοί πεφ. (fr. 166), which Wilamowitz (ap. Kaibel) had already conjectured should instead be attributed to Sophron. But the sense here is presumably '[we were no longer] inflated wineskins' (ἀσκός = belly, as at Archil. fr. 119), a joke either on the Epicharmean phrase or on a popular expression which lies behind both quotations (cf. the use of γαστέρες to describe mankind at Hes. *Th*. 26).

At line 44 the papyrus punctuates ]δεπανδύϲ· βιηται (Doric βιᾶται cj. Norsa–Vitelli). Kassel–Austin remove the stop, and it certainly seems oddly placed, though elsewhere the papyrus tends to punctuate correctly. The revised supplement to LSJ cites ἐπανεδύcω from Eustathius (*Op. min.* p. 303. 19 Wirth), and supposes that ἐπανδύϲ = *ἐπαναδύϲ (with apocope). ἀναδύομαι can mean 'rise up'; probably the speaker rises up (again) from the flood of excrement.

In line 45 we must divide ]αμερον ὅπερ ἧϲ (Dor. = ἦν; see on fr. 59). More sense may be gained by reading μαλερον (though Kerényi, 16, suggests ἐπ]άμερον = ἐφήμερον); only half of the first letter is legible, an angled down-stroke, which could be the last stroke of either α or μ; the next traces could be either μ or αλ (the cross-bar of the alpha is not visible).

For υδρηρον in line 46 Olivieri conjectures ὑδρηλόν, an apt word for describing the speaker's watery excrement; but the form ὑδρηρόϲ is attested in the fourth-century tragedian Diogenes of Sinope (*TrGF* 88 F 7. 6 ὑδρηροῖϲ . . . ποτοῖϲ) and alternation of liquids (ρ/λ) is common enough (cf. e.g. fr. 26). ἐκεραύνω[ϲ]εν at line 47 need not be literal.

### [Fragments *5–*9]

**Title and Subject:** Three of these fragments derive from the arguments and scholia to Theocritus 2. Much of this is likely to go back to Apollodorus' commentary, and there is little reason to doubt at least the gist of the statements. The other two (frs. **8 and *9) are ascribed to the same mime because they contain related material. According to one scholion (fr. *6), Theocritus derived the whole subject of magic from Sophron,[4] and though we need not think the ritual details were precisely similar, it seems a fair assumption that Sophron's mime, like Theocritus' poem, dealt with erotic magic. Fr. 4A is sometimes thought to belong here; the extant passage depicts a purification ritual, but purification can sometimes feature as an element in erotic magic (see ad loc. and Hordern (2002a) ). However, the relationship is by no means assured, and in part depends on the authenticity of fr. **8: the invocation of Hecate found there is difficult to

---

[4] Deubner's suggested reading τὴν τῶν Φαρμακευτριῶν ὑπόθεcιν does not materially alter matters.

imagine after the (successful) summoning depicted in fr. 4A. See also on frs. 3, 4A, for more detailed discussion of this problem.

Fr. \*5 says that Thestylis, Simaetha's servant, was taken from Sophron's mime. Clearly Sophron's magician was also assisted by a servant. She may not actually have been called Thestylis (as Gow, *Theocritus*, ii. 35 n. 1, suggests), though the name is only found in Theocritus, and so is presumably intended to be Sicilian (so O. Masson, *ZPE* 102 (1994), 179[5]). But the text implies a more significant debt on Theocritus' part.

The Argument qualifies its statement with the adverb ἀπειροκάλως, which only occurs once elsewhere in the Theocritean scholia, in a note on *Id.* 5. After the abusive exchange between Lacon and Comatas at 5. 116 ff., Comatas accuses Lacon of losing his temper and tells him to go and gather squills from an old woman's grave (5. 120 f.). Lacon's response, κἠγὼ μὰν κνίζω, Μόρcων, τινά· καὶ τὺ δὲ λεύccειc, | ἐνθὼν τὰν κυκλάμινον ὄρυccέ νυν ἐc τὸν Ἄλεντα (122 f.), is understood by the scholia as abusive as well (cf. schol. 5. 121a, 121d, 123/4c). Gow and Dover (ad loc.) more plausibly think the plants here are apotropaic: Lacon and Comatas are to collect plants which will save them from their own loss of temper. But another scholion makes a different point (schol. 5. 123/4b)· κυκλάμινοc οὐχὶ πάντωc χαλεπῶc ὀρύccεται. ἀλλ᾽ ὥcπερ ἀπειροκάλωc (the adverb is Wilamowitz's correction; codd. have ἀπειρολόγωc (G) and ἀπρολόγωc (K)) ἐκεῖνοc κατηράcατο, οὕτω καὶ οὗτοc ἀπὸ τοῦ παραπεcεῖν εἰc τὴν κυκλάμινον. Here the scholion refers clearly enough to Comatas' abusiveness, but not to the fact that this abusiveness is out of place. To take the scholion's statement as an accusation of plagiarism thus looks doubtful, and it may mean no more than that Sophron's character was portrayed as somehow obscene or indecent (though this is not a feature of Theocritus' characterization of Simaetha).

Fr. \*7 indicates that Sophron's mime contained an address to Hecate, and includes what seems to be a phrase from it (see also on fr. 152). The similarity in the phrasing of these two notes no doubt points to dependence on a common source, probably Apollodorus' commentary. The phrase πρύτανιc νερτέρων will thus be Sophron's (cf. also on fr. 152), though whether the dead

---

[5] -υλιc is a common feminine suffix; Masson derives the first term from a putative \*θεcτόc 'desiré, demandé' (cf. ἀπόθεcτοc, πολύθεcτοc; < θέccαcθαι).

in particular or infernal spirits generally are meant is uncertain. The epithet would evidently be apt for a figure also identified with Persephone. Perhaps Sophron also hinted at the syncretism of Selene-Hecate; it is a common feature of later magical texts, and there is some evidence for syncretism of various goddesses in Sicily itself, particularly in connection with the sanctuary of Demeter at Gaggera (cf. Hordern (2002*a*), where, however, my assertion that Sophron identified the two was more than a little cavalier). Part of an address to Hecate may be preserved in the Doric prose invocation quoted by Plutarch (= fr. \*\*8), though Sophron is not an explicit source.

Finally, fr. \*9 recalls Hecate's arrival in Theocr. 2, and is attributed to Sophron on the strength of this: at Theocr. 2. 12 dogs are said to shiver before Hecate; shortly afterwards the goddess's arrival at the crossroads is marked by the howling of the dogs in the town (2. 35). Also relevant is Vergil's apparent echo in the punning half-line, *et Hylax in limine latrat*, in his imitation of Theocritus (*Ecl.* 8. 107). Sophron's dog is probably howling because, as in the other two pieces, the goddess is suddenly present.

## Fragment \*7

πρύτανιν: not with special reference to any magistracy that she might be supposed to hold there; for the word used of (normally male) deities in a variety of phrases, cf. Stesich. *PMGF* 235 ἵππων πρύτανιν (Poseidon), Pi. *P.* 6. 24 (Zeus), [A.] *Pr.* 170 (Zeus), Ion fr. eleg. 26. 13 Διόνυϲε . . . ϲυμποϲίων πρύτανι (cf. *PMG* 744. 4 f. οἶνον . . . ἀνθρώπων πρύτανιν), E. *Tro.* 1288 (Kronos).

## Fragment \*\*8

Plutarch says this is an invocation of Artemis, but given its contents this either must be a careless error or reflects syncretism of the two goddesses. The passage is corrupt, but the fact it is both prose and has Doric elements suggests Sophron as the author. Wilamowitz restored Doric forms throughout and ascribed it to this mime (*Gr. Lesebuch* I 2. 336, II 2. 210; *Kl. Schr.* IV. 160). The lines are strongly reminiscent of Simaetha's words at Theocr. 2. 11 ff. The language suggests an exploitation of 'the goddess's pollution for shameful ends' (Parker, 223), but love magic evidently cannot be ruled out.

## [Women watching the Isthmia]

**Title and Subject:** The mime clearly depicted two or more women (probably Syracusan) at an Isthmian festival; no doubt, as in Theocritus 15 and comparable works, they commented on what was to be seen as part of the spectacle. The Argument to Theocr. 15 rounds off its brief summary of that poem's contents with the assertion that τὸ ποιημάτιον was taken over from Sophron's *Women watching the Isthmia*, though it differed in poetic character. The exact wording of the title is uncertain; that used in the Argument may be a paraphrase, and at least needs Doric colouring, but ταὶ θάμεναι τὰ Ἴσθμια is unobjectionable enough. There are verbal forms in others of Sophron's titles. Theocritus' poem deals with the adventures of two Syracusan women, Gorgo and Praxinoa, at the festival of Adonis in Alexandria. Possibly the similarities extended to no more than (Syracusan) women in a festival context, and the general subject of ecphrasis (cf. Gow's *Theocritus*, ii. 265).

According to a scholion on Pindar (schol. *O.* 13. 158a, c), Syracuse and Aetna celebrated Isthmian games, named after the famous Isthmian festival at Corinth, the Syracusan mother-city. Possibly these are meant, though as one of the major Panhellenic festivals (held every other year: cf. Pi. *N.* 6. 39–41) the Isthmia at Corinth was obviously a popular destination for tourists. That Theocritus has his women visiting Alexandria may further indicate a foreign context for Sophron's mime. Aristophanes refers to the tents put up there by festival-goers (*Pax* 879–80, with further references provided by Olson ad loc.), and possibly his play Cκηνὰc καταλαμβάνουcαι featured women attending the festival (see Kassel–Austin ad loc.). The Corinthian festival was sacred to Poseidon, and so presumably was that in Syracuse. Poseidon is mentioned in two other fragments (frs. 125, 131), which may belong here; the mime perhaps included an internal prayer or hymn, like the song to Aphrodite at Theocr. 15. 100 ff. or the short invocation of Asclepius by the temple attendant at Herod. 4. 83–5. A fragment of this prayer may be preserved as fr. *171 (see ad loc.).

The sacred procession and the games themselves will have been objects of interest, but the mime may rather have focused on the offerings in the sanctuaries. Several hundred years later Pausanias thought the Corinthian theatre and race-course, and the numerous statues and sculptures, worth a visit (ii. 1. 7–2. 2). Theocritus' tourists comment on the wonderful tapestries to be seen (78 ff.). Herodas' poem 4, possibly also influenced by Sophron, portrays women sacrificing to Asclepius and discussing the various sculptures and paintings on display in the sanctuary. Callimachus' *Iamb* 6 described Zeus' statue at Olympia for the supposed benefit of an acquaintance on the point of visiting it, thus cleverly inverting the 'visiting tourist' genre (cf. Kerkhecker, 167–79). Ecphrasis in the context of a festival is still an established topos as late as Ach. Tat. 5. 2 (Cleitophon at the festival of Zeus Sarapis in Alexandria; cf. also 1. 1. 2).

There were earlier models. Epicharmus' *Thearoi* depicted people attending the Pythia and describing the offerings displayed there; the largest surviving fragment is a list of votive objects including tripods, chariots, spits, and mixing bowls (fr. 68). More dramatic action must have featured in Aeschylus' satyric *Theoroi* or *Isthmiasts* (frs. 78a–82 Radt). Similar ecphrases can of course also form part of larger units; cf. esp. the behaviour of the tourist-chorus at Delphi at E. *Ion* 184 ff. See in general R. Hunter, *Papers of the Leeds International Latin Seminar*, 10 (Leeds, 1998), 131–56.

Possible further fragments: frs. 31 (see ad loc.), 77, 81, 85, *93 (cf. Theocr. 15. 65), 95 (see ad loc.).

## Fragment **10

Sophron is not the explicit source for this fragment (though dialect makes his authorship likely), and it is ascribed to this mime only because of Theocr. 15. 2 ὅρη δρίφον, Εὐνόα, αὐτᾶι, where Praxinoa provides Gorgo with a chair. But clearly similar expressions could easily have appeared in any number of mimes (cf. e.g. also Herod. 6. 1 κάθησο, Μητροῖ. τῆι γυναικὶ θὲς δίφρον, 7. 4–5 τῆις γυναιξὶν οὐ θήσεις | τὴν μέζον' ἔξω cανίδα;).

ὦ: see fr. 4A. 7 n.

δρίφον: a type of light stool or chair, often associated with women elsewhere, as in both passages cited above, and also Herodas 1. 37, 77; cf. δίφρος of the earth-woman's stool at Semon. fr. 7. 26. The word appears again at fr. 88.

## Busied about the Bride

**Title and Subject:** Both fragments quoted by Athenaeus describe the activities of a group which includes at least some men (τοί, βαλλίζοντεc; cf. Sect. II, n. 9). The subject of προῆχε is also male (λαβών). Athenaeus, however, makes the title feminine, and Hesychius glosses νυμφοπόνοc (ν 725) as ἡ περὶ τὴν νύμφην πονουμένη; the main character will have been a woman, who may be speaking here.

A natural inference is that the mime described the festivities surrounding a wedding. A similar subject may have featured in *Promythion* (frs. 50–1; see ad loc.). The results of the celebrations here recall the scene in fr. 4D, possibly the result of excessive drinking. Much the same could be implied here. If θάλαμον means the bridal chamber itself, the celebrations have clearly got seriously out of hand. Perhaps the groom's friends are running riot.

Greek wedding ceremonies could be quite elaborate, if Athenian practice is anything to go by. The bride and bridegroom took a ritual bath before the wedding, and were anointed with oil; after the feast, there was a procession ending with the introduction of the bride to the bridegroom's house (Henderson on Ar. *Lys.* 378; Gomme–Sandbach on Men. *Sam.* 713, 729; Olsen on Ar. *Pax* 842). Practices in other parts of the Greek world probably differed only slightly.

Epicharmus described, in two versions and apparently in some detail, the wedding of Heracles and Hebe. At least in the second version, *Muses*, he mentioned Athena playing the enoplion for the Dioscuri to dance to (fr. 92), which implies sympotic revelry as a theme. The remaining fragments are largely concerned with the different fish and other foods provided by the Muses and Poseidon (cf. fr. 48). Possibly Sophron's fr. 12 relates to the food or drink consumed during the feast (for the varieties of food served at weddings, see Olson on Ar. *Pax* 1195–6); but the plate may have been something broken by the revellers' riotous behaviour.

## Fragment 11

**προῆχε:** = Att. προεῖχε. Someone (the door-keeper? see next n.) holds up an object to protect himself from the thrown excrement. There are probably mock-military overtones in the use of the verb here (cf. Dover on the expression τὴν ἀcπίδα τῆc κωλῆc προέχων at Ar. *Nub.* 989), but the object itself was perhaps something like a chamber-pot. The probable sympotic context perhaps evokes the idea of a scatological version of cottabus.

**ἐβάλλιζον:** 'Ulpian' (the speaker in Athenaeus) wants the word to mean 'dance' here, but in the next line, and at fr. 31, the required sense is clearly 'throw'. Similarly, at Alexis fr. 112 βαλλιcμόc appears to refer to throwing in a sympotic context, though there the word also has 'a penumbra of associations evoked by the behaviour of a rampaging κῶμοc, associations which include the music of cymbal, drum and pipes, singing and doubtless drunken dancing' (Arnott ad loc., whose excellent note should be consulted for a fuller account). The context and sense of βαλλίζοντεc at Epich. fr. 68. 4 (*Thearoi*) is unclear. Throwing stones and other objects is an attested sympotic activity (e.g. Ar. *Vesp.* 1253, Eub. fr. 93). Anacreon says cινάμωροι πολεμίζουcι θυρωρῶι (*PMG* 351), where the θυρωρόc may be the person who, at least at weddings in Lesbos, was supposed to prevent the bride's friends from rescuing her (cf. Sa. fr. 110a); but Anacreon's cινάμωροι are no doubt the bridegroom's friends, up to unwelcome mischief.

**θάλαμον:** properly an inner-room, therefore a bed-chamber, and often more especially the bridal chamber. Given the mime's title, the latter is probably meant here.

**cκάτουc:** cκῶρ was slang on the Attic stage, and has an equivalent earthiness at Epich. fr. 48. 3 (καὶ cκάρουc, τῶν οὐδὲ τὸ cκὰρ θεμιτὸν ἐκβαλεῖν θεοῖc 'whose shit even the gods aren't allowed to throw away'). Contrast the elaborate metaphors used by Sophron for sexual activity. For scatological humour in Sophron and elsewhere, see on fr. 4D.

## Fragment 12

Hesychius (α 8453) glosses αὐτοποίητον as εὐτελέc 'well-made', but 'home-made', in any case the more obvious sense, seems more attractive here.

For the word πατάνα, see above p. 23.

## Mother-in-Law

**Title and Subject:** The subject, one with obvious comic poten-
tial, may have been traditional. An Athenian terracotta lamp of
the 3rd cent. BC with a painting which depicts three mime-actors
connects them with a mime called ἑ(ι)κυρά (an inscription on
the back of the lamp reads μιμολόγοι | ἡ ὑπόθεcιc | ἑ(ι)κυρά: C.
Watzinger, *Ath. Mitt.* 26 (1901), 1–8). Terence's *Hecyra* had a
Greek model in Apollodorus of Carystus' comedy of the same
name, but the relevance of either here is doubtful.

## Fragment 13

The Mother-in-Law is probably speaking or being spoken to.
Theoretically it could be she who has sent the food for the
children (her grandchildren?), but this seems unlikely if we
assume that the titles of mimes usually referred to the central
figure. One would expect the Mother-in-Law to be present most
or all of the time.

τ': Kaibel emends to γ'; but for τε as a connective between
clauses, cf. fr. *136, and see Denniston, 497 ff. The usage is more
common in, but not restricted to, verse. A pronoun would be
nice, but cυμβουλεύω requires a dative (Cobet obligingly proposed τιν).

ἄρτον . . . τυρῶντα: (< τυρόεντα) Sicilian cheese was famous
(Pollux 6. 63). For bread made by mixing cheese in and baking it,
see Gow on Theocr. 1. 58; Aristophanes mentions cakes backed
with cheese (*Ach.* 1125 πλακοῦντος τυρόνωτον . . . κύκλον, cf. Olson
ad loc.). While references to cakes and bread possibly have
obscene overtones elsewhere in Sophron (see on fr. 28), clearly
nothing of the sort is implied here.

γάρ: see on fr. 4A. 8.

## [Koikoa: Fragments 14–*17]

**Title and Subject:** The title can only be a matter for guesswork
(I use [*Koikoa*] for convenience only), but these fragments
clearly come from the same mime. Admittedly, the repetition of
the name Koikoa may not be conclusive; the same characters
appear more than once in Herodas (poems 6 and 7 both feature

Metro and Cerdon). But the similarity of context which frs. 14 and 15 require, and the information in fr. 16 that Koikoa was a foreign slave-girl, all point to the same setting: a mime in which Koikoa provided the speaker and her friend(s) with food and drink. She will not, of course, have been the main character.

Herodas 9 depicts women breakfasting together; no more than the first few lines are preserved, and those rather lacunose, but they seem to include criticism of a maid-servant (see Headlam–Knox on Herod. 9 tit.). Menander's Cυναριcτῶcαι (frs. 335–44 K–A with addenda, vol. i p. 395) may also be relevant, since it too depicted women having an early meal together (cf. esp. fr. 385. 1 ἂν ἔτι πιεῖν μοι δῶι τιc κτλ.). Women in classical Athens occasionally had morning meals together, if Ar. *Eccl.* 348–9 is anything to go by (μῶν ἐπ' ἄριcτον γυνὴ | κέκληκεν αὐτὴν τῶν φίλων; where the joke is that even for such a meal, no woman would leave the house before dawn (see Ussher ad loc.)).

The name Koikoa is not otherwise known. Demetrius (= fr. 16) says that she was called Koikoa because she was foreign (ξενίζ[ουcαν]), and possibly makes a direct connection with the verb κοικύλλειν ('gape vacantly') in col. 60.[6] If the verb was actually used in a speech to Koikoa (προφοραῖc could mean 'rebukes'; cf. LSJ *s.v.* IV), then there may be an implied etymological connection between κοικύλλω and Κοικόα; cf. a similar etymologizing alliteration at fr. 48. At Ar. *Thesm.* 852 the verb is used of Euripides' relation gazing this way and that in search of aid. Kaibel compares the name Κοικυλίων, mentioned at Ael. *V.H.* xiii. 15 as someone so stupid that they would try to count the waves. More relevantly, at Herod. 4. 41 ff. the slave-girl Cydilla is told off by her mistress, Cynno: οὐ coὶ λέγω, αὕτη, τῆι ὧδε κῶδε χαcκεύcηι; At Semon. fr. 7. 110 κεχηνότοc is used of a man who pays no attention while his wife freely plans adulteries (see Lloyd-Jones ad loc., with further references there), and Solon fr. 13. 36 says χάcκοντεc κούφαιc ἐλπίcι τερπόμεθα, when he means *thoughtless* enjoyment of empty hopes. The name would therefore be apt for an inattentive slave-girl slow to carry out her mistress's wishes, and thus give particular point to fr. 15.

---

[6] Romeo, however, approvingly cites earlier attempts to derive the name from onomatopoeic words such as κοάξ (E. Hauler, *Verhandlungen der 42. Versamml. Deutsch. Philol. u. Schulmänner in Wien* (Leipzig, 1894), 257) or κοῖ/κοΐζειν (Führ; cf. Olivieri, 89).

Slaves appear not to have kept their native names in captivity; note the name *Αἴθων* ('Darky') at Thgnd. 1209 f., and the numerous 'ethnic' slave-names (e.g. *Θρᾶιττα*, frequently of Thracian slave-girls in Attic). But Koikoa, as an otherwise unattested name, may have sounded exotic to a Greek ear. She may be imagined as a Sicel, who evidently had a typically poor reputation among the Greeks (cf. esp. Epich. fr. 207).

Foreigners are frequently portrayed as intellectually inferior in comedy and elsewhere; cf. esp. the Scythian archer in Ar. *Thesm.*, whose wit is as defective as his Greek. See in general E. Hall, *Inventing the Barbarian* (Oxford, 1989), and, on comedy in particular, T. Long, *Barbarians in Greek Comedy* (Carbondale and Edwardsville, 1986). Possibly Demetrius' interpretation (if correctly reconstructed) goes back to Apollodorus' commentary (for Apollodorus' interests in etymologizing, see Sect. V. A). As a Laconian, however, Demetrius would have been better placed than most to read Sophron without assistance, and he could easily have had independent knowledge of the mimes.

There is some similarity to Praxinoa's criticism of Eunoa at Theocr. 15. 27 ff.: *Εὐνόα, αἶρε τὸ νῆμα καὶ ἐc μέcον, αἰνόδρυπτε,* | *θὲc πάλιν· αἱ γαλέαι μαλακῶc χρήιζοντι καθεύδειν· | κινεῦ δή· φέρε θᾶccον ὕδωρ. ὕδατοc πρότερον δεῖ, | ἃ δὲ cμᾶμα φέρει. δὸc ὅμωc. μὴ δὴ πολύ, λαιcτρί κτλ.* (cf. also the criticism of male slaves at e.g. Herod. 7. 4–7). Possibly therefore the Koikoa fragments belong with the [*Women watching the Isthmia*], but this is far from certain, and Theocritus could well have been influenced (if influence this is) by more than one mime in any given poem.

As a literary topos, the 'lazy slave-girl' can be traced back at least as far as a humorous Sumerian composition (ed. B. Alster, *Journal of Cuneiform Studies*, 27 (1975), 215–16; cf. also J. van Dijk, *La Sagesse suméro-accadienne* (Leiden, 1953), 98) in which a slave-girl is ironically encouraged to do no work by an unidentified speaker (but surely to be imagined as the girl's master or mistress), who then outlines the probable consequences of this behaviour (destitution).

## Fragment 14

*cκύφον*: of wine. The drunken habits of women are a repeated subject of humour in Aristophanes and elsewhere (see on fr. 1). A skyphos was particularly a rustic cup (e.g. Alcm. *PMGF* 56. 3,

Theocr. 1. 143), usually without a stem, and with semicircular horizontal handles at the level of the rim. At Herod. 1. 79 ff. Metriche's Thracian slave pours a cup of wine for Gyllis.

## Fragment 15

At a Greek meal the tables were loaded with food outside the room, and only brought in when those eating had taken their places; for the verbal sequence and language here, cf. esp. Ar. *Vesp.* 1216 ὕδωρ κατὰ χειρός· τὰς τραπέζας εἰcφέρειν, and see MacDowell ad loc.

  τάλαινα: also addressed to a slave-girl at e.g. Herod. 6. 3.

  ποχ': i.e. ποκα, the West Greek and Boeotian equivalent for Attic-Ionic ποτε (as also ὅκα = ὅτε, τόκα = τότε).

## Fragment 16

The text is based on my own examination of the papyrus; Demetrius' argument in connection with Sophron and suggested readings are discussed in greater detail in Hordern (2002c). Here I largely restrict my comments to the fragments themselves.

Demetrius appears to be concerned with mime throughout these six columns of *On Poems 2*, and given προεκκειμέ[νοιc at col. 55. 6, earlier sections of the treatise must also have mentioned the subject. However, whether this was anything more substantial than a brief reference, perhaps in the extremely fragmentary col. 54, is unclear. Certainly there are no obvious connections with mime in what can be made of the surviving sections of the text. The presence of Koikoa's name clearly indicates that Sophron is under discussion in col. 55, and his own name appears in col. 60; despite obscure references to Aeschylus and Euripides, it is probable that the larger part of the intervening material is concerned with the mimes, and perhaps just with the Koikoa mime throughout. The bulk of the discussion in cols. 56–9 deals with various figures of speech: synecdoche is mentioned briefly in col. 56, but Demetrius' main interest appears to be in vocabulary and word-choice, a prominent subject in poetic manuals generally. Romeo identified references to word-order at cols. 56. 6–11 and 59. 3–6, but neither is particularly clear and other readings are possible. My own text assumes that word-choice (ἐκλογή) is in view throughout.

However, while Demetrius' discussion throws some useful light on ancient views of Sophron's style, the most important aspects for us are the quotations, beginning in col. 57. There is no certainty, of course, that all belong to the Koikoa mime, but one of the women's mimes looks likely to be the source for fr. 16A and B, and thus also for 16C (which clearly belongs with them). The reference to 'slow learners' in col. 60 is readily understandable if Koikoa is meant there, and if the emphasis in cols. 55 and 56 is on Koikoa's linguistic barbarism (ξενίζουϲαν could be taken to mean 'because she speaks a foreign language'), then Demetrius' reference to the τόποϲ περὶ ποιημάτων at col. 60. 6 points to a further connection. The reference is probably to the Stoic τέχνη περὶ φωνῆϲ, of which the second subdivision (called τόποι) was περὶ ϲολοικιϲμου καὶ βαρβαριϲμοῦ καὶ ποιημάτων καὶ ἀμφιβολιῶν (Diog. Laert. 7. 44). Particularly interesting, then, is the apparent quotation of λειοκόνιτε from fr. 74 in col. 59, which could well be imagined as something addressed to Koikoa by her mistress.

Col. 57 (fr. 16A) mentions Sophron's use of an invented word instead of the common μῶλυ 'garlic'. Romeo's ingenious supplement τη[γανιϲτ]όν is almost certainly correct: Demetrius' point appears to be that Sophron could use this as an equivalent for μῶλυ because it is derivable from the verb τηγανίζω, just as μῶλυ is (fancifully) derivable from μωλύ(ν)ω. The phrase νωθρὰν [ϲ]ύνεϲιν further suggests Koikoa (for the adjective, suggesting her reluctant servitude, cf. Callim. *Hec.* fr. 68 Hollis with his note). Romeo makes the attractive suggestion that this 'garlic' was something prepared for the women's meal, its partially cooked state a matter of reproach for the hapless slave-girl. The quotation which commences in line 14 (fr. 16B) is regrettably beyond reconstruction, but the form ϲοι is noteworthy: it can be paralleled in Sophron by first person μοι, but we do not necessarily expect these in Syracusan and it is just possible that the usage is meant to reflect Koikoa's foreign status. Certainly there seem to be deliberate errors in fr. 16C, despite the lamentably lacunose state of the text. Here the garlic is again in question. R. Janko (per litt.) suggests κα 'ποήϲα and then perhaps κα 'ζέο (the ending suggests an uncontracted second-person middle imperfect; < ζέω 'boil'?), which would perhaps refer to its preparation: but the forms are odd, and we must assume either that the

scribe has grown even more careless than usual at this point, or
that they are deliberate errors: Koikoa, as a non-Greek, is drop-
ping her augments and perhaps also the iota of καί. This would
agree well with the apparent references to linguistic barbarism
elsewhere in Demetrius' discussion. Or they may be hyper-
doricisms: we expect καὶ + ἐ- to produce κῆ- in West Greek
(above, p. 19), but given that long α for Att.-Ion. η was characteristic of Doric, a scribe may have felt the forms with alpha
appropriate here.

   The sense of the discussion at the beginning of col. 59 is disputed. Romeo thinks that Demetrius is discussing word-order,
twice reading ἄρθ⟨ρ⟩α κινῶν. But however we emend αρθα in line
3, it can only with difficulty be made the object of the following
κινῶν, which, given the position of δέ, must be the first word in its
sentence or clause. Moreover, it is striking that the scribe wrote
αρθα twice. In Hordern (2002c), I suggested ὀρθά in both places:
changing the styles (εἴδη) of the mimes is achieved by changing
the 'proper' words (for the sense to be given to ὀρθά, see my discussion there, and cf. e.g. Ar. *Ra.* 1181, and Pl. *Phaedr.* 267 c,
*Crat.* 391 B on Protagoras' interest in linguistic ὀρθότης). The
scattered quotations from Sophron in cols. 59 and 60 are, however, disappointing. Apart from the quotation of fr. 74, only one
of them (fr. 16D) is anything like complete, where someone
(Koikoa again?) said 'I tend the . . .' and substituted another
word for the expected ὄϊεσσι 'sheep'. τάc in the quotation shows
that the object was feminine, and perhaps the line was a com-
plaint about having to serve her ovine mistress (but we expect
dative after αἰπολῶ, and should perhaps read τα⟨ῖ⟩c; or is this
another deliberately barbarous error?).

## Fragment 17

We expect πίμπλημι to have imperative πίμπλη, but the comparison with the imperative ὅρα (< ὅραε) indicates that Herodian
understood the verb here as the less common semantic doublet
πιμπλάω (for the contraction α + ε > η, see above, p. 18).

## Unplaced Women's Fragments

### Fragment 18

We can readily imagine an apodosis; e.g. 'the cakes would remain flat and tasteless; you know what slaves are like. . .'. The fragment may be connected with the scholion on Ar. *Pax* 28 (= fr. 39), where ἑαυταῖc is almost certainly an error for τὸ cταῖc (Meineke). Several fragments from the women's mimes deal with cookery, or types of food. Cheese-bread was mentioned in the *Mother-in-Law*, and baking is referred to at fr. 27 (and fr. 28?). These fragments need not all have belonged to the same mime; we may readily imagine any of these statements as asides in a variety of contexts. But a mime dealing predominantly with women talking about cooking is certainly a possibility.

Cookery is not prominent in either Archilochus or Hipponax (though various foods and foodstuffs are frequently mentioned), but may have featured at some length in Semonides. The knowledgeable sacrificer of fr. 24 is a cook (μάγειροc) according to Athenaeus, and sacrificing or cooking is probably alluded to at frs. 23, 28, and 30. Possibly these fragments belong together (with frs. 26–7, 32, 39) in an iambus which described a banquet or revel. Hermippus (fr. 2) mentions white figs in an unknown context, and Ananias (fr. 5) recommends the right time of year to eat certain animals in a passage recalling the sort of advice later given by Archestratus. A revel was probably described in an iambus (doubtless quite different from his other trimeters) by Solon (frs. 38–41). Cooks are characters from the lower end of the social scale whom we expect to find in iambus and mime, and they feature prominently in Attic comedy. See the detailed studies by J. Wilkins, *The Boastful Chef* (Oxford, 2001); H. Dohm, *Mageiros* (Munich, 1964). However, there they are usually men; that the speaker here is a woman indicates a more domestic context than anything found in comedy.

**αὑταυτᾶc:** = ἐμαυτῆc (see pp. 21–2).

### Fragment 19

Normally one's heart leaps with love. Alcibiades at Pl. *Symp.* 215 E claims that his heart leaps when he listens to Socrates (ὅταν γὰρ ἀκούω, πολύ μοι μᾶλλον ἢ τῶν κορυβαντιώντων ἥ τε καρδία πηδᾶι), and at Ach . Tat. 5. 27 Cleitophon's sexual arousal is also marked by his heart leaping; contrast E. *Hipp.* 1351–2 διά μου κεφαλῆς ἄιccουc' ὀδύναι | κατά τ' ἐγκέφαλον πηδᾶι cφάκελοc (the dying Hippolytus).

**μεθέν**: Apollonius says ἐμέθεν is Syracusan as well as Aeolic, and cites this fragment in support; it does not in fact illustrate his point, which is indeed good reason *not* to restore ἐμέθεν. μεθέν is hapax in Sicilian literature, and we may wonder whether Apollonius had any further authority for his statement. An alternative is that someone is speaking a dialect other than Syracusan. Sophron probably depicted the slave-girl Koikoa as a speaker of barbarous Greek (cf. frs. 14–*17), foreign dialects were a feature of the Spartan δεικηλιcταί, and their representation is common in Old Comedy (see Colvin, *passim*, for a detailed account of non-Attic speech in comedy, as well as his briefer treatment in D. Harvey and J. Wilkins (eds.), *The Rivals of Aristophanes* (London, 2000), 285–98; also Hordern, *Timotheus*, 204–6). But the contraction α + ει > ηι is certainly Doric (cf. also imperative πάδη in Laconian at Ar. *Lys.* 1317 with Colvin, 134–5).

### Fragment 20

The verb (Dor. = Ion. λωβέομαι) is a forceful one. According to Semonides even the woman who seems respectable, αὕτη μέγιστα τυγχάνει λωβωμένη (fr. 7. 109), since she is planning secret adultery. Such a situation might be imagined here, though ἀμέ would have to be her children as well as her husband. Sometimes physical maltreatment is in question: Herodas' schoolmaster Lampriscus uses the verb when he speaks of chastising his wayward pupils (3. 68–9). Since the subject is here a woman, perhaps we may instead imagine a slave (e.g. Koikoa?) complaining about her mistreatment, and that of her fellow slaves, at the hands of their mistress (cf. also the (male) slave's prayer at Hippon. fr. 40: Μαλὶc †κονιcκε, καί με δεcπότεω βεβροῦ | λάχοντα λίccομαι cε μὴ ῥαπίζεcθαι).

For the contraction -βῆτο (< -βά -ετο), see p. 18.

### Fragment *21

ἐκλεπυρόω means to remove the λεπύριον, a thin outer husk or peel (so at Theocr. 5. 95, acorns are said to have a thin λεπύριον and are thus eatable).[7] Here it probably refers to the foreskin of the penis; κριθή ('barley') can refer to the erect penis in Attic comedy (e.g. Ar. *Pax* 965 ff.; *Av.* 506 with Dunbar; Henderson, 119 f.), and there is a related double entendre in Sophron at fr. 38. 'Drawing back the foreskin' may be a sign of incipient sexual activity at Hippon. fr. 12. 3 (reading δαρτόν with Masson for the codd.'s meaningless ἄρτον; cf. also Archil. fr. 39 with Bossi, 123–6). The image at Hippon. fr. 84. 17 ἐπ' ἄκρον ἕλκων ὥσπερ ἀλλᾶντα ψύχων may be somewhat similar (Knox suggests ψήχων; but see R. Rosen, *TAPA* 118 (1988), 38 f.).

ἀποκαθάραcα is transitive. Women cleaned themselves before sex (cf. Ar. *Pax* 868), but the verb here may refer to cleaning something, such as semen, off the penis (cf. Hauler, 106 n. 3); if so, the scene here is clearly post-coital.

For the accent of καλῶc, cf. p. 25.

## Fragment *22

The name Physka is not otherwise attested, but there are various related masculine forms, concentrated largely in Boeotia and Locris: Φύcκων (2nd cent. BC Boeotia); Φύcκιον (twice in Locris, 2nd–3rd cent. BC; once in 2nd cent. BC Thessaly); Φυcκίων (2nd cent. BC Locris); and Φουcκίων (five times in 2nd–3rd cent. BC Boeotia). Bechtel (*Personennamen*, 481) cites ΦύcϘων on an archaic Corinthian vase, and compares names such as Γάcτριc, Γάcτροc etc. based on γαcτήρ. It will originally have been a nickname (cf. Bechtel, *Spitznamen*, 31). Pittacus was mocked as Φύcγων 'pot-belly' by Alcaeus (frs. 129. 21; 429), and Φύcκων was also the sobriquet of Ptolemy VIII.

## Fragment 23

The razor-fish, with its long, cylindrical shape (cf. Thompson, 257 f.), was thought to be visually similar to the penis, and so cωλήν probably refers to the penis at Archil. fr. 46 (cf. Hsch. c 3069). Here however the cωλῆνεc are dildoes. In comedy as in iambus women are naturally lascivious, and the use of dildoes is a concomitant of male absence; cf. e.g. Cratin. fr. 354 μιcηταὶ δὲ γυναῖκεc ὀλίcβοιcι χρήcονται, and see Henderson, 221–2. The women mentioned in line 2 may be genuinely widows, or

[7] At Hesych. λ 689 λεπυριῶcαι· ἐξαχυριῶcαι, Kaibel suggests restoring -ίωcε or -ύρωcε· ἐξηχυρίωcε.

perhaps they are called 'widowed' simply because their husbands are absent, as at Herod. 1. 21 f., κόσον τιν᾽ ἤδη χηραίνεις; where Metriche is 'widowed' because Mandris is away in Egypt. Dildoes also appear in fr. 25 (see ad loc.), and Herodas gives the subject extensive treatment in poems 6 and 7. Epicharmus is said to have used the expression γέρρα Νάξια 'Naxian wickers' (fr. 226); this is explained by most sources as a euphemism for the genitals, both male and female, but γέρρα is more plausibly understood at Et. Orion. p. 42,25 as τὰ δερμάτινα αἰδοῖα.

**ἐντί:** = Att. εἰсί.

**ποκα:** = Att. ποτε (cf. fr. 15 n.).

**φίλα:** a common form of address in Sophron (cf. frs. 25, 31). According to Dickey, 135, the masculine φίλε expresses 'genuine, indisputable affection only in combination' (i.e. with a name or equivalent). This also seems valid for the feminine in Herodas. His women use it at 1. 73 (Metriche to Gyllis), 4. 20, 56 (both Phile[8] to Cynno: φίλη Κυννοῖ), 6. 12, 18, 86 (all Metro to Coritto: φίλη Κοριττοῖ), and 23 (Coritto to Metro: φίλη Μητροῖ). Thus, only Metriche certainly uses it without a name, and she and Gyllis are hardly genuine friends. But we do not know to what extent this applied in Sophron.

**τοὶ μακροὶ κόγχοι:** codd. have μακραὶ κόγχαι, and the feminine κόγχη, like the masculine, can refer to several types of shellfish. But here a masculine is needed to support the joke (the shellfish are masculine because they are fulfilling the function of men), just as the feminine form supports a different obscene joke at fr. 24 (see ad loc.). Kaibel's τοίδε τοὶ μακρογόγγυλοι is a bold, but ultimately unjustified, emendation on the basis of Epich. fr. 40. 7 τούς τε μακρογογγύλους cωλῆνας.

**cωλῆνέc:** the razor-shell, so-called because of its long, cylindrical shape (Thompson, 257–8).

**θην:** an intensive particle almost exclusively confined to Homer and Sicilian literature (Sophron, Epicharmus, Theocritus), though it is found in Attic at [A.] *Pr.* 928. 'It is equivalent in sense to δή, but perhaps rather weaker in force' (Denniston, 288–9).

**λίχνευμα:** only here.

---

[8] Cynno simply addresses her interlocutor as φίλη (4. 27, 39), which is probably a name rather than an endearment; but we can hardly expect Cynno to address her as φίλη Φίλη.

## Fragment 24

Here the κόγχαι are feminine. Names of different shellfish are frequent slang-terms for the female genitalia, and κόγχη in particular, which properly refers to the pink cavity of a seashell, is evidently an apt image for the vagina (Henderson, 142). It may have been a common slang word ('. . . all the cunts . . .'). The mime perhaps included a description of a sexual adventure like those described in several iambi; e.g. Archil. fr. 192a; Hippon. frs.12, 16–17, 56–7 (see West, *Studies*, 142), 70 (note especially τὸν βρύccον of the female genitals), 84. This fragment no doubt preceded a bawdy description of actual intercourse, clearly involving several male and female participants (ἁμίν).

γα μὰν: μάν = Att. μήν; see Denniston, 328 ff.

αἴ κ': in Doric we expect αἴ κε(ν) or αἴ κα instead of ἐάν; in later West Greek inscriptions εἴ κα is more common (Buck, 106), but Epicharmus has several examples of αἴ κα with both subjunctive and optative (e.g. frs. 18 αἴ κ' . . . ἴδοιc; 32. 5 καἴ κα . . . λῆι, 10 etc.); cf. Gow on Theocr. 11. 73.

κεχάναντι: like mouths, in anticipation; cf. e.g. Hippon. fr. 9 πάλαι γὰρ αὐτοὺς προcδέκονται χάcκοντεc | κράδαc ἔχοντεc ὡc ἔχουcι φαρμακοῖc.

κρῆc: here the inner labia. For κρέαc of the female genitals, cf. Ar. *Pax* 717, *Ach.* 795, though it can also refer to the male genitals (*Eq.* 428); see Henderson, 144. For the contraction, see p. 19.

## Fragment 25

A woman is speaking to her friend. κουρίδεc and καμμάροι are both varieties of shellfish, and καμμάροι in particular are usually described as 'red' or 'purple'. I suppose that the women could be at a fish-market, but redness and smoothness are also typical characteristics of dildoes (see the individual lemmata). At Herod. 7. 60 καρκίνια ('crabs') refers to a type of dildo. The situation may have been similar to that in Herod. 7, where women discuss the variety and quality of dildoes on display (cf. also fr. 23).

κουρίδων: identified by Chantraine (1963) as the *squilla palaemon* (cf. Thompson, 103). Epich. fr. 78 has κωρίδαc, but fr. 28 κουρίδεc; the Att.-Ion. form is καρίc.

The partitive genitive after other verbs of perception is

common, but not after ἰδεῖν. Three other alleged cases are cited
by Kidd on Arat. *Ph.* 430 (Ar. *Ra.* 815–16; Pl. *Rep.* 558 A; X.
*Mem.* 1. 1. 11), but none of these is an uncontested instance of the
usage (see Dover on *Ra.* 815–16). Kaibel thinks of ἴδε καμμαρίδων
φῦλα, where φῦλα would also govern the genitive κουρίδων, but
favours keeping the vocative φίλα; however, the frequency of the
vocative could itself be responsible for corruption here.

**καμμάρων**: 'les καμμάροι sont des grosses crevettes roses dont
les dimensions vont jusqu'à 15 centimètres et qui sont plus
grandes que le *palaemon*' (Chantraine (1963), 137).

**θᾶcαι**: cf. fr. 31, Epich. fr. 114, Theocr. 1. 149, 3. 12.

**μὰν**: = Att. μήν.

**ἐρυθραί**: the κάμμαρος is conventionally red, but this is also a
typical quality of dildoes; cf. the term κοκκίδεс ('crimsons') at
Herod. 7. 61, and Coritto's scarlet one (κόκκινος) at 6. 19
with Headlam–Knox ad loc. for further references. The comic
phallus was probably also red (Ar. *Nub.* 538–9 with Dover;
*Suda*, φ 60).

**ἐντὶ**: = Att. εἰcὶ.

**λειοτριχιῶcαι**: Coritto praises the smoothness of Cerdon's
dildo at Herod. 6. 71, and λεῖα describes a variety in his catalogue
at 7. 57.

Verbs formed in -όω are chiefly factitive, denoting 'to cause' or
'to make' (cf. esp. ἐκλεπυρόω at fr. 21). Thus, λειοτριχιόω means
not 'having smooth hair', but 'being smoothed of hair', or 'with
the hair removed'. Contrast the related but independent formation at Arist. *H.A.* 8. 8. 595ᵇ26 ἡ δὲ κράстιс λειοτριχεῖν ποιεῖ ὅταν
ἔγκυος ἦι: grass gives (horses, mules etc.) a smooth coat, but the
verb is λειοτριχέω 'to be possessed of smooth hair'. λεῖα is
common of depilated skin (e.g. Herod. 2. 70).

Chantraine (1963), who takes λειοτριχιῶcαι to mean 'smooth-
or shining-haired' (with reference to the lobster's shining cara-
pace or its tentacles?), thinks that there is a pun on κούρη (or κόρη,
κώρη) and κουρίс; the shellfish are like smooth-haired girls (and
the hair perhaps pubic). But this interpretation seems less likely
if it is right to take the shellfish to stand for dildoes.

## Fragment 26

**θείαιс**: 'mira est haec materterarum et Hecatae coniunctio' (A.
Meineke, *Analecta Alexandrina* (Berlin, 1843), 50); indeed, and

so Blomfield ((1826), 341; followed by Wilamowitz, ap. Kaibel) proposed θειαῖς 'for the goddesses', which makes the fragment refer to ritual offerings (cf. fr. 4A. 17). Hecate might be a person's name at Herod. 7. 86, though I doubt that there we can rule out the hypothesis that the goddess is meant (cf. Cunningham, Headlam–Knox ad loc.). Ahrens solves the difficulty by writing ἑκά⟨ς⟩ται 'for each'.

**κριβανίτας:** here with κρ-, which Athenaeus and others describe as Attic against Doric (and Ionic) κλ-, which Athenaeus also cites for Sophron (fr. 27; cf. Epich. 137). His text must therefore have presented both forms, but it is unlikely that we should conclude that fr. 26 was spoken by an Athenian. Athenaeus also credits Epicharmus with a form in κρ- (fr. 46), and it is possible that both forms were in use in Syracusan; the liquids ρ and λ are in any case frequently exchanged.

**ἡμιάρτιον:** not an amount of bread, but a type of semi-circular loaf (Hsch. η 485: εἶδος ἄρτον ἡμικυκλῶδες). For the phrasing, cf. esp. Epich. fr. 113. 241 ὅμωρος οὐδέ χ' ἡμιά[ρ]τιον.

## Fragment 27

Henderson (144) thinks πέσσειν, the usual verb for baking bread or cakes, could be (Attic) slang for sexual intercourse, though none of the instances he cites is certain; and while 'flat-cakes' could be a double entendre for the female genitals in fr. 28, there is no obvious obscenity implied here. The Greeks delighted in descriptions of food for their own sake, and in particular Epicharmus' *Marriage of Hebe* seems to have been little more than a list of the different foods, mainly fish, consumed at the wedding-feast. For the form κλιβ- against κριβ-, see on fr. 26.

## Fragment 28

εἰς νύκτα may encourage a sexual interpretation. The speaker is not certainly a woman, nor is the subject of the verb (whatever lies behind αἰτίαι σύν) definitely feminine, though the fragment comes from the γυναικεῖοι. 'Flat-bread' (πλακοῦς) perhaps refers occasionally to the female genitals in Aristophanes (Henderson, 144), though none of the cases (Ar. *Pax* 869, 1359, *Eccl.* 223, *Pl.* 995) is particularly convincing.

**με †αἰτίαι σύν:** Hauler, following the various restored versions of Casaubon, Meineke (μ' ἑστιάσειν), and Botzon (μ' ἱστ-), wanted μ' ἱcτίαcεν, a plausible form. One or other of these corrections looks likely to be right. Kaibel's μελίτειον or μελιτίταν cὐν, though these are less attractive options (we would expect the quotation to contain a verb), could also easily be given an erotic sense (e.g. referring to vaginal secretions).

ἄρτωι πλακίται: the phrase only here, and πλακίται is hapax, though a fifth-century *defixio* from Selinus (Dubois, no. 38. 10) gives Πλακίτας as a man's name; πλακοῦς, however, is a generic word for a round, flat loaf of bread.

## Fragment 29

This slightly recalls Alc. fr. 140 μάρμαιρει δὲ μέγαc δόμοc | χάλκωι, παῖcα δὲ †ἄρηι κεκόcμηται cτέγα | λάμπραιcιν κυνίαιcιν κτλ. (describing a hall equipped with weapons ready for war, though this is unlikely to be the context here), and Ba. fr. 20B. 13 χρυcῶι δ' ἐλέφαντί τε μαρμαίρουcιν οἶκοι (the halls of Alexander of Macedon). These, and similar passages, may account for the variant ἐμάρμαιρεν here.

The scene is most likely sympotic. Day-to-day utensils would not be made of precious metals, but at elaborate banquets more expensive items would be displayed. Bacchylides' poem for Alexander is sympotic, and at the fantastic feast described by Philoxenus in his *Deipnon* (*PMG* 836), the tables are λιπαρῶπεc and λιπαραυγεῖc ((b). 1, (e). 1), the water-vessels silver ((a). 2), and the cups gold ((d). 1). Bronze tables (perhaps small bronze models rather than actual tables?) feature in the catalogue of temple contents at Epich. fr. 68. 1 (*Thearoi*), but οἰκία seems not to be used of temples. The internal rhyme χαλκωμάτων . . . ἀργυρωμάτων is noteworthy.

ἐγάργαιρεν: a rare verb, largely restricted to comedy (Cratin. fr. 321, Ar. fr. 375; cf. Timoth. *Pers.* 96 with my note), and so more likely to be changed to the common ἐμάρμαιρεν than the reverse.

## Fragment 30A

Both πελειάc and περιcτερά can be used as a generic name for a pigeon or dove, though the two are distinguished at Arist. *H.A.* 544^b2 and 597^b3, where the πελειάc appears to be the wild rock-pigeon (*Columba livia*) and the περιcτερά the domestic pigeon (*Columba livia domestica*).

## Fragment 31

Other instances of φίλα as a form of address in Sophron, and those in Herodas, suggest one woman is addressing another. Though Demetrius is not explicit, the fragment is therefore likely to be from the γυναικεῖοι.

Two main proposals have been suggested: (1) Wilamowitz (*Kl. Schr.* V 2. 64) thought of the custom of throwing leaves and garlands at a victorious athlete (cf. e.g. Pi. *P.* 9. 123 f. πολλὰ μὲν κεῖνοι δίκον | φύλλ᾽ ἔπι καὶ στεφάνους, of Alexidamus, the legendary ancestor of Telesicrates, for whom the ode is meant; also Callim. *Hec.* fr. 69. 11 Hollis with his note), and assigned the fragment to the [*Women watching the Isthmia*]. Epicharmus wrote a play called *Epinik(i)os*, but nothing is known about it except that it was in anapaestic catalectic tetrameters (Heph. *Ench.* 8. 2). (2) Botzon (1856), 7, and others think of nuptial rites, comparing e.g. Stesich. *PMGF* 187, where apples, myrtle leaves, violets, and roses are thrown in the way of a chariot probably to celebrate the marriage of Menelaus and Helen (cf. further Chariton 8. 1. 12, where the 'second wedding' of Chaereas and Callirhoe is celebrated in similar fashion). This may suggest a connection with *Busied about the Bride* (which also featured sympotic throwing; see ad loc.). Slightly against this suggestion is the plural ἄνδρας, though it could possibly refer to the bridegroom together with his party of friends.

In either case, the mythological comparison, probably intended by the speaker to imbue the event (s)he is describing with a poetic, heroic quality, deflates it by its actual content. The episode is mentioned in the Hypothesis to Sophocles' *Ajax*: περὶ δὲ τοῦ θανάτου τοῦ Αἴαντος διαφόρως ἱστορήκασιν. οἱ μὲν γάρ φασιν ὅτι ὑπὸ Πάριδος τρωθεὶς ἦλθεν εἰς τὰς ναῦς αἱμορροῶν, οἱ δὲ ὅτι χρησμὸς ἐδόθη Τρωσὶ πηλὸν κατ᾽ αὐτοῦ βαλεῖν (cf. also Dictys 4. 20; schol. Hom. *Il.* 14. 405b). R. C. Jebb (*Sophocles: Ajax* (Cambridge, 1896), 6) thought that it might derive ultimately from a satyr-play or comedy, but the source need not be so literary.

θᾶcαι: cf. fr. 25 n.

βαλλίζοντι: see fr. 11 n.

## Fragment 32

Perhaps of love or desire (cf. e.g. Theocr. 30. 21 τῶι δ᾽ ὁ πόθος καὶ τὸν ἔσω μύελον ἐσθίει), though the sense need not be metaphorical

164 Commentary

(e.g. X. *Eq.* 4. 2 ἐπειδὰν ἐνϲκιρωθῆι . . . τὰ νοϲήματα). M.L.W. suggests reading dative αὐτᾶι (cf. τῶι in the Theocritean passage) for αὐτάν.

## Fragment 33

ὑγιώτερον as if from *ὑγιόϲ; Athenaeus (2. 59 C) cites the same proverb for Epicharmus (fr. 152, in the correct form ὑγιέϲτερον (cod. C; -ώϲ- in E, but corrected to -εϲ-)). Epich. fr. 181 (cited by Eustathius from Philoxenus, *On Comparative Forms*) has several unexpected comparative (ἀλλιοέϲτερον, ἐπιηρεϲτέραν) and superlative (ἀναγκαιέϲτατον, ὡραιέϲταταν) forms; these may also be deliberate mistakes, unless forms in -έϲτεροϲ, -έϲτατοϲ were a particular feature of Syracusan or Sicilian Greek (note also Dinoloch. fr. 10 γενναιέϲτατον).

The saying is possibly attested again for Sophron at fr. *103. The gourd, a juicy fruit not unlike a watermelon, was not considered to provide much nourishment, but was thought valuable for dietary purposes on account of its moisture (e.g. Diphilus and Mnesitheus ap. Athen. 2. 58 B C).

## Fragment 34

For the sloppy hanging participle as an intentional solecism intended to imitate the realities of female speech, see above, pp. 14–15. The present ending -ει in the perfect seems, by contrast, to have been relatively standard for Syracusan. Herodian claims perfects in -ει for Epicharmus (fr. 188), which is partially borne out by e.g. γεγάθει in fr. 108. Forms in -ε are, however, attested elsewhere (frs. 11 πέποϲχε, 18. 3 τέτριγε, 158. 6 ἔοικε). Even the papyrus texts fluctuate: fr. 113 *fr.* 1. 10 has δέδοικ᾽ (i.e. δέδοικα) against δε]δοίκω at fr. 113 *fr.* 16. 157. Both forms were probably in use. Sophron himself has the pluperfects ἐπεπείγει and ἐπεποιήκει (not -ε) in fr. 4D. 39, 41.

For the form κιτών rather than χιτών, see J. Wackernagel, *Sprachliche Untersuchungen zu Homer* (Göttingen, 1916), 23, and cf. Greg. Cor., *De dial. Dor.* 151 (= gloss. 228 K–A ἰδίωϲ δὲ λέγουϲιν οἱ Ϲικελοὶ τὴν χύτραν κύτραν, τὸν χιτῶνα κιτῶνα).

## Fragment 35

'Desiring children', she engaged in copious amounts of sex? Obtained φάρμακα for fertility or potency?

ἅμα looks odd. Wilamowitz wanted ἄλλα (an easy scribal error), and this is printed in the Teubner editions (Paton–Pohlenz–Sieveking, 1929; Sieveking–Gärtner, 1997). But read perhaps ἃ γα: for the combination γα θην, cf. Epich. fr. 31. 2, and for θην see on fr. 23. The contracted participle δευμένα is paralleled by δεύμενος in a Thessalian inscription (*BCH* 59 (1935), 38). Sophron has δῆcθε from δέομαι at fr. 45, and uncontracted δεήcηι at fr. 155. In Attic the contraction of δεόμενος would produce δοῦμενος.

## Fragment 36

The δεκάλιτρον was equivalent to two drachmas (see on fr. 71).

## Fragment 38

Although the sources offer various confused readings, this is clearly a single fragment capable of being read in two ways. The scholia to *Acharnians* cite the fragment for the barytone Doric accentuation of the name Phales (perispomenon in Attic); but since the point is that the expression is a pun we cannot be sure that there is any basis to this.

ἀμφ' ἄλητα 'over the barley-meal' (ἄλητα is a syncopated form of ἀλήατα or ἀλείατα) is the primary reading. But κυπτάζει can have obscene overtones, as apparently also in fr. 40. Hipponax has the simple verb of Arete bending over (fr. 17 κύψαcα 'towards the lamp'), so that the speaker, probably imagined as Hipponax himself, can penetrate her sexually from behind (cf. Ar. *Thesm.* 488). The position was a popular one (Henderson on Ar. *Lys.* 231). The related adverb κύβδα at Archil. fr. 42 refers to a woman bending over and performing fellatio, and this is also the sense here (cf. further Ar. *Lys.* 17 with Henderson; Archil. fr. 45 κύψαντεc ὕβριν ἁθρόην ἀπέφλυcαν has also been taken to refer to fellatio, but see Bossi, 135–7). The joke thus depends on hearing ἀμφ' ἄλητα as ἀμ φάλητα 'over the penis'. Kaibel is suspicious of ἀνα with the accusative after κυπτάζω, but jokes do not always follow strict grammar.

## Fragment 39

See on fr. 18.

## Fragment 40

For the verb, see on fr. 38. Where ἐνθάδε refers to is unclear (another city? A part of Syracuse? Or simply a brothel?).

# II. MEN'S MIMES

## Messenger

**Title and Subject:** The title is preserved only by the Latin scholion on Aratus, not the Greek of which that is in large part a translation. The Latin scholion's authority is unknown, but *Nuntius* must translate Greek ἄγγελος. This suggests a connection with a little story told in a scholion to Theocr. 2. 12. After commenting on the relationship between Simaetha's invocation of Hecate and a passage in Sophron (= fr. *7), the scholion continues:

Ἥραν μιχθεῖσαν Διὶ γεννῆσαι παρθένον, ὄνομα δὲ αὐτῆι θέσθαι Ἄγγελον. ταύτην δὲ μετὰ τὴν γέννησιν ταῖς Νύμφαις δοθῆναι παρὰ τοῦ Διὸς τρέφεσθαι. αὐξηθεῖσαν δὲ κλέψαι τὸ τῆς Ἥρας μύρον, ὧι τὸ πρόσωπον αὐτῆς ἐθὰς ἦν χρίεσθαι, καὶ δοῦναι Εὐρώπηι τῆι Φοίνικος θυγατρί. αἰσθομένην δὲ τὴν Ἥραν ἐφορμῆσαι βουλομένην αὐτὴν κολάσαι. τηνικαῦτα μὲν τὸ πρῶτον εἰς γυναικὸς τετοκυίας οἶκον καταφυγεῖν, ἐκεῖθεν δὲ πρὸς ἄνδρας νεκρὸν φέροντας. ὅθεν τὴν μὲν Ἥραν ἀποστῆναι, τὸν δὲ Δία τοὺς Καβείρους κελεῦσαι ἀναλαβόντας καθᾶραι αὐτήν. ἐκείνους δὲ ἐπὶ τὴν Ἀχερουσίαν λίμνην ἀπαγαγόντας ἁγνίσαι. ὅθεν τὴν θεὸν ἀποκεκληρῶσθαι τοῖς τεθνεῶσι καὶ καταχθονίοισι φασίν.

(He relates that) Hera lay with Zeus, gave birth to a girl, and gave her the name *Angelos*. After her birth this girl was given by Zeus to the Nymphs to bring her up. When she was fully grown, she stole the myrrh with which Hera was accustomed to make up her face, and gave it to Europa, the daughter of Phoenix. When Hera discovered this, she flew at her and wanted to punish her. When this happened, Angelos sought refuge first at the house of a woman who had just given birth, then with some men who were carrying a corpse. And when Hera relented, Zeus ordered the Cabiri to take and purify her; so they took her and made her holy in the harbour Acherousia. So, they say, she was assigned as goddess to the dead (but perhaps we should emend to e.g. ταῖς τοκάσι 'to those in child-birth' (M.L.W.)) and those beneath the earth.

Ἄγγελος seems a strange name for a girl, but the scholion's suggestion that it was another name for Hecate appears to be supported by her association with the dead, and Hecate is also κουροτρόφος at Hes. *Th.* 450–2 (though see West ad loc. for doubts about the genuineness of these lines).[9] However, Hesychius (α 391) thinks that Ἄγγελος was a Syracusan name for Artemis, and it is possible that a local Sicel deity was variously assimilated to familiar Greek gods. The name need not be originally Greek at all.

The story is clearly paraphrased from somewhere, possibly Apollodorus' commentary, which could explain its presence in the scholia at this point. However, the mythological content would be surprising for one of Sophron's mimes, and Apollodorus may simply have related the story in passing, to explain or call attention to a particular detail. The fact that the one fragment quoted evidently begins an invocation (and perhaps a narrative) with heroic overtones does not mean that the mime contained a mythological story.

Fragment 41 may have been the opening line; it certainly looks like the beginning of a speech, and the scholion's point is that such openings were common in hymns. Messenger-speeches in tragedy do not begin in this way, but if the Ἄγγελος was indeed a real messenger, the line may have been intended to give a mock-heroic dignity to his narrative (whatever its content). The language is traditional, and there are suggestions of dactylic rhythm (note esp. ἀρχόμενος καλέω –⏑ ⏑–⏑ ⏑–). We find comic prayers and invocations with traditional elements elsewhere in Sophron (see on fr. 4A). That this may have introduced a suitably comic narrative (for example, like that in fr. 4D) is very possible.

### Fragment 41

ἐξ Ἑστίας ἀρχόμενος: it was usual to pray to Hestia first in prayers addressed to a large number of gods (MacDowell on Ar. *Vesp.* 845–6; Dunbar on *Av.* 865; Diggle on E. *Phaethon* 249–50; cf. Pi. *N.* 11. 6–7). Consequently, the phrase, more usually in the form ἀφ᾽ Ἑστίας, often had a simple metaphorical sense, 'beginning right from the start' (as at Ar. *Vesp.* loc. cit). Here it combines the

---

[9] A fifth-century inscription from Selinus (Arena no. 38) may read [τᾶ]ι [Ἀ]νγέλōι τᾶι hεκάται ἀνθέθεκε (M. T. Manni Piraino, *Kokalos* 21 (1975), 137–53, no. 53), but the supplement is doubted by Dubois (pp. 62 f.), who reads more tentatively [   ]‥ελοι.

language of traditional ritual with familiar colloquial under-
tones.

ἀρχαγέταν: often especially of gods in their role as founders of
a city, but Zeus πάντων ἀρχαγέτας is really just another way of
saying 'Zeus, ruler of all' (even though the epithet may have had
special resonance for an audience in the colonies of Magna
Graecia). [Terpander], *PMG* 698. 1 (= fr. 3 Gostoli) has Ζεῦ
πάντων ἀρχά, πάντων ἀγήτωρ, with much the same meaning (these
lines are almost certainly not by Terpander, and probably date to
the fifth century BC; see Gostoli ad loc.).

### The Fisherman against the Countryman[10]

**Title and Subject:** The title implies a debate between two
characters. We may infer that it focused on an argument between
a fisherman and a rustic farmer, each extolling the virtues of his
own way of life and criticizing the other's. This hypothesis seems
supported by the few fragments, two of which mention lowly
types of fish, and a third appears to be an abusive epithet for a
fisherman. Although one fragment is cited simply as appearing ἐν
τῶι Ἀγροιώτηι (fr. 44), doubtless the same mime is meant. Sicily
was particularly famed for its seafood (cf. A. Dalby, *Siren Feasts*
(London and New York, 1996), 113–29). The treatment of fish in
Attic comedy is covered in some detail by J. Davidson,
*Courtesans and Fishcakes* (London, 1997), 3–35.

Debate poems have a substantial history. There are several
Akkadian and Sumerian examples of debates which take place
largely between non-human participants,[11] like the olive and the

---

[10] For the form of the title, Kaibel compares the proverb ὁ Σικελὸς τὰν
θάλασσαν (Zenob. Ath. 2. 18 Bühler = Zenob. vulg. 5. 51), though the sense is of
course somewhat different. Dunbabin, 192 n. 1, suggests that ὁ Σικελός is not the
Greek Sicilian but the landlubberly Sicel; the analogous proverb 'the Cretan
(against?) the sea' is said to have been used of those who had knowledge but
pretended not to (Schol. Ael. Arist. *or.* 46. 138. 4; cf. Alcm. *PMG* 164), and is
there explicitly compared to ὁ Σικελὸς τὰν θάλασσαν.

[11] A Sumerian dispute (a genre which, like the Akkadian poems, more usually
involves non-human participants) opposes a Herdsman and a Farmer, as we
might expect for that region, and mythological competitions probably reflect
similar debates; cf. e.g. the familiar biblical story of Cain and Abel, the dispute
between the Sumerian gods Emesh and Enten for the favour of Enlil and the
position as the divine patron of farmers (S. N. Kramer, *Sumerian Mythology*
(Philadelphia, 1972), 49 ff.), or the conflict between Lahar and his sister Ashnan
(Kramer, 53 ff.).

laurel of Callim. *Iamb.* 4 (for the probable oriental origin of
which, see M. L. West, *HSCP* 73 (1969), 118 f., and *Melammu*,
1 (2000), 93–7; Kerkhecker, 86 with n.15). Non-human participants also probably featured as the speakers of Epicharmus'
*Earth and Sea*, which seems to have staged a debate between
those two elements. The remaining fragments are regrettably
largely uninformative, but there may have been some similarities
to Sophron's mime; certainly a large number of fish appear to
have been mentioned. The subject of Epicharmus' *Logos and
Logina* is even less clear; a contest between male and female
reason is possible, though the play was set in the mythological
world (fr. 76; cf. Pickard-Cambridge, 272) and the exact formation of *Λογίνα* unclear (see most recently Cassio, 69 f.). A
connection with Sophron's men's and women's mimes is tanta-
lizing, but impossible to substantiate. Moschus, poem 5, contains a comparison between the land and sea which Wilamowitz
(ap. Kaibel) conjectured derived in part from Sophron's
fisherman, but no clear point of contact can now be established.
P. Oxy. 425 is a little song in which the Nile boatmen compare
the sea unfavourably to their beloved river; cf. Ach. Tat. 4. 12.
1–4, which describes in mock-epic terms the conflict between the
Nile and the surrounding land.

## Fragment 42

Blennies 'are little fishes common in the rock-pools, often called
Butterfishes from the slime or mucus which they exude. Hence
their name, from βλέννοc = μύξα, slime or spittle' (Thompson,
32). They are rarely mentioned elsewhere, and were evidently
not a delicacy. The reference may therefore have been uncom-
plimentary; for example, the rustic mocking the fisherman's diet
or catch.

Fr. 144 claims for Sophron the form πλέννα rather than βλέννα
'slime', and possibly we should restore πλέννωι here.

## Fragment 44

The goby is a type of small, worthless fish, 'seldom eaten except
in the Mediterranean, and there only by the poor' (Thompson,
137). The second element in the compound derives from πλύνω
(though this is not elsewhere used of cleaning fish). But to
describe a fisherman as one who cleans or guts fish is clearly

insulting, even more so when the fish is a cheap one; the phrase would fit well in the mouth of a hostile landsman.

## The Tunafisher

**Title and Subject:** The Tunafisher himself was no doubt the main character;[12] his son with the punning name Cothonias was at least mentioned (fr. 46), but we do not know if he played a more developed role. The precise content of the mime is of course uncertain. Something is mixed in fr. 47; this may be poison, which is mentioned as a means of catching fish at e.g. Philostr. *Imag.* 1. 13 ἰδέαι μὲν οὖν καθ᾽ ἃς ἁλίϲκονται μυρίαι· καὶ γὰρ ϲίδηρον ἔϲτιν ἐπ᾽ αὐτοὺς θήξαϲθαι καὶ φάρμακα ἐπιπάϲαι καὶ μικρὸν ἤρεϲκε δίκτυον ὅτωι ἀπόχρη καὶ ϲμικρόν τι τῆϲ ἀγέληϲ. In the account of fishing with poison in Oppian, the fisherman is said to take white clay and cyclamen, μίξαϲ ἐν παλάμηιϲι δύω φυρήϲατο μάζαϲ (*H.* 4. 660); these he smears in the caves where the fish are to be found. This may account for fr. 48: the effect of poison on the eyes of fish is explicitly mentioned at Opp. *H.* 4. 666 f. ἀχλύϊ δ᾽ ὄϲϲε | καὶ κεφαλὴ καὶ γυῖα βαρύνεται. But A. fr. 308 R. τὸ ϲκαιὸν ὄμμα παραβαλὼν θύννου δίκην suggests the tuna was thought to possess a peculiar glance, and Sophron may be referring to no more than this. Fr. 45 clearly refers to greediness; perhaps the fisherman means the tuna's greediness in eating the bait left for them. The ancient literature on the tuna-fish is vast: for a summary, see Thompson, 79–90.

It is intriguing that Aelian (*N.A.* 15. 6) refers to this mime as τὸν ἡδὺν θυννοθήραν.

Possible further fragments: fr. 94 (see ad loc.), 113 (addressed to Cothonias?).

## Fragment 45

For the animal comparison, see on fr. 49. For criticism of gluttony in iambus, cf. Archil. fr. 167, and esp. Hippon. fr. 118b, where a greedy person is likened to a heron: λαιμᾶι δέ ϲοι τὸ χεῖλοϲ ὡϲ ἐρωιδιοῦ (cf. 118a. 2 καὶ γαϲτρὸϲ οὐ κατακρα[τεῖϲ).

ὄκκα is equivalent to Attic ὅταν, contracted from ὅκα + κα (for ὄκα as the West Greek equivalent to ὅτε, cf. fr. 15 n. and see Colvin, 203). For δῆϲθε (< δέ-εϲθε), see on fr. 35. On ὑμέων, see fr. 85.

## Fragment 47

εἴω is subjunctive (= Att. ἴω); see p. 22.

## Fragment 48

**λογάδαϲ:** of uncertain derivation; the word can refer to uncut stones (whence Hesychius' gloss ψήφουϲ λευκάϲ), and so to the eyes probably because of some notional similarity (Chantraine, s.v.). The fanciful derivations offered in the sources clearly begin very early, and Soranus' suggested connection with λοξόω is perhaps implied by Sophron himself.

### You'll frighten off boys

**Title and Subject:** ποιφύϲϲω can mean 'puff, snort', as of the dolphin at Anyte *HE* 710 f. (*AP* 7. 214), but Hesychius glosses ποιφύξειϲ as ἐκφοβήϲειϲ, and the context in which the title is quoted implies the same sense. Titles with such verbal elements are also found in Varro's Menippean satires.

The future verb in the title may suggest that the mime was a description of a person so ugly that he scares off any boy he happens to fall in love with, but the phrasing of fr. 49 perhaps implies that homosexuality in general was under attack; cf. esp. Callim. *Iamb.* 5, which advises a pederastic schoolmaster against seducing his pupils, but the theme is a frequent one in Greek literature. For criticism of adult pathic homosexuals on the Attic stage, see Henderson, 209–15, and for general attitudes, K. J. Dover, *Greek Homosexuality*[2] (Cambridge, Mass., 1989).

Possible further fragments: frs. 62, 63 (criticism of someone's homosexuality), 162? (see ad loc.).

## Fragment 49

The red mullet has distinctive barbels hanging from its mouth (Thompson, 264–8), rather like a beard (cf. fr. 30). Having a chin like a red mullet's therefore means to be bearded, and thus of mature age. The reference to the τριγόλα, an unidentified fish (mentioned again in fr. 66), is adequately explained by Tryphon (even if here 'a mere comic word', as Thompson, 268, suggests), and we may compare the many jokes in Attic comedy about anuses worn rough and thin by over-frequent buggery.

Animal comparisons are characteristic of iambus (e.g. Archil. fr. 43, Semon. frs. 7 *passim*, 18, Callim. *Iamb.* 2), and invective contexts generally (cf. *Il.* 1. 225; Cratin. fr. 314 = Eupol. fr. 120; Eupol. fr. 368).[13] A similar comparison appears in Sophron at fr. 45. But for the abusive phrases here, cf. esp. Epich. fr. 79 τὰς πλευρὰς οἶόνπερ βατίς, | τὰν δ' ὀπισθίαν †ἐχῆϲθ' ἀτενὲς οἶόνπερ βάτος, | τὰν δὲ κεφαλὰν ὀϲτέων οἶόνπερ ἔλαφος, οὐ βατίς, | τὰν δὲ λαπάραν ϲκορπίος †παῖς ἐπιθαλάττιος τεου. Corruptions in the text, and the lack of context, make this less than clear, but it almost certainly describes a person (cf. Kerkhof, 130). Closely parallel seems the description of Cleon at Ar. *Vesp.* 1034–5 = *Pax* 757–8 φωνὴν δ' εἶχεν χαράδρας ὄλεθρον τετοκυίας | φώκης δ' ὀϲμήν, Λαμίας δ' ὄρχεις ἀπλύτους, πρωκτὸν δὲ κάμηλου (on which see the commentators).

For the form ὀπιϲθίδια, which existed alongside the more common ὀπίϲθια (e.g. Epich. fr. 79. 3), see W. Schulze, *Kl. Schr.* (Göttingen, 1934), 72–3 n. 5, who compares the variation between ἐνδοϲθίδια and ἐνδόϲθια.

### Promythion

**Title and Subject:** Wilamowitz (*Kl. Schr.* IV. 161) compares the Sicilian word προμυθίκτρια, said to be an equivalent for προμνήϲτρια (Gloss. 250 K–A); these were women who assisted in arranging marriages. If this connection is correct, the mime may in fact have belonged to the γυναικεῖοι. Kassel–Austin object that the masculine participle μηλαφῶν in fr. 50 implies a male speaker, but see Sect. II for the presence of male characters in the women's mimes. Further attempts at establishing content are largely hopeless. Cataudella speculated that the *promythion* may have been sexual instruction of the sort provided for Daphnis by the old woman Palaestra in Longus' *Daphnis and Chloe*. In fr. 50 a sexual interpretation is perhaps not out of the question, but is hardly required, and is not the sense our source implies. More

[13] Cf. also the splendidly abusive Sumerian composition 'He is the Good Seed of a Dog' (ed. Å. Sjöberg, *Journal of Cuneiform Studies*, 24 (1972), 107–19), which begins: 'He is the good seed of a dog, a descendant of a wolf, | with the stench of a mongoose, a hyena cub . . ., a fox with the back of a crab, | A monkey from the mountain (whose) judgment is not good . . .'.

relevant than Palaestra could be Cleinias' instructions to Cleitophon on how to gain a woman's love at Ach. Tat. 1. 10. 1–7. Fr. 51 obviously suggests abuse or criticism (of a bride-groom?).

## Unplaced men's fragments

### Fragments 52, 54–6

All four fragments take as their subject the problems of old age. The sources for frs. 52 and 55 explicitly state that old men are talking, and so much may be inferred for the other two. I see no reason to connect fr. 53 with this group. Possibly we should imagine a single mime to which all four passages belong; one in which, for example, an old man lamented the state age had brought him to. Fr. 52 may imply a sympotic or feasting setting. The theme, however, recurs in Greek literature with depressing frequency from Homer and the archaic poets on; cf. e.g. Mimn. frs. 1–6, Semon. fr. 1. 11 ff., Anacr. *PMG* 395 etc., and see in general F. Preisshofen, *Untersuchungen zur Darstellung des Greisenalters in der frühgriechischen Dichtung* (Wiesbaden, 1977); U. Mattioli (ed.), *Senectus: La vecchiaia nel mondo classico* (Bologna, 1995).

### Fragment 52

ἄγκυρα is said at Epich. fr. 189 to be a slang word for the penis. The image obviously depends on the visual similarity of the anchor with its two arms and central stock, and the (erect?) penis and testicles (on ancient anchors, see L. Casson, *Ships and Seamanship in the Ancient World*² (Baltimore and London, 1995), 250–8). A similar innuendo probably applies at Herod. 1. 41–2. The adjective ὁμότριχας no doubt reflects the frequent reference to grey or white hair as a sign of age; cf. e.g. Sa. fr. 58, Anacr. *PMG* 358, 395, and of course many other passages. For τηλίκος of old age in particular, cf. e.g. Thgnd. 578.

Henderson (p. 161), noting that nautical metaphors are common for sexual activity, suggests that sex is also at issue here. But 'putting *into* port' would be a more natural image for sexual intercourse (e.g. Ar. *Eccl.* 1106), and a joke about the incontinence of old men is perhaps more likely; for the subject in Aristophanes, cf. Ar. *Lys.* 402, 550; *Vesp.* 807 ff, 858, 935, 940,

946, 1127 f.; *Thesm.* 611 f. etc. 'Putting out to sea' could well be a metaphor for urinating. ποντῖναι is clearly corrupt; it cannot be an error for a form of πόντιος (or its feminine ποντίας). M.L.W. suggests the sense should be 'weak, rotten'; this is attractive, though it is hard to see what word the corruption would conceal. Ποντικαί is perhaps another possibility: 'men of a certain age have Pontic pricks'; their penises, like Pontus, are seemingly full of an endless supply of water. R. Janko wonders (per litt.) whether the nautical language may indicate that the old men are fishermen.

ὦν = Att. οὖν (although the words may not be etymologically related; cf. Denniston, 415 f.). There are several attestations of ὦν in Epicharmus (frs. 35. 6, 35, 113. 110 and 251, 122. 3), to be contrasted with non-Doric forms in the Pseudepicharmea (οὖν four times in fr. 277).

## Fragment 53

A ξυσμά is an itch or irritation, equivalent to ξυσμός (the more common word), and it is the itch which is causing the speaker to scratch himself so violently (κνυζοῦμαι is middle rather than passive). The verb ἱππάζεται is striking, but may be intended to suggest the activity of e.g. a flea jumping from one place to the next.

At fr. 147 a choregos (which may mean here the poet rather than the chorus-leader; cf. Epich. fr. 13) scratches himself (again the verb ξύεται is more probably middle than passive). The same source quotes immediately before this the phrase from Sophron: 'if someone scratches the scratcher . . .'. While these two phrases may belong to the same mime, there is no reason to think they are protasis and apodosis. Possibly there is a hint here of a mime which involved an unforeseen bout of itching (due to fleas or lice?) attacking a chorus, with predictably comic results. (Epicharmus' *Choreuts* or *Dancers* may be relevant, but we know nothing of its content.) The expression τὸν ξύοντα ἀντιξύειν was proverbial, at least in later times, and could be used either of returning a favour ('you scratch my back . . .'), or of requiting an evil (see the passages cited by Kassel–Austin on fr. 147. 1). But τις as the subject sits slightly uncomfortably with a proverbial usage; we must allow for the possibility that Sophron was the originator of the expression, and that here it had a literal force.

## Fragment 54

Old age can be said to pickle or preserve one because of the imaginative connection between youthfulness and moisture in Greek (see A. Lorenzoni, *Eikasmos*, 3 (1992), 80 n. 19).

## Fragment 55

ξύcιλοc is hapax, and of uncertain meaning. LSJ gloss it as 'shaven, smooth', and Chantraine explains 'teigneux (?), dit d'un vieillard, terme expressif bâti sur un radical ξυc-'. There may be, but is not certainly, a connection with ξύω, as the sources imply. However, even granted that ξύcιλοc alludes to a skin condition of some sort, the sense of the exchange is still unclear. Our main sources imply that cῦφαρ refers to wrinkled skin, which would also account for Hesychius' gloss (c 2820) cῦφαρ· γῆραc, τὸ ὑπέρτατον· οἱ δὲ τὸ τοῦ ὄφεωc καὶ τὸ ἐρ⟨ρ⟩υτιδωμένον cῦκον. καὶ τὸ ἐπὶ τοῦ γάλακτοc τροφῶδεc (schol. Nic. *Alex.* 91 also says that the Siceliotes used cῦφαρ for the skin on milk; cf. further Callim. *Hec.* fr. 74. 11 Hollis with his note). Perhaps the skin meant is the old man's penis; δέρμα alludes to the foreskin at Ar. *Eq.* 29, and 'fig' is a slang word for the male genitals at e.g. Ar. *Pax* 1351 and elsewhere. This may explain ἀντ' ἀνδρόc; the man has become impotent with age, and this is represented by his permanently limp and shrivelled penis.

Kaibel took the exchange between the two old men to be abusive, and suggested that something like ξύcιλοc τύ γ' ἐccί preceded the quoted fragment. But it is just as (if not more) likely that one of the old men is talking self-pityingly about himself or that a third person is being abused.

For τί γάρ 'what else', see Denniston, 84–5.

## Fragment 56

Sophron has genitive τῶ and -ω here and in fr. 86, but τοῦ and -ου at frs. 82, 96, and perhaps *171. The evidence from Epicharmus is mixed: in papyrus we find τοῦ Λευκάρου at fr. 113. 249, and τῶ corrected into τοῦ at fr. 135. 1. Of course, it is possible that Epicharmus' (or Sophron's) own text would have made no orthographic distinction between these two forms (above, III. B, introd.), in which case the 'genuine' Syracusan form, while we would prima facie expect it to be -ω, is difficult to guess. See also Cassio, 61.

For the particle θην, see on fr. 23, and for τῆνοc (= (ἐ)κεῖνοc), cf. p. 22.

## Fragment 57

The speaker is calling to someone just sighted; the question is provoked by something about his appearance. This need not be anything genuinely martial (military expeditions seem unlikely to play a part in Sophron's mimes); δόρυ and other such words were common slang for the (erect) penis.

For ὦ οὗτοc, cf. e.g. Ar. *Vesp.* 1364 ὦ οὗτοc οὗτοc, τυφεδανὲ καὶ χοιρόθλιψ (interestingly, but probably only coincidentally, also in an erotic context).

## Fragment 58

επικαζε is hopelessly corrupt. Botzon (1867), 15, suggests ἐπίαζε (Dor. πιάζω = πιέζω 'press upon'); Guttentag (in Schneider's edition of Apollonius) ἐπείκαζε 'guess' (perhaps the easiest solution), Kaibel ἐπείραζε 'attempt', and there are other possibilities. But without a context we cannot begin to imagine what the sense should be.

The position of τυ further complicates matters. We expect enclitics to attract themselves to the second position in a sentence ('Wackernagel's Law'), and Doric τυ seems to be no exception. In almost all literary instances it is attracted to the second main position, or as close as possible to it (frs. 4A. 17, 78; Epich. fr. 44. 1 ἐκάλεcε γάρ τυ τιc; Alcm. (?) *PMGF* 168 καί τυ φίλιππον ἔθηκεν; Ar. *Ach.* 730 (Megarian); Theocr. 1. 82, 5. 74; and elsewhere) and the meagre inscriptional evidence supports this (e.g. Collitz 3339. 70 αἴ τύ κα ὑγιῆ ποιήcω (Epidaurus)). Only Callim. epigr. 46. 9 Pf., οὐδ' ὅcον ἀττάραγόν τυ δεδοίκαμεc, breaks the rule. See Wackernagel, *Kl. Schr.* I. 12. Guttentag suggests τι, but this would still be enclitic and does not solve the problem at all.

ὁ δεῖν(α) is colloquial, 'so-and-so' or 'that chap' (cf. Dover on Ar. *Ra.* 918).

## Fragment 59

The peripatetic Chamaeleon used a very similar phrase in response to the abuse of Seleucus in 370/1 BC (Mnem. ap. Phot. *Bibl.* 224 = *FGrH* 434 F 7):

Σέλευκος παροξυνθεὶς τούς τε πρὸς αὐτὸν ἀφικομένους πρέсβεις ἀπειλητικοῖс
ἐξεφαύλιζε λόγοις καὶ κατέπληττεν, ἑνὸς τοῦ Χαμαιλέοντος οὐδὲν
ὀρρωδήсαντος τὰς ἀπειλάς, ἀλλὰ φαμένου· Ἡρακλῆς κάρ⟨ρ⟩ων, Σέλευκε
(κάρρων δὲ ὁ ἰсχυρότεροс παρὰ Δωριεὺсιν). ὁ δ' οὖν Σέλευκος τὸ μὲν ῥηθὲν οὐ
сυνῆκεν, ὀργῆс δ' ὡς εἶχε καὶ ἀπετρέπετο.

Kaibel (*Abh. Kgl. Ges. Wiss. Gött.* II 4 (1898), 49 n. 2), followed
by Wilamowitz (*Die Textgeschichte der griechischen Lyriker*
(Berlin, 1900), 28) and Jacoby (ad loc.), thought that this was a
direct quotation of Sophron. Wehrli (on Chamaeleon, fr. 1)
expresses doubts, and the phrase could easily have been proverbial; cf. Theophr. *Char.* 16. 8 (adduced by Kassel–Austin),
where the Superstitious Man exclaims Ἀθηνᾶ κρείττων to avert
the ill omen caused by an owl's hooting.

ἦс was the original form of the third person singular, with a
corresponding plural ἦν (contracted from earlier ἦεν). Both
forms were retained in West Greek, whereas in Attic the third
person plural was reformed with -сαν from the *s*-aorist, producing ἦсαν, and the form ἦν replaced singular ἦс. Epicharmus
has plural ἦν in frs. 58, 85, 52, 122. 6, and singular (ἐν)ἦс at fr. 58;
cf. Cassio, 56 f. (who, however, also seeks to defend παρῆсαν as
genuine Epicharmus in fr. 275. 1, which Kassel–Austin more
reasonably treat as Pseudepicharmea).

κάρρων (also at fr. 116, Epich. fr. 163, Alcm. *PMGF* 105, and
the little Spartan song at *PMG* 870. 3) is equivalent to Att.
κρείссων.

## Fragment 60

Cf. ἐγγυάсαсθαι . . . θōκέοντας in a Gelan inscription of the fifth
century (Dubois, no. 134a. 2, 4). For ὑμές, see on fr. 4A. 12; for
θωκεῖτε, on fr. 4A. 6.

## Fragment 61

Archonidas is a common enough name in Sicily as elsewhere,
and the character here is probably not the Sicel king mentioned
at Thuc. 7. 1. 4 as a friend of the Athenians, and recently dead in
414 (cf. also Diod. Sic. 12. 8. 2).

ὑμέ is the standard West Greek form as opposed to Attic ὑμᾶс
(Colvin, 195), and is also cited by Apollonius for Alcman
(*PMGF* 85) and attested for West Greek in Cretan (F. Halbherr
and M. Guarducci, *Inscriptiones Creticae* (Rome, 1935), I 7. 3).

We find it as a marker of Megarian at Ar. *Ach.* 737, 739, and of Laconian at *Lys.* 87, 1076.

## Fragment 62

The murex is a greedy carnivore, but 'greediness' here perhaps refers to sexual appetite (so R. Janko (per litt.) ); cf. fr. 63. For λίχνος in this sense, cf. e.g. Callim. fr. 196. 45 (*Iamb.* 6) with Kerkhecker, 162 with n. 80. Ahrens (p. 446) proposed reading λιχνοτέραν, and thus linking this fragment with fr. 63 (an accusation of lechery).

## Fragment 63

καταπύγων does not always imply homosexuality: K. Dover (in Willi, 94) notes that it is simply an antonym of cώφρων at Ar. *Nub.* 529, and is used of female sexual insatiability at *Lys.* 137. But here the connection with male homosexual activity is obviously effective, and a connection with *You'll frighten off boys* is tempting.

We would expect the comparative to be -πυγονεcτέραν, but occasional stems in -ον substitute -ο for -ον (thus producing the form here -πυγο-τέραν), as with e.g. πίων, but πιότεροc and πιότατοc. Aristophanes has an irregular comparative καταπυγωνέcτεροc at *Lys.* 776.

## Fragment 65

'Well-fed' translates Kaibel's τραφεράι (for which he compared [Theocr.] 21. 44 καὶ τιc τῶν τραφερῶν ὠρέξατο, of fish nibbling at a fisherman's bait). Casaubon's ῥαφίδι is inappropriate (although a word for fish at Epich. fr. 45) for the sprat. The datives recall those in fr. 42, and the two fragments were joined by Botzon (1867), 12.

## Fragment 66

For the unidentified τριγόλα, see on fr. 49. The relevance of the epithets here is unclear.

## Fragments 67–8, 72

Epial(t)es is the personification of nightmare. The demon's name was probably originally ἐφιάλτηc, which popular etymology connected with ἠπίαλοc by way of the doublet ἐπίαλοc, since nightmares bring on a cold sweat like that caused by fever. An image strikingly similar to Sophron's appears at Ar. *Vesp.* 1037 f. where Cleon is said to have taken in hand the ἠπιάλοιϲ . . . | οἳ τοὺϲ πατέραϲ τ᾽ ἦγχον νύκτωρ καὶ τοὺϲ πάππουϲ ἀπέπνιγον. Nightmares throttle their fathers because the dreamer is imagined as the father of the dream (Sommerstein ad loc.); as Demetrius indicates, the image was a standard one, and we need not see a direct connection between Aristophanes and Sophron. See further W. H. Roscher, *Ephialtes, Abh. Sächs. Ges. Wiss.* XX 2 (1900), 48–53; Chantraine s.v.

Roscher (op. cit. 52–3; cf. *RhM* 58 (1898), 179) speculates that fr. 68 reflects a myth in which Heracles fought with and defeated Epial(t)es, just as in other accounts he wrestled with old age or with death (Hesiod, *Th.* 212, makes both Death and Dreams children of Night), as in Euripides' *Alcestis*; and thus that in the passage from Aristophanes' *Wasps* Cleon is being presented as a second Heracles. It is unlikely that Sophron would have told such a myth (if it existed) in any detail. Crusius (p. 88) more plausibly links the two fragments in a hostile exchange: 'Are you (like) Nightmare who strangles his father? Then I'll be (like) Heracles . . .'. This hardly requires a current myth to make sense; Heracles was a well-known defeater of such monsters.

Fr. 72 could also belong in such an exchange: the hedgehog is λαβεῖν μὲν ῥᾴδιον, ϲυνέχειν δὲ χαλεπόν, according to Aelian (*V.H.* 4. 14), in a passage which owes something to Archilochus, though the comparison is probably Aelian's own (= Archil. fr. 302; see West, *Studies*, 138, on the problems associated with the text). Kaibel rightly notes that strangling a hedgehog could be thought more dangerous to the strangler than to the hedgehog itself: 'you'll find you're strangling a hedgehog' would thus mean roughly 'you'll get more than you bargained for'.

Heracles was a popular figure in Magna Graecia, with which he had close mythological connections. No fewer than six of Epicharmus' plays dealt with his adventures (*Alcyoneus, Busiris, Marriage of Hebe, Muses,* and two *Heracles* comedies), he was the hero of three of Stesichorus' poems (*Geryoneis, Cerberus, Cycnus*), and Rhinthon also wrote a *Heracles*.

### Fragment 71

The λίτρα was a local weight, like the νοῦμμος (νόμος) and οὐγκία/ὀγκία, perhaps of Sicel origin and borrowed thence into Latin and Sicilian Greek (see above, p. 23), where it acquired standard status. It was worth one-fifth of the Syracusan or Attic drachma. Larger amounts were thus also calculated in *litra* rather than drachmas (so a *dekalitron* = didrachm; *pentekonta-litron* = decadrachm); see Pollux 4. 174–5; Diod. Sic. 11. 26. 3; Dunbabin, 190.

### Fragment *73

Morychus was a Sicilian epithet of Dionysus, allegedly because his face was smeared with wine (< μορύccω; see Bechtel, *Spitz-namen*, 53, Chantraine, Frisk, s.v.), and Polemon wrote on Syracusan matters ἐν τῶι περὶ τοῦ Μορύχου. The anecdote looks as if it belongs in the realm of folk-narrative, a popular, rationaliz-ing attempt to explain why the statue of Dionysus Morychus (cf. Lippold, *RE* III A 1 (1927), 158) stood outside his temple rather than inside the sanctuary as was usual.[14]

Ahrens (p. 467) made the attribution, which, if right, requires Kaibel's restoration of ἐccί and κάθηι (or εἰμί and κάθημαι, if the first person is preferred from Photius to the second-person forms in other sources).

## III. UNPLACED FRAGMENTS

### Fragment 74

For the sense of λειοκόνιτοc, cf. Hesych. λ 532, who glosses it as ἡ τελείωc εἰc κόνιν διαλελυμένη; λείωc stands for τελείωc as at Archil. fr. 226. The line could be addressed to Koikoa or another unfor-tunate slave. The reading [λε]ι[ο]κό[νε]ιτε is difficult to avoid in fr. 16 (ει for ι is so common in papyrus texts that we hardly need to cite parallels), which encourages the view that Koikoa is meant.

For πεῖ = ποῦ, cf. fr. 4A. 8. ἐccί is the usual West Greek form of the second person singular (= Att. εἶ).

---

[14] In Attic comedy Morychus is the name of a glutton (see Ar. *Pax* 1008 with the references provided by Olson ad loc.); he appears to have been a real person (cf. Pl. *Phaedr.* 227 B).

## Fragment 75

M.L.W. suggests 'where are you burrowing into the inner place', to which we could possibly give an obscene sense. The language slightly recalls the imagery at frs. 38, 40. μυχός could in this case perhaps refer to the vagina, though it is not so used anywhere else. Wünsch (pp. 112 f., 118), on the other hand, assigns the line to the *Women who say they are expelling the goddess*, seeing similarities to the abuse of Thestylis at the start of Theocr. 2.

πῦϲ is equivalent to Attic ποῖ, and we find relative ὗϲ(περ) in papyrus at Epich. fr. 97. 11. Ahrens (p. 474) suggested the form should instead be ποῖϲ (an expanded form of the basic ποῖ), but for the derivation, see Schwyzer, i. 621 n. 10, Cassio, 77 n. 80.

## Fragment 77

For the form, cf. Hesych. ω 522 ὤψεον· . . . ἰδεῖν ἐβούλοντο.

## Fragment 78

For the position of τυ, see on fr. 58.

## Fragment 79

Perhaps the denouement of a mime? LSJ translate δυϲθαλίαι as 'misfortunes', which must be the rough sense. Archytas ap. Stob. 3. 1. 107 has εὐθάλεια metaphorically of the 'bloom' of happiness, with the second term from θάλεια (as opposed to θαλία). But even if we read δυϲθάλεια here, as Kaibel tentatively suggested, the word would still most naturally mean an unfortunate state of affairs.

## Fragment 80

For ἥϲϲων (= Att. ἥττων), see p. 20.

## Fragment 82

Archestratus praises the head of the conger-eel, and it features frequently in culinary catalogues (see Archestr. fr. 19. 1 (*SH* 149) with Olson–Sens; Thompson, 49–50).

The genitives in -ου here contrast with those in -ω at frs. 56 (see ad loc.) and 86.

## Fragment 83

Translation uncertain. The manuscript does not accent οι δω, and the articulated forms (οἱ δῶ) are Blomfield's ((1826), 357). δῶ would be aorist subjunctive, but the force remains unclear. In his edition of Apollonius, Schneider suggests future δωcῶ 'I won't give' (cf. Theocr. 3. 36 καὶ δωcῶ οἱ) or 'I won't let . . .', a simple correction, especially given the fact that Cώφρων follows immediately in the text. The question mark is Kassel's.

## Fragment 84

For the aorist ἐcτράφθη, cf. Hesych. c 1975. Theocr. 7. 132 has (Doric) cτραφθέντεc (Att.-Ion. would have cτρεφ-).

## Fragment 85

Cf. Theocr. 15. 68 (a poem based on Sophron) ἀπρὶξ ἔχευ . . . ἁμῶν, where Praxinoa advises her slave Eunoa to stick close to her and Gorgo as they make their way through the Alexandrian crowds, but the context need not be the same here.

Apollonius' distinction between the two forms is contradicted by possessive ὑμέων at fr. 45.

## Fragment 86

The verb should mean either 'hits, strikes' or the exact opposite, but the form is quite unclear. None of the suggested emendations really convinces. While it seems somewhat improbable that the first term should be connected with ζυγόν, no other word readily suggests itself. 'Shooting in the dark' was also an expression of Alcaeus' (fr. 437), but it is unlikely that we have a direct allusion here. The phrase can easily be understood as a common, probably proverbial metaphor. Neither passage is provided with a context.

Apollonius claims that ὧν is possessive (= αὐτῶν, 'any one *of them*'). Wilamowitz (*Kl. Schr.* II. 134 n.) suggested that this interpretation was in fact erroneous, and proposed reading ὧν (= Att. οὖν, as at fr. 52). For the genitive τῶ, see on fr. 56 (on the gender of cκότοc, see Barrett on E. *Hipp.* 192).

## Fragment 88

Apollonius is illustrating the use of ὑμίν, but the translation is unclear. The δίφροc (or δρίφοc?) is probably a woman's stool as at fr. \*\*10 (see my note), and ἐπημμένον looks as if it could be a form of ἔφημαι, equivalent to the standard ἐφήμενος. Alcaeus has ἐπήμενοι in an uncertain sense at fr. 58. 14, though 'sitting' does not there seem very appropriate.

For τοι . . . ὑμίν, cf. fr. 96.

## Fragment 89

The meaning of the fragment is beyond sensible conjecture. For the form ψιν, see p. 21.

## Fragment 90

For the form ψε, see p. 21. We expect West Greek dialects to have -μες in the first-person plural rather than -μεν, and the usage is widely attested in literary texts (e.g. Alcm. *PMGF* 1. 12, Theocr. 15. 15) as in inscriptions (see Colvin, 210 f.). Ahrens' correction here is hardly to be doubted.

## Fragment 91

τὸ λᾶιον is literally the crop at Theocr. 10. 21, 42 (and see Wilamowitz, *Kl. Schr.* V 1. 374 n. 3), but here we may have a reference to depilation. The verb, ἐκτίλλω, is common in such contexts; cf. esp. fr. 167 (depilation of the female genitals) and perhaps Hippon. fr. 114a (plucking the anus). But the practice was not restricted to the genitalia. Wealthier women at least employed slaves (called παρατιλτρίαι: see LSJ s.v. and cf. e.g. Cratin. fr. 275), one of whom may be addressed here, who were charged with the rather unpleasant task of plucking their mistress's limbs. For the practice of depilation generally, see further Olson on Ar. *Pax* 892–3, Henderson on *Lys.* 87–9.

## Fragment \*93

As a form of address, μᾶτερ is primarily used to one's mother, though it can occasionally be used in other contexts as a general term of respect (see Dickey, 78 f., who cites Alexander's use of μῆτερ to the mother of Darius at Diod. Sic. 17. 37. 6 with Diodorus' own remarks on the usage). The use of πάτερ from Homer onwards as a rough equivalent to 'sir' is comparable (see Dickey, loc. cit., and e.g. Timoth. *Pers.* 154 with my note).

## Fragment 94

The expression is probably jocular (so Kassel–Austin), like the comparable 'unbacchic water' at Timoth. *Pers.* 62–3 (with my note). In Antipater of Thessalonica (*AP* 9. 305 = *GP* 267 ff.) Dionysus humorously advises the poet against water-drinking (ὕδατος ἀκρήτου κεκορημένωι ἄγχι παραστάς | χθιζὸν ἐμοὶ λεχέων Βάκχος ἔλεξε τάδε κτλ.), and at Ach. Tat. 4. 18. 4–5 the water of the Nile is praised because it is pure enough to drink without wine; this may also be humorous, though the purity of Nile water is a topos going back at least to [A.] *Pr.* 812 (cf. also Heliod. 2. 28, where Calasiris explains why the Nile is so good to drink). Hauler (p. 125 n. 2) saw a connection with the Tunafisher of fr. 47.

## Fragment 95

ἐλίγματα are wraps or wrappings which one wears on the head, thus 'some form of coif or snood' (Gow–Page on Ephippus, *HE* 1960); Botzon (1867), 7, saw a connection with [*Women watching the Isthmia*], comparing Theocr. 15. 78 f. τὰ ποικίλα πρᾶτον ἄθρησον, | λεπτὰ καὶ ὡς χαρίεντα, but these are *tapestries* which Gorgo is praising. Instead, cf. perhaps 15. 21, where Praxinoa puts on a shawl and wrap (ἀμπέχονον; for the sense see Gow ad loc.); ornately embroidered wraps may at first sight seem odd for lowly folk like Theocritus' (and presumably Sophron's) women, but Theocr. 15. 36 emphasizes the decoration and cost of Praxinoa's dress.

## Fragment 96

The context of this is quite unclear; there were two harbours, a larger and a smaller, at Syracuse (Thuc. 7. 22. 1; Diod. Sic. 14. 7. 3). Perhaps a fisherman or even fishmonger is speaking, describing either his catch or his wares; Kaibel thought of a connection with *The Fisherman against the Countryman*. It is just possible that these shellfish are metaphorical like those in frs. 23–4, since λιμήν would obviously be an apt word to describe the female genitals. But what sense should then be given to μελαινίδες is in that case unclear.

For τοι . . . ἐμίν, cf. τοι . . . ὑμίν at fr. 88, and see Schwyzer, ii. 581.

## Fragment 97

A type of sea-urchin (Thompson, 249; F. Skoda, *Rev. Phil.* 111
(1985), 77–85).

## Fragment 98

Archestratus praises the moray caught in the Sicilian straits
(fr. 17 Olson–Sens (*SH* 147); cf. Plin. *N.H.* 9. 169), and it is
also mentioned as a food at e.g. Epich. fr. 89. But the word could
also be used as an abusive term to describe people (e.g. A. *Ch.*
994, adesp. com. fr. 156), since the eel was notoriously aggressive
and unpleasant (Ar. *Ra.* 474–5; Nic. *Th.* 823–5; Opp. *H.* 1.
141–2). Either could be the case here, though the invective fish-
comparisons at fr. 49 (also fr. 45?) may encourage the latter interpretation.

## Fragment 100

Alexis (fr. 120. 2) says κάνθαρον καταστρέψοντα of draining a cup,
and cf. also Hor. *Sat.* 2. 8. 39 f. *invertunt Allifanis vinaria tota* |
*Vibidius Balatroque* (they empty whole wine-flasks into their
cups). However, wine may not be meant here. Sophron's fragment is probably addressed to a child, since unlike παῖς, τέκνον
was not normally used to slaves (Dickey, 65–72): note also the
address to someone's mother at fr. *93 and the presence of
children in Sophron's mimes is perhaps implied by Choricius at
fr. 102.

## Fragment 101

ἐκρατηρίχθημες is aorist of κρατηρίζειν (for the form, see
Wackernagel, *Kl. Schr.* ii. 860 ff.; Schwyzer, i. 772), literally 'to
drink from a krater' but in some contexts with a ritual sense,
referring specifically to consuming a sort of sacramental drink
(cf. Dem. 18. 259 with Wankel, and the expression κρητηρισμός
in an Erythraean inscription of the second half of the fourth
century BC relating to the cult of the Corybantes (H. Engelmann
and R. Merkelbach, *Die Inschriften von Erythrai und Klazomenai*
(Bonn, 1972–3), no. 206. 6–12 = F. Sokolowski, *Lois sacrées de
l'Asie Mineure* (Paris, 1955), no. 23), with H. Wankel, *ZPE* 34
(1979), 79–80). It is at least possible that the joke in Sophron also
belongs in a ritual context ('we got drunk on sacramental wine').

### Fragment *103

The second phrase, 'healthier than a gourd' is attested for
Sophron at fr. 33 (see ad loc.), but also for Epicharmus (fr. 152),
and was clearly proverbial. There is no guarantee that Sophron
also used the first. 'Balder than a clear sky' (also at Phot.
p. 638,14 = *Suda*, φ 38) evokes the image of a sky with only a few
wisps of cloud, like the few wisps of hair on a bald man's head.

### Fragment 104

The idle chatterer is a Theophrastan type (*Char.* 3). Boulias may
belong in the lawcourts (cf. the proverb Βουλίας δικάζει; Zenob.
vulg. 2. 86; cf. Zenob. Ath. 3. 26 = vulg. 2. 67), and Battarus'
defence speech in Herod. 2 is often compared; but Hutchinson
(p. 243 n. 47) points out that while Battarus rambles a little and
his material is poorly organized, he sticks closer to the point than
Demetrius implies Boulias did.

### Fragment 105

Those who cut up cumin are mean and parsimonious people (e.g.
Ar. *Vesp.* 1357 with MacDowell, Theocr. 10. 55 with Gow); and
a person who 'scrapes the ladle' (with his tongue or another
implement?), a proverb otherwise unknown, will equally be one
who ensures that absolutely nothing goes to waste. Alcaeus (fr.
438) used the expression 'he drew the lion from its claw' with the
sense of someone judging a large matter from a small and
insignificant part of it (and the expression is widely attested elsewhere: see Leutsch on Diogen. 5. 15); Sophron's use will not of
course be a reminiscence, and there is no reason to doubt that he
could have used the same phrase with a different meaning. Since
Demetrius is illustrating Sophron's tendency to collocate
proverbs, it seems most likely that all three sayings should be
given the same sense and be assumed to come from the same
mime.

For the genitive τοῦ, see on fr. 56.

### Fragment *106

Herodian's account of the verbal form is difficult to believe.
Wilamowitz (ap. Kaibel) suggested πλαδ- (cf. πλαδαρός 'damp'
and related words).

## Fragment 107

The use of ἐρυθραί as an epithet for dildoes at fr. 25 may be relevant: see ad loc.

## Fragment 115

θαύμακτρον should mean 'money paid to see a conjurer's trick' (LSJ); cf. the parallel formations δίδακτρον, μήνυτρον, μαυλιστήριον (Hippon. fr. 160), but it is hard to see how this relates to the second half of the sentence. Blomfield (1811), 387, thought that the first element should perhaps be understood as θυμ-, comparing the formation θυμιατήριον 'censer', and assigned the fragment to the *Women who say they are expelling the goddess*. Kaibel suggested writing θύμακτρον, which would refer to the money paid to hired sacrificers or exorcists (cf. frs. 3, 4A?, though the fragment probably belongs with neither). But θαύμακτρον could be meant to be deliberately dismissive of the abilities of such persons.

## Fragment *116

Kaibel's καὶ κάρρων ⟨ὁ⟩ βῶς is appealing. For κάρρων, see on fr. 59.

## Fragment 117

The whole of this is very confused. Apollonius (*pron.* p. 64,10 Schn.) refers to comic formations in -τερος (ἕνεκα γελοίου ἡ κωμωιδία cχήματά τινα ἔπλαcεν, ὥcτε οὐ κριτήριον τῆc λέξεωc τὸ αὐτότεροc, ἐπεὶ καὶ Δαναώτατοc ὑπερτίθεται παρὰ Ἀριcτοφάνει, τῶν κυρίων οὐ cυγκρινομένων; see also on 'intentional solecisms', pp. 14f., and cf. Epich. fr. 5), and R. Renehan (*HSCP* 87 (1983), 22), defending Sappho fr. 111. 6 ἄνδροc μεγάλω πολὺ μέζον ('much taller than a tall man', i.e. extremely tall), thinks that Sophron could have said οἶοc οἰότερον or προβάτου προβάτερον (following conjectures by Ahrens) and meant 'more sheepish than a sheep' (cf. LSJ, s.v.); cf. Sa. fr. 156 χρύcω χρυcοτέρα (and we say 'whiter than white'). But Herodian's text is too corrupt for any certainty.

## Fragment 118

For the form χρέομαι, see p. 19.

## Fragment 122

The reference is to a board game like draughts or chess, the rules of which are no longer known. Clearly, however, one playing piece was positioned on a line from which it would be moved only in special circumstances, when the player had no other option left. The phrase thus came to describe an act of desperation. The saying is mentioned by various authors (e.g. Alcaeus fr. 351, Men. fr. 205, Theocr. 6. 18 and see Gow ad loc. with the further references given there), including Epicharmus (fr. 202).

ἱαρᾶς: Eustathius has ἱερ-, but we expect ἱαρ- in West Greek dialects generally, and the form hιάρο͞ν is attested in early Syracusan inscriptions (Dubois, nos. 94a, 96).

## Fragment 123

Eudaemon's point is that the name Myrilla is masculine, though in form it looks feminine, just like the Illyrian name Kopaina, and words like τοξότα. We cannot know how much of this narrative depends on Sophron, but if his, the fancifully historicizing account seems to point to past rather than contemporary events.

There was a theatre at Syracuse in the archaic period, probably dating from the late sixth century. It possibly already had a raised stage, perhaps used for rudimentary dramatic performances, but this was later replaced, probably already by the time of Epicharmus, by a more substantial structure. Epicharmus' near-contemporary Phormis is credited with introducing φοίνικα δέρματα as a backdrop for the stage, which implies a building of some elaborateness (cf. Pickard-Cambridge, 289; *Suda*, φ 609). The orchestra of this second theatre is relatively small (there is little firm evidence for the presence of a chorus in Epicharmus' plays, though it is hard to doubt a chorus for plays with titles such as *Atalanta and her companions, Dionysus and his companions*, or *Revellers* and *Dancers* (or *Choreuts*)), but the theatre had proper parodoi and other elements of the classical theatre. It will also, of course, have been used for dithyrambic and other choral performances. See generally L. Polacco and C. Anti (eds.), *Il teatro antico di Siracusa* (Rimini, 1981; Padua, 1990), i. 160 ff.

## Fragment 124

Kaibel suggested ⟨ἐν⟩ τοῖc τρημ., but the verb is also construed with the dative at Ar. *Ach.* 24, 844, *Lys.* 330. ὠcτίζομαι is itself restricted to comedy (cf. Olson on *Ach.* 24). Presumably the speaker either jostles with the (other) dicers in order to get a good place, or is an entertainer being pushed out of the way. For the dative plural -εccι in consonant stems, cf. Epich. fr. 18. 4 ῥίνεccι and see Thumb–Kieckers, 212 f. (also a feature of Corinthian: Thumb–Kieckers, 131).

## Fragment 125

Dialects with ποτί also tend to preserve original τ in words like 'Poseidon'; in other dialects it is weakened to c (Buck, 107 f.). The form ποτίδα (codd.) in fr. 125 must underlie either Ποτιδᾶ or Ποτειδᾶ; a 5th-cent. BC inscription from Selinus supports the form with epsilon (Dubois, no. 78. 3 Π[οτ]ε[ιδ]ᾶνα). Equally at Epich. fr. 48. 1 ποτιδαν (A) underlies Ποτειδάν, and at fr. 70 ποτιδάν underlies Ποτειδᾶν. (For the later coalescence of pronunciation of ει and ι, cf. Allen, 94.) Simonides has Ποτ[ιδ]ᾶνοc (*PMG* 519 fr. 77. 6; see Poltera, 532 f.), and Ποτιδᾶ is the genitive at Eupol. fr. 149, probably in the mouth of a Laconian (Colvin, 272).

The first half of the compound, δραcτο-, is meaningless; Ahrens suggests πραco- or πραcιο- 'green-haired'. Poseidon is κυανοχαίτηc (later understood as 'blue-haired' rather than 'dark-haired', the original sense; cf. E. Irwin, *Colour Terms in Greek Poetry* (Toronto, 1974), 108 ff.) in Homer and often thereafter. Greenness can be a quality associated with rivers, usually with reference to the surrounding plant-life, but it is not usually a characteristic of the sea in Greek, though Timoth. *Pers.* 31 has cμαραγδοχαίταc . . . πόντοc (for which see my note ad loc.).

## Fragment 126

Comparison with Modern Greek (τρέλα 'madness', τρελόc 'insane') indicates that this is another punning name, with the sense 'crazy, mad'. The related Τρέλλοc appears as a personal name in *IG* 2². 12552.

**Fragment 127**

The meaning of the word is unknown.

**Fragments 128, 130**

Photius (p. 315, 10) gives ὀδαῖος as an epithet of Hermes equivalent to ἐνόδιος, but elsewhere the form is the more easily understood ὅδιος (Phot. p. 315, 15; Hesych. *o* 88), and ὀδαῖος should almost certainly be emended in the first passage. Kaibel suggests reading ἀδαῖος in Herodian, 'you are far too much', comparing fr. 130 (where he also reads, and I translate, ἄγον for the manuscript's senseless ἔργον). Less appealing, though clearly semantically possible, is Ahrens's ὀδαγός 'guide' (p. 474). For ἐccί, see on fr. 74.

**Fragment 129**

All three passages evidently depend on the same source, though there have been various additions, omissions, and corruptions. Nevertheless, it seems clear enough that Sophron's phrase was ἀγροῦ πυγή and that he meant prosperous and fertile areas of land generally, the 'rump' perhaps in fact because they are fatter and richer and the part on which the poorer regions can expect to depend.

**Fragment 131**

Ἁλικαύων is suspect. Botzon (1867), 24, suggests Ἁλικύμων; Kaibel Ἁλικλύδων. Perhaps ἁλικύων, i.e. 'Dog-fish' Poseidon (for the dogfish, see Thompson, 136–7), would be suitably comical.

**Fragment 133**

For the sense, cf. a *defixio* from Selinus of the 5th cent. BC, in which the writer binds ἐπ' ἀτελείαι 'to inaction' the tongues of his legal opponents (*DGE* 167ᵃ with Schwyzer's note ad loc. (p. 461)).

**Fragment 134**

No doubt in a comic prayer or oath (so Crusius, 88: ⟨μὰ τὸν⟩ Ἡρ.); cf. the diminutives Ἡρυλλος, which featured in satyr-plays (*TrGF* adesp. 590), and Ἡρακλεί⟨διον⟩, restored at Achaeus *TrGF* 20 F 26. 2, from that playwright's satyric *Linus*. Possibly the form here should rather be Ἡράκυλλον (M.L.W.) or something of the sort (Ἡράκυλον Latte: Ἡρυκλον R. Janko, per litt.). For Heracles elsewhere in Sophron, see on frs. 67–8, 72.

## Fragment 135

Tattooing was a form of punishment and overt humiliation. The foreheads of runaway slaves could be tattooed, in which case it was as much a deterrent against future escapes (Ar. *Av.* 760 with Dunbar). In Herodas, poem 5, the slave Gastron expresses his fear of tattooing in line 28, a suggestion which his mistress Bitinna takes up at line 65 (see Cunningham ad loc.), and shoulder-tattoos for slaves are mentioned at Callim. Iamb. 13. 56, on which see Kerkhecker, 266 with n. 96. In Sophron those who were tattooed were presumably mutinous or deserting soldiers (given ἀτακτούντων), who would be marked with the name of their commander (see further Headlam–Knox on Herod. 5. 66).

## Fragment *136

For the form ἦνθες (= Att. ἦλθες), see p. 19.

## Fragment 137

The whole entry is corrupt. The form of the lemma itself is uncertain, but the first word in the gloss proper looks as if it should be ἐπίχαλκα 'covered with bronze' (Musurus), after which we can without much difficulty recognize παρὰ Ϲώφρονι. But what follows is all very unclear.

## Fragment 139

The form is evidently comparable to κυνάγχης (e.g. Hippon. fr. 3a. 1) and λεοντάγχης, and Kaibel suggests that butchers (and here butchers' shops) are meant (LSJ's gloss ὑάγχη is clearly erroneous). But while one may well throttle a dog or lion, it seems an odd, and somewhat difficult, thing to do to a pig, even for a butcher, and I wonder whether 'pig-stranglers' might not be an abusive term for villains in general.

On πεῖ, see p. 23; εἶ is here the equivalent relative form (= Att. οἶ ~ ποῖ).

**Fragment 140**

According to a scholion on *Il.* 10. 511 the whole phrase became
proverbial (schol. (T) παροιμιῶδες γέγονε), and it is thus difficult
to treat Sophron's 'imitation' of the line as a reminiscence or
allusion in the proper sense. The fragment more correctly
belongs with the numerous other proverbs used in the mimes.
μιμεῖ]ται is restored by Lobel (ed. pr.), and the fact that the
papyrus commentator went on to quote Sophron's words
suggests that his was not a straightforward use of a well-known
proverb. It is regrettable that the papyrus breaks off at what was
presumably the vital point.

**Fragment 144**

See also on fr. 42 βλεννόc.

**Fragments 146, 148**

See on fr. 71.

**Fragment 147**

See on fr. 53. For the possible sense διδάcκολοc to be given to
χοραγόc, see Epich. fr. 13.

**Fragment 149**

Cf. the loss of γ in ὀλίγοc > ὀλίοc (the result of γ becoming a glide
and then being dropped), which Herodian says is Tarentine
(Rhinth. fr. 2). Plato com. fr. 183, satirizing Hyperbolus, mocks
this pronunciation as non-Attic, together with δηιτώμην for
διηιτώμην, though such pronunciations may well have been
heard in Athens itself (cf. Colvin, 282); in Attic inscriptions
forms such as Ἰγερων- (= Ἰερων-) show that already in the fifth
century γ could represent a glide between ι and a following front
vowel (cf. L. Threatte, *The Grammar of Attic Inscriptions*, i:
*Phonology* (Berlin and New York, 1980), 441).

**Fragment 151**

The stem ἡρων- is paralleled by ἥρωνα in a Coan inscription
(R. Herzog, *Arch. für Religionswiss.* 10 (1907), 402); cf. Thumb–
Kieckers, 200.

## Fragment 152

The secret things the busybodies want to know are presumably those pertaining to the underworld. The full text of the passage notes that the thirtieth of each month was sacred to the dead, and offerings were made to Hecate (cf. also Athen. 7. 325 A):

τὰς ἐν Ἅιδου τριακάδας· τιμᾶται ἐν Ἅιδου διὰ τὴν Ἑκάτην μυστικώτερον, ἧι καὶ τὰ τρία ἐπιθύεται, ἐπεὶ καὶ αὐτὴν τὴν Ἑκάτην φασι τριτογενῆ εἶναι ‖ τὸ γοῦν μυστικὸν Ἑκάτη ἡ Περσεφόνη καλεῖται, τῶν ὑποχθονίων δεσπότις‖ ὅθεν καὶ ἀφιδρύματα Ἑκάτης πρὸς ταῖς τριόδοις ἐστί, καὶ τὰ νεκύσια τριακάδι ἄγεται. τὰ γὰρ †νεώματα οὐκ ἀρχαῖα ὡς πάνδημος†. λεχθείη κτλ. (fr. 152 follows).

Wilamowitz (*Hermes* 34 (1899), 209) suggests reading ὡς Φανόδημος in the last line, since Phanodemus, an Attic historian of the fourth century BC, is known to have been interested in religious matters (= *FGrH* 325 F 28), but the correction is very doubtful. Alternatively, Cohn (*BPhW* (1896), 1096) proposed ὡς πάνδημος ⟨ἑορτή⟩, which is equally suspect. The intrusive gloss (in line 3 above) is interesting; it is faintly reminiscent of Sophron's description of Hecate in fr *7, and may be meant as a quotation.

Epicharmus wrote a play *Triakades*, but there are no hints to its content.

## Fragment 153

The presence of a schoolmaster recalls Callimachus' pederastic teacher (Iambus 5) and also Herodas' Lampriscus (poem 3), but there is no evidence how Sophron treated the subject.

## Fragment 154

The context is unclear, but the cawing of crows is associated with bad omens at Hes. *Op.* 747, where they are said to sit on unfinished buildings; elsewhere their cawing usually presages bad weather (Theophr. *Sign.* 39, Arat. 1022, etc.), though in Hesiod it probably foretells a death (see West ad loc.). Perhaps we are to take the crows as unlucky here as well. Other birds could be considered unlucky; Festus preserves a little verse which was supposed to ward off the misfortune brought by the screech-owl (*PMG* 859; and cf. Theophr. *Char.* 16. 8), and

Hipponax mentions a charm or remedy against swallows (fr. 172, with Degani, *Studi*, 287–9).

## Fragment 156

The form suggests a popular saying of the sort typically used elsewhere in Sophron to describe moral or physical characteristics (cf. frs. 33 (health); 62 (greed or lewdness); 63 (lechery); 73 (stupidity); 103 (baldness); fr. 169 is an exception). The phrase may simply describe a person with a pronounced squint. (But cf. also Herod. 4. 70 f. οὕτω ἐπιλοξοῖ . . . τῆι ἑτέρηι κούρηι, of a threatening ox, and see Gow on Theocr. 20. 13 on the emotions which can cause one to look askance.) 'Crow' can be a nickname, possibly applied to people with a squint (cf. Bechtel, *Spitznamen*, 23 n. 1).

## Fragment *158

Wilamowitz, *Kl. Schr.* IV. 158, restored Sophron's name in both texts, and assigned the fragment to his '*Women at breakfast*' (= [*Koikoa*], frs. 14–17). But Kassel–Austin rightly hesitate over the presence of both Sophron's name and 'in Doric' in the scholion, and wonder whether cώφρον could instead be an adjective.

## Fragment 161

Cf. νόμος at Epich. fr. 134; on Diogenian of Heraclea, see Wendel, *RE* s.v. Pamphilos no. 25, XVIII 3 (1949), 341 f.

## Fragment 162

Perhaps a description of an old-fashioned person: in Athens, at least, the wearing of the cicada fell out of fashion shortly after the Persian Wars, though equivalent customs may have persisted longer elsewhere. Intricate coiffeuring is also often seen in Attic comedy as a mark of effeminacy because of its connections with an aristocratic life-style (e.g. Ar. *Vesp.* 466 with MacDowell, 1068–70), and Archilochus dislikes his no doubt aristocratic general's well-kept locks (fr. 114).

## Fragment 163

A non-Greek word, perhaps of Italic or Punic origin. One of the Aeolic isles was Πορδοcιλήνη. Cf. Maas, *Kl. Schr.* 214–18;

Chantraine, Frisk, s.v. Cf. also Posidon. 253. 46 E–K and mod. Gk. τσιληπουρδῶ.

## Fragment 164

The medieval manuscripts have the singular κύμβου, and contain the gloss ἀντὶ τοῦ ϲκυφοειδοῦϲ ποτηρίου, while the papyrus copy of the scholia has plural κυμβέων, preceded by ]ων, for which Cazzaniga (ed.) plausibly suggests supplementing ξυλίν]ων '[wood]en (cups)'. The plural is probably preferable, though whether ὄγκοϲ should then mean simply 'weight' or perhaps 'heap' is unclear without further context.

## Fragment 165

Crusius (pp. 86 f.) and Kaibel (1899) saw that the leaves here are chewed as a form of magical protection (as the context implies, and cf. the chewing of laurel discussed in my n. on fr. 4A. 4), against the wilder speculations of e.g. Reich, who posited a mime involving a magical transformation into donkey-form. A connection with *The women who say they are expelling the goddess* (so Blomfield (1811), 389) is doubtful. For the magical properties of the thorn, see further E. Rohde, *Psyche. Seelencult und Unsterblichkeitsglaube der Griechen*[2] (Freiburg, 1898), i. 237 n. 3.

For the verb, cf. Cypr. *ka-ra-si-ti* = ἔϲθιε; but no doubt here, where it is used of humans, it has comic overtones.

## Fragment 166

The adjective does not obviously have anything to do with Artemis' connection with horses, or the spring Arethusa. There were several springs with this name, including one in Syracuse (Strabo 6. 2. 4), and here we might perhaps read e.g. Ἀρεθούϲιην (more correctly -αν with Doric alpha).

## Fragment 167

All are relatively common slang words for the female sexual organs; the direct obscenity which they imply contrasts with the complicated and humorous euphemisms found in e.g. frs. 23–5. Whether Sophron (or Hipponax) actually used all these words, or whether they are simply named as writers with a well-known taste for lascivious subject-matter, is uncertain. For the

possibility that genital depilation featured in Sophron, see also
on fr. 91.

## Fragment 169

The saying refers to a battle, of uncertain date, but clearly before
the early fifth century, fought between Croton and Epizephyrian
Locri at the river Sagra (perhaps the Allaro, the largest river
between Locri and Caulonia). The various accounts (Paus. 3. 19.
11–13; D. S. 8. 32; Justin 20. 2–3; Strabo 261; Conon 18) have
much that is mythological, and the genuine historical elements
are somewhat uncertain. The Locrians were allegedly heavily
outnumbered, but were victorious with the aid of the Dioscuri,
to whom they attributed their success, and who had been 'sent'
as assistance by the Spartans, to whom the Locrians had appealed
for help. Locrian Aias was also supposed to have made an
appearance on behalf of his native city, wounding the opposing
general.

 A rumour of the victory percolated to mainland Greece (to
Olympia, as the games were being held according to Strabo 261;
to Corinth, Sparta, and Athens according to Justin 20. 2–3) on
the same day as the battle, but was generally disbelieved until
further confirmation was provided later; from this detail came
the proverb, with the sense 'absolutely true (even if difficult to
believe)'. See in general Arnott on Alexis, fr. 306, Dunbabin,
358–9. Zenobius' account itself may go back to a western Greek
historian like Timaeus (so Arnott).

## Fragment *170

Zenobius' reference to Apollodorus encourages a connection
with Sophron. It is unclear why the mantis ('seer') was so called,
though a scholion to Theocr. 10. 18 (pp. 229 f. Wendel) claims
that its appearance prophesied famine, and the *Suda* (s.v.) that
prophecies were made on the basis of its movements. The latter
account in particular looks like a popular, etymologizing explanation of a late date. The idea that the praying mantis's gaze
causes ill was evidently a familiar one, but again of uncertain
origin. The *Suda*'s connection with the 'old lady wormwood'
(γραῦς cέριφος; cf. cέριφον, a type of wormwood) is more informa-
tive; the forms ἔριφος and ἔριθος -η make sense as corruptions
of cέριφος. Old maids are notoriously noxious persons, and we

could have here a Sicilian joke (first in Sophron?) comparing
old women to the insects 'either because of the effects of the
creature's stare . . . or because of a supposed resemblance
between old woman and insect' (M. Davies and J.
Kathirithamby, *Greek Insects* (London, 1986), 170 ff.). Women
are in any case often thought possessed of the Evil Eye, and old
women in general, not just old maids in particular, are prover-
bially a source of malice.

## Fragment *171

No continuous sense can be gleaned from this little scrap, but
Sophron is a very good candidate for authorship of any passage
of literary Dorian prose. μεδέων is a rather surprising poeticism
(cf. Willink on Eur. *Or.* 1690), certainly not what we would
normally expect in Sophron's prose, and used almost exclusively
of gods (in the *Iliad* always of Zeus); hence we probably have to
do with a prayer or invocation. If Kassel's tentative θαλ]αccίου
(for the genitive in -ου, see on fr. 56) is correct in line 1, the god
will be Poseidon (cf. e.g. Corinna *PMG* 654 col. iii. 14–15 πόντω
. . . μέδων Π[οτιδίων] ), and the passage perhaps belongs to the
[*Women watching the Isthmia*]; see ad loc. and Hordern (2002*b*).
Poseidon is also mentioned in frs. 125 and 131.

For πότ as the apocopated form of ποτί (= πρός), see on fr. 4A.
16.

## Fragments **172A–D

These fragments were ascribed to Sophron by Wilamowitz
(*Platon*² (Berlin, 1920), 386 f.), but the arguments for his authorship are very weak. Although it is possible that his mimes
included criticism or satire of philosophers, he nevertheless
seems a startling choice of author for Plato to choose to illustrate
the hostility between poetry and philosophy, unless the fragments have been quoted out of context.

Fragments A and B have Doric colouring in δεcπόταν and
κενεαγορίαιcι (the first term from κενέος, Dor., Ion., and Ep. =
Att. κενός), though this would not be out of place in Doric or
Doricizing lyric and we would need to restore πὸτ δεcπ. for
Sophron. Nothing internal to the fragment requires it to refer
to philosophy, although there appears to be an allusion to the
same phrase at *Lg.* 12. 967 CD, where Plato again refers to poets

comparing philosophers to 'bitches barking in vain'. P. Murray (*Plato on Poetry* (Cambridge, 1996), 231) suggests that since the attack seems to be aimed at atheistic views on the heavenly bodies, 'Anaxagoras must have been a prime target'. Nothing in such an attack suggests Sophron. A heroic context can easily be imagined for fr. B. Fragment C is more of an oddity. διαϲόφων, if from a hapax compound διάϲοφοϲ, shows an emphatic use of the prefix most closely paralleled in the archaic use of Aeolic ζά = διά in epic compounds (see Chantraine, *Grammaire*, i. 169). This would surprise in Sophron. Murray (loc. cit.) compares διαϲοφίζομαι at Ar. *Ra.* 1619, but the preverb there is not emphatic (cf. Dunbar ad loc.). Also in fr. C we might have κράτων (with Adam) 'the crowd of know-all heads', though it has no firm advantage over κρατῶν.

Fragment D refers most clearly to philosophical thought. λεπτόϲ is a common word for intellectual refinement, at least in Attic, first at E. *Med.* 529 (431 BC) and often in Aristophanes (Dover on *Nub.* 153; Dunbar on *Av.* 318). Whether the sense was current outside Attic is less clear. μεριμνάω is also a popular word to use for philosophers. Dover states that it is not common in prose (though noting that Xenophon uses it 'unselfconsciously'; Dover on *Nub.* 101). The Sicilian Empedocles uses it several times (DK 31 B 2. 2, 11. 1, 110. 7). But there is nothing especially Doric about the phrase, which raises further doubts about the attribution.

Metre is uncertain throughout, but verse should not therefore be ruled out as a possibility. T. Bergk (*Poetae Lyrici Graeci*[4] (Leipzig, 1882), 731 (= fr. 135)) thought frs. A and B lyric, the others perhaps from comedy or tragedy.

# INDEX LOCORUM

References given for fragments of Sophron are exclusive of the main entries in the commentary.

# GENERAL INDEX

allusions 140, 141, 182, 186
Alcaeus 182
Apollodorus of Athens 26, 30–2,
    142
Archilochus 8
Archonidas 177
Aristotle 3–4, 15–16
Artemis 6, 144, 167, 195
Atellan farce 27

biography 2–4

Callimachus 28–9, 146, 193
Chamaeleon 176
Choricius of Gaza 29, 32
coins 23–4, 180, 194
cookery 5, 155, 161
    as a metaphor for sex 149, 161,
    162
crasis 132

debate poems 168–9
Decimus Laberius 27, 123
δεικηλικταί 6, 123, 156
depilation 183, 195–6
dildoes 5, 28, 157–8, 159–60, 187
Dinolochus 2–3
Dionysus 6, 180
divine epiphany 134, 136
doctors, foreign 123
drunkenness 185

ecphrasis 145–6
Epiales 6, 178–9
Epicharmus 3–4, 6–7, 11 ff.,
    18 ff., 23, 128, 146, 147, 169,
    188

fellatio 5, 165

foreigners, doctors 123
    intellectual inferiority of 151
    linguistic errors of 149, 152 ff.,
    156

Gorgias 11 ff.

hairstyles 194
Hecate 6, 125–6, 127, 136, 144,
    166–7, 193
Heracles 5–6, 179, 190–1
Herodas 1, 4–5, 8, 14, 28–9, 129,
    146, 149, 158, 193
Hieron 4
Hipponax 6, 23, 128–9, 139
homosexuality 5, 171, 172, 178

iambus 139, 159
incontinence 173–4
invective, animal comparisons
    used in 170, 172, 185
invocations 167
Isthmian games 145–6

Koikoa 31, 149 ff., 180

language 16–25
    accentuation 24–5
    adverbs 23
    apocope 22, 129, 131
    lexicon 23–4
    morphology 20–2
    phonology 18–20
laurel, used in purification 130

magic 125, 126–7, 127 ff., 133,
    142–3
magodists 8
marriage, as a theme in mime
    147, 149, 163, 172–3